REASON, REVELATION, AND
THE FOUNDATIONS OF POLITICAL PHILOSOPHY

REASON, REVELATION, AND THE FOUNDATIONS OF POLITICAL PHILOSOPHY

JAMES V. SCHALL

LOUISIANA STATE UNIVERSITY PRESS
BATON ROUGE AND LONDON

Copyright © 1987 by Louisiana State University Press
All rights reserved
Manufactured in the United States of America

10 9 8 7 6 5 4 3 2 1

Publication of this book has been assisted by a grant from the Andrew W. Mellon Foundation.

Designer: Diane B. Didier
Typeface: Garamond #3
Typesetter: G & S Typesetters, Inc.
Printer: Thomson-Shore, Inc.
Binder: John H. Dekker, Inc.

Library of Congress Cataloging-in-Publication Data
Schall, James V.
    Reason, revelation, and the foundations of political philosophy.

    Bibliography: p.
    Includes index.
    1. Political science—History. 2. Political science—Philosophy. I. Title.
JA82.S26   1987   320'.01   86-27624
ISBN 0-8071-1303-4

CONTENTS

Acknowledgments   vii
Preface   1
Introduction   9
1. The Statement of the Problem of Political Philosophy   16
2. Aristotelian Political Theory: Immortality and Happiness   38
3. From the Stoics to Augustine: Practical Philosophy, Neo-Platonism, and Revelation   63
4. Thomas Aquinas and the Proper Life of Man   93
5. The Humanization and "Historicization" of the Practical Order   129
6. The Intellectualization of Political Reality   143
7. The Practical Order Materialized   163
8. Jerusalem, Athens, Rome   182
Conclusion   225
Bibliography   241
Index   251

ACKNOWLEDGMENTS

For the opportunity to reflect on political philosophy, I am grateful to several of my mentors, particularly Heinrich A. Rommen and Father Charles N. R. McCoy, both now deceased, and Clifford G. Kossel, S.J., at Gonzaga University. Michael Jackson, during his graduate studies in our department, was of particular help. Joyce Kho has given me many suggestions for the technical preparation of and improvements in the manuscript. I also appreciated the use of the Gleeson Library and the many facilities at the University of San Francisco. I especially thank Joseph Fessio, S.J., and the staff at the St. Ignatius Institute. A sabbatical year of leave from the Department of Government at Georgetown University made it possible for me to complete the project. Finally, I am grateful to Beverly Jarrett, Catherine Barton, and the members of the Louisiana State University Press for their encouragement and guidance.

James V. Schall, S.J.

REASON, REVELATION, AND
THE FOUNDATIONS OF POLITICAL PHILOSOPHY

PREFACE

Aristotle remarked that a gentleman ought to be able to play the flute in order to understand properly what music is. Music is an occupation of leisure and pertains to the highest things. But a gentleman ought not to be able to play the flute too well, as this would require all the time he had, so that, if he played too well, he would sacrifice a balanced understanding of the highest things to his routine work of flute playing. *Reason, Revelation, and Foundations of Political Philosophy* proposes itself as an "academic" essay in political philosophy as such. That is, it is not directly about metaphysics, history, theology, psychology, or economics. It will, of course, as is proper in connection with the "highest of the practical sciences," presume that the educated political philosopher is familiar with the whole scope of his own field. But it will assume that the political philosopher will also understand the major details and elements from these other areas of knowledge, including the revealed tradition.

Thus it should be possible to speak of Hebrew, Christian, or Muslim religious self-understanding as a normal cultural accomplishment of a fully educated man without the necessity of elaborate apology or repetitive explanation, no matter what one's personal persuasions might be. It has not often been possible to do so in modern times, particularly in the schools, but I believe that, for a number of reasons, political philosophy is today much more prepared to accept the fact that an intelligent understanding of revelation and metaphysics can also be acknowledged as necessary for a full understanding of particularly political philosophy without inevitably implying that political philosophy itself is somehow revelation, dependent directly on it, or corrupted by the effort.

To "believe" in the doctrine of the Incarnation or Trinity or creation, then, may or may not be an intelligent choice. But not to know what these doctrines might mean in themselves or how they related to political speculations in the great tradition is merely a matter of ignorance, not necessarily to be praised, since this knowledge is in general easily available to and operative in that culture in which the universities originally arose and still, it is to be hoped, continue. The great thinkers knew about these doctrines, however they were understood. I do not mean to be argumentative or condescending here; I mean merely to suggest the sort of academic culture required if a full and broad understanding of the reaches of political philosophy is ever to be achieved. Perhaps the most crippling thing that can happen to a student of political philosophy is to have no notion of religious belief and how it might even intellectually influence those who hold it—in practice by far the majority of mankind.

Invariably, lacking the broader understanding, the political philosopher will attempt to explain religious truths in terms of his own discipline alone, falling prey to a reductionism that will pervert both his own discipline and that which he seeks to explain. Political philosophy as it is today, for both historical and intellectual reasons, includes the adequate comprehension of revelation's influence upon political philosophy and of political philosophy in its relation to revelation, for better or for worse. The studied inattention of the professional political philosopher to theological questions has in part been responsible, ironically, for a dangerous politicization of religion itself, something of great potential damage in the city as well as to religion.

Likewise, the present essay holds that political philosophy is an intelligible discussion continuing over the centuries about certain basic issues arising in human living to which varied responses have been posed, beginning particularly with—and constantly returning to—the Greek classical writers and those who have and still do comment on the abiding questions they posed. I do not directly, however, make a detailed "exposition" of the text of Plato, Aristotle, Cicero, Augustine, Aquinas, Machiavelli, Hegel, Marx, Voegelin, or Strauss, all necessary work, to be sure.

Preface

Rather I acknowledge that these and other writers in political philosophy—well studied in the schools—are engaged with each other and ultimately with us in an ongoing reflection about the meaning of life in the city; its limits, if it has any; and how this political life relates to particular human beings who compose and, in some sense, transcend the city. Obviously much more can be presented at every step. I have rather sought to stick to the essential argument, as I see it, following it where it goes and considering what it means. Other political philosophers ancient, medieval, and modern have argued differently perhaps. But their very arguments can be thought about—where they come from, what they signify. The first order of business for the political philosopher, I would suggest, is to clarify what it means for philosophers to speak of the city and of that which may be beyond it. Philosophers need all the relevant information, from whatever source. Only when this is understood will the city itself be able to be a city—the limited but real home for mortal men yet a home in which the full meaning of what it is to be human is not exhausted. This is the burden of my overall argument. Contemporary political philosophy, I think, needs a sustained argument about its origin and nature that would include how the revelational tradition responds to its own legitimate questions and to problems not solved by its own arguments.

This particular effort to understand the foundations of political philosophy began with the view that politics, to be politics, ought not to seek to explain all reality by itself. This basic truth, no doubt, can best be learned by reading Aristotle. To state the case differently, I noticed that one of the primary effects of authentic revelation on political philosophy itself seemed to be, paradoxically, to free the city from the burden of becoming itself an ontology. When religion remained itself—if and when it did—it allowed politics to be only politics, but on the condition that the questions posed about the highest things were themselves properly formulated and freely addressed in their own order, which was not necessarily or exclusively political. I was always struck by the extreme, quasi-religious character of political philosophy when it claimed for itself something more than its limited competence. On the other hand, politics did have its own legitimacy, which made it something more than a mere tool of metaphysics or theology, however valid these latter might also be. I found, in other words, that often when the political philosopher thought he was talking about political philosophy, he was in fact speaking of revelation or metaphysics.

In their earlier stages these reflections began during my work under Heinrich Rommen, Charles N. R. McCoy, and Clifford G. Kossel.¹ At that time I had understood that the argument of political philosophy revolved around the peculiarly unideological nature of particularly American political practice, as compared with the more speculative nature of much European theory.² I believe this major issue still manifests itself in the unsettlingly ideological nature of religious views on the economy.

But I suspected then, and continue to do so now, that the reason for the practical nature of classical American politics was that politics officially allowed ultimate questions to be formulated among the citizenry largely by religion. This point was particularly important because a religion, for example the Judaeo-Christian one dominant in American culture, had the distinction of reason and revelation in its own intellectual background in various ways. Likewise, there was prevalent a sense of Aristotelian practical reasoning, which implied that sensible people could know, after a fashion from experience, the right order of things not infrequently better than the philosophers themselves.

American politics, I felt at the time, was peculiar. The pragmatic relation of American religious and classical education to the medieval and classical traditions seemed to have in a large degree protected the United States from that form of philosophical discourse and its direc-

---

1. James V. Schall, "Immortality and the Foundations of Political Theory" (Ph.D. dissertation under Heinrich Rommen, Georgetown University, 1960). Leo Strauss reviewed Rommen's *State in Catholic Thought* in his *What Is Political Philosophy?* (Glencoe, Ill., 1959), 281–84.

2. See James V. Schall, "Theory in American Politics," *Modern Age*, IV (Spring, 1960), 150–159.

tion which political philosophers now call, variously, "modern political philosophy," insofar as that discipline had come to represent a conscious break with the classical and medieval views. The difference between the French and American revolutions, with particular attention to Edmund Burke and John Adams, seemed to be the most graphic example of this real difference.

The broader intellectual understanding of developments in political philosophy (and in American political life) as well as in the rest of the world, especially in the Marxist world and in developing countries, during the past quarter of a century has suggested rather that neither the American tradition nor Christianity itself in particular was as immune as I had suspected from autonomous political metaphysics as it had developed in the classical modern European writers and experiences. The question was why? And was the public life of the American experiment turning itself, albeit democratically, into just another version of theoretically autonomous man presupposed to no order but his own?

In the meantime, political philosophy itself was, at least in some key quarters, largely on the basis of this same sort of questioning, revitalized, partly because of the peculiarly graphic nature of World Wars I and II and partly because of Leo Strauss, Eric Voegelin, Hannah Arendt, and their schools together with a persistently vigorous attention to Burke in other quarters. These writers and many others—such as Heinrich Rommen and others of my professors such as Rudolf Allers, Goetz Briefs, and Josef Solterer—bore virtually in their lives the marks of the relation of American thought to European as America itself apparently shifted more and more in the direction of ideology.

At about this time too I went to spend over a decade in Rome at the Gregorian University, where the question of the nature of particularly Christian political philosophy was a major concern, with its relation to the history and nature of political philosophy as such. This seemed the element in Western intellectual tradition least addressed by modern political philosophy. But the world of Christian intelligence seemed curiously inattentive to the work of the political philosophers who recognized the need to criticize the very legitimacy of much modern political philosophy. Yet it also seemed clear during this time, symbolized perhaps best by the fate of Jacques Maritain, that Christian philosophy, as articulated in its Augustinian and Thomist forms, was itself coming under attack from within, from the very forces to which Strauss in particular had felt that Catholicism especially might be immune, the forces of modern political philosophy itself presenting themselves also in theological terms.

In arguing for a return to the classical foundations of political philosophy, an argument with which I generally agreed, Strauss and Voegelin, I began to think, did not sufficiently attend to this very tradition of Augustine and Aquinas (something that could be said more recently to be true to an even greater extent of many Christian writers), to how revelation addressed political philosophy itself. With Strauss, I found less disagreement than a certain incompleteness in the midst of great profundity and good sense about both metaphysics and revelation as well as political philosophy. Voegelin, who was more attuned to the Christian culture, seemed to me less attentive to the side of political philosophy which would be able to control properly a revelational tradition that admittedly could and sometimes did become extreme. Voegelin seemed to look for a revelation beyond the traditional one which seemed to present itself in direct relationship to the questions of political philosophy.

It became clear, then, that Christianity in particular, much less than Judaism (Islam has not changed its theory, but has only gained power), starting in Protestantism and continuing on to certain elements of Catholicism, began in fact more and more to be tempted, as Voegelin well understood, to accept the "modern project" or "Gnosticism," as he called it, in some form and to try to baptize it in religious terms. I would agree with Strauss and Voegelin that this cannot be done. Thus it seems to me that a reformulation of the position of Augustine and Aquinas in particular is necessary to understand why the "modern project" is itself the undermining of revelation as a possibility and therefore, I would argue, of the possibility of a politics limited to this life. Proposals to return to the classics are not in themselves fully able to provide this reformulation. The forgetting or rejecting of how

Augustine and Aquinas addressed the classical questions seems to have made it possible for political enthusiasm to enter religion. That is, the energies of religion combined with a completely man-made theoretic order made the totalitarianism of the twentieth century much more dangerous than even the extreme tyranny of the classics. And on the basis of theory I do not believe we can rule out the possibility of a species of "democratic totalitarianism," something present in our theory since at least Rousseau.

Because of these factors, we can and should now present a new theory about the unity of political philosophy which has heretofore been almost impossible to elaborate because of the neglect by the political philosopher of revelation and what has happened to it. The new theory is to be not merely "stating" a thesis, however, but likewise addressing factors in the general culture which can be of great danger if they continue to add a religious enthusiasm to the extremes of the modern political theory, which allows in the public forum only the view of man and his dignity that is presupposed to nothing but his own powers. Here arises the question of the unity and relation of the highest things, including political things, to each other. The argument at least needs to be posed, bluntly and sparely, perhaps, yet forcefully and completely.

Political philosophy has come to be the first line of defense not merely of the limited city but also of a revelation that does not conceive its task to be one of building a city based implicitly on the denial of the norms of nature. This is the argument in its development and meaning that I have endeavored to set forth in the present essay, which holds that, for the foundation of political philosophy, for its completeness, even in its own order, certain questions found in human experience and reflection need to be confronted, questions to which intelligence can be addressed. When political philosophy understands why it is not itself metaphysics or a revelation, it can tell us most what we need to know about why politics is limited, why it is about what is proper to mortal man but not necessarily about all that man is in his given being.

For the answers to such questions, however, we also need to know how revelation itself has responded to questions arising validly for the political philosopher. In a sense, "modern" political philosophy has been an unfortunate attempt to answer these higher questions presupposing nothing but itself. For this reason the record of the endeavor's outcome is also a part of political philosophy that causes us once again to reopen the questions the classical political philosophers posed and to see how the whole tradition, including the revelational, responded to them.

INTRODUCTION

The nature of political philosophy is itself a philosophical problem. In one sense, what political things are, for the most part, seems to be self-evident. They are known before we reflect in any detail on how they are and what they are. Otherwise there is no beginning. Aristotle taught us well to begin with commonsense things, things which everyone recognizes as belonging to this or that category of reality, which contains within itself differentiations, grades of being, and particular beings. On the other hand, a time finally arrives when it is not sufficient to rest content with commonsense knowledge of things. Rather we must seek to understand where a discipline or an experience falls in the totality of things, of *what is*. When Aristotle defined man as a "political" animal, he did not intend to suggest that man was nothing more than political, for Aristotle also called him a "rational" animal, the animal who laughs and speaks. But he did intend to say that man's "political-ness" was unique about him in relation to other beings also found in the cosmos, gods or beasts (*Politics*, 1253a1–3).

The thesis of this book concerns the relation of lived political life in existing states to transcendent questions. These latter questions from Greek political philosophy, such as the location of final happiness, the immortality of the soul, friendship, and the contemplative life, have been constantly deepened and clarified throughout Western philosophical and religious history for the sake of understanding political life properly. Also, I argue herein that, if we do not "understand" what political life is, we will in the end destroy or distort it, because we humans cannot live without "understanding" what politics is. Aristotle, we should recall, wrote not just *The Politics* but also *The*

Metaphysics. A right understanding of metaphysics, then, was presupposed to a right understanding of politics, but a well-ordered city needed to allow for the possible existence of speculative knowledge within its confines without the destruction either of itself or of philosophy or of the citizen who bore both.

This ever-present lesson of *The Apology* of Plato for political philosophy was not lost on Aristotle. It was, in turn, directly related to the final book of *The Nichomachean Ethics*, in which human happiness as such was discussed in relation to political life. Here Aristotle suggested that there were two kinds of happiness, one of which had to do with the being of man insofar as he lived a full life on this earth, in which he understood and activated all the powers and faculties he discovered already in existence within himself, in the context of communication and confrontation with those things which were most "for themselves," for their own sakes (1178a8–1178b23).

But there was also a higher kind of life, which usually required for its pursuit the right ordering of the city, though sometimes a solitary philosopher such as Socrates might by divine calling receive the capacity for it (1177b1ff.). This higher kind of life consisted in understanding the proper order of things and their natures in existence. To this latter life, as far as possible, Aristotle thought, we should devote all our energies, because these were the things that were highest in themselves, things to which the human intellect was in some sense open without having them under its control or dominion. Aristotle called these the things that could not be "otherwise." He suggested that they were to be pursued "for their own sakes" rather than for any particular use or pleasure we might derive from them. Both use and pleasure, however, were good, and we, in some sense, do experience them, even in the highest things, especially in fact in the highest things. But to understand the "lower things" did not mean that the "higher things" were merely reducible to them, to use or to pleasure.

The "intellectual" history of political philosophy may be regarded as consisting in an effort, analogous to Gilson's *Unity of Philosophical Experience,* to understand why politics had a limited—"moderate," to use Leo Strauss's phrase—role to play in human life.[1] From a negative point of view, what is at stake here is the effort to prevent politics from claiming to be itself a metaphysics, which, if put into existence as a "political metaphysics," would deprive man of a real intellectual or spiritual life apart from the complete control of the polity. That is to say, how is it possible, while acknowledging the validity of politics, to prevent it from claiming that it could, by its own methodology and efforts, explain the intelligibility of all reality? The "moderation" of politics needed adequate philosophical argumentation based on openness to all reality.

How, indeed, was it possible for political philosophy even to think of becoming a "metaphysics," an explanation of *all that is?* The present study, finally, is about the answer to this question. But initially, it was possible in the history of thought to think of this problem because of the Greek discussion about immortality with its relation to the Christian doctrine of "the resurrection of the body." These questions, together with the others addressed to reason from revelation, were at least intelligible to the philosophers insofar as they themselves formulated their own inquiries about man, the cosmos, and the causes of being. One of the primary reasons for the elevation of politics to the post classically held by metaphysics had to do with the ultimate status of each individual member of the human race. This question, in turn, related to the status of the whole human race itself and of each member of which it is historically composed with regard to any transcendent meaning and existence that could directly or indirectly be given to each member of this same human totality. This theme was familiar to Augustine and was brilliantly reproposed by Dante Germino in his *Political Philosophy and the Open Society.*[2]

During the past thirty years or more, a number of factors have arisen in political philosophy and experience which, I think, render

---

1. Etienne Gilson, *The Unity of Philosophical Experience* (New York, 1937); Strauss, *What Is Political Philosophy?*
2. Dante Germino, *Political Philosophy and the Open Society* (Baton Rouge, 1982).

this approach to political theory of especial importance. The first of these is, no doubt, the work of Leo Strauss, Hannah Arendt, and Eric Voegelin, with their schools. They have forcefully raised the question about the relation of reason and revelation, of modern and classical political philosophy to each other. They have challenged the very philosophy upon which the modern state has rested, since it seems based in certain fundamental aspects on a deviation from *what is*. These writers, at least, along with certain writers in the neoconservative and Thomist schools, permit us to discuss the deeper questions of the relation of reason and revelation as an issue in political theory, a question that has received little adequate presentation in contemporary political philosophy, though Strauss and Voegelin in particular have acknowledged its importance.

In this context too, it is necessary, I think, to ask again whether Thomas Aquinas did not in fact properly interpret Aristotle while at the same time going far beyond him.[3] In recent years this issue becomes as important for revelational religion as for political philosophy itself. Indeed, the neglect of political philosophy seems to have been more harmful to religion than to political philosophy. Religion has sometimes permitted itself to be used as the means to achieve the ends of "modern" political philosophy, ends presupposed to nothing but politics. One of the unusual vocations of political philosophy, then, seems to be the very intellectual effort to save reason from revelational language and movements, which base themselves, directly or indirectly, on "modern" political philosophy. Thus political philosophy seemingly needs attention on the part of religion in order to save itself from being merely an echo of the modern ideologies. The intellectual wars of our era are fought primarily in the area of political philosophy.

Medieval political philosophy has a particular role to play here, since it is often the missing element in contemporary discussions of the nature of political philosophy. (Its neglect is itself a further problem in political philosophy.)[4] The revival of classical political philos-

---

3. See Harry Jaffa, *Thomism and Aristotelianism* (Westport, Conn., 1956).
4. See James V. Schall, *The Politics of Heaven and Hell: Christian Themes from Classical, Medieval, and Modern Political Philosophy* (Lanham, Md., 1984).

ophy has often slighted or been otherwise directed against not merely "modern" philosophy but also medieval theory, which is said to be valid only insofar as it preserved Plato or Aristotle and not in that it continued and deepened the very philosophical bases of the classics in their own terms.

That medieval theory was reason addressed by revelation, then—reason influenced by faith—was considered the primary reason for its corruption or lack of credibility in the modern mind. However, the question can still be asked whether it is its "corruption" or "salvation." Has the drift of philosophy into ideology proved the validity or the invalidity of revelation? In this area the historians of thought, manners, and ethics have much to tell us. The great influence of ideology in religion, in any case, returns thought to the other side of the issue. Will revelation remain authentic if it is not addressed by a reason itself not derived from the ideologies—that is, from reason not originating in "modern" theory as such, which began with Descartes and Machiavelli, with the separation of the speculative and practical orders?

Political philosophy therefore needs to be rethought less in terms of its past than in terms of its own "theory" of itself. In other words, the record of political philosophy, to be intelligible, must be viewed against the questions directed to it by revelation and by the historical results of *not* following classical and revelational norms. In one sense, we can indeed test the value and validity of ideas in a laboratory, namely, that to which ideas have led us. Rethinking political philosophy too involves, naturally, will. We shall never see what we "choose" not to see. For this reason political theory itself is also a branch of moral philosophy, a study in part dependent upon the virtue of the investigator (or the lack thereof) as well as upon that of the investigated.

But political philosophy has as a primary task the understanding of itself and its limits—of what it is open to—and is in this sense its own legitimate enterprise. That everything seems open to political philosophy is an exhilarating feeling for the thinker, although often deceptively so. Political philosophy does not and ought not, on the other hand, to substitute for theology or metaphysics or for any study of what properly *is* in its own right, including the individual person as something not exhaustively political. Yet control of the city in large part decides whether anything but the particular order or constitution of this or that individual city, Thebes or Athens, will be allowed public or private expression. Frontiers, in this sense, in principle prove to be as much moral and metaphysical as geographical. For the city can itself claim, or can at least exact, absolute allegiance to its laws, themselves presupposed to nothing but themselves, to nothing but their own will. Openness as such is not a virtue without its dangers. For we can be open to disorder and evil, which can exist, though they should not, and can form the constitution of a polity, though, again, they should not. In the completely disordered polis—a central theme of classical political thought—the wise and the good will be silent, will perish, or will do both.

Political philosophy, moreover, ought to be open even to revelation. For too many, the mere affirmation of this statement will itself be ambiguous or even a sort of anathema, though it is no more than a statement of honesty and reality, of *what is*. Human beings can evidently be addressed not only by good spirits but also by bad ones. That is, openness to revelation does not mean adherence to everything that is "revealed" *ipso facto*. The spirit needs testing. One of the principal functions of political philosophy itself is indeed the negative function of deciding whether what is revealed is also reasonable, credible. For this reason there must be political philosophy even with the fact of a revelation. For this reason, too, by neglecting revelation, political philosophy has often appeared as a counter "final vision."

Such, then, is the service that politics pays to revelation. We must begin, however, with questions that do already occur to the human mind and arise in human experience before there is a question of revelation, even though in fact there may not be a purely "natural" world, a world presupposed to no revelation, and there may never have been one. Creation is not praised by denying to rational creatures their own legitimate powers and functions. "To hold creatures cheap," Aquinas said, "is to slight the divine power."⁵ The prior understanding, either in time or in conception, that unsolved, perplexing questions arise from human living, particularly political living, to challenge us, must exist before there can be any talk of the relation of reason and revelation to political philosophy itself, which addresses and formulates such questions.

Though there may be, moreover, several sources for answers to such questions, themselves in need of being related in an orderly fashion, the questions nevertheless exist legitimately and independently. Political philosophy does thus stand guard at the gates of the city in order both to preserve the city as it is and to open individual members to what lies beyond, to resources that the polity does not, and *knows* it does not, possess in itself. The foundations of political philosophy lie in the endeavor to clarify and understand how questions that do arise in the individual, the family, and the polity lead both to answers that are adequate for the polity and also to answers that transcend it. The endeavor to comprehend why questions are posed which are not fully to be answered in the polity likewise limits what we can and ought to expect from politics. This endeavor alone will ultimately protect political life from being subsumed into an activist metaphysics in which the only openness to "being" has become that formed by and for the polity, presupposed to nothing but itself.

5. Thomas Aquinas, *Summa contra Gentiles*, III, 89. Translation in *St. Thomas Aquinas, Vol. I, Philosophical Texts,* Selected and translated with notes and an introduction, by Thomas Gilby (Durham, N.C., 1982), N. 380. (Henceforth translations from this edition will be cited as follows: I [or II: *Theological Texts*] and the citation number in the text, i.e., I, N. 56.) In the absence of such a citation, translations of Thomas Aquinas are my own.

1

THE STATEMENT OF THE PROBLEM
OF POLITICAL PHILOSOPHY

The medieval researcher and philosopher Albertus Magnus (Albert the Great, who died in 1280) began his commentary on *The Politics* of Aristotle with a proof for the immortality of the human soul, whereas his main endeavor in his commentary on *The Ethics* was to discover "the proper life of man."[1] The significance of these two ideas, when applied to political theory, requires that they both be located within the history and intelligible argument of Western thought. In placing the proof in this particular commentary, Albert provided, if we reflect deeply on it, a key to understanding what political philosophy is about and what has happened to it. We must see these ideas as they developed and produced results in ancient, medieval, and modern thought. That a medieval thinker reproposed in his own way these points familiar to the Greeks and the Romans provides a guide and a key to the completion of a basic side of political philosophy which has been lacking in the contemporary discipline.

The real issue that Albert confronted with the two ideas of immortality and the proper life of man is the intelligible meaning of political life and political theory. If man is immortal and his ultimate goal is not in this life, however these notions are to be rightly and completely understood, what effect does this position have on political life itself? Must man consequently abandon the practical, political life in favor of the contemplative life? Are religious and philosophical doctrines about the contemplative life or the immortal life intrinsically opposed to the political life, so that the real task of political theory is to seek to eliminate them as destructive of the political order itself? Must reli-

---

1. Alberti Magni, *Opera omnia*, ed. A. Borgenet (Paris, 1890), Vol. V. *De anima*, Lib. I, t. i, c. 1, p. 118. Albert's commentary on Aristotle's *Ethics* is found in Vol. VII; the commentary on *The Politics* is in Vol. VIII.

gion and philosophy destroy politics in order to exist? Yet if the proper life of man is really associated with this political life, can there be any place for the contemplative life or the doctrine or reality of immortality? And how adequate is this doctrine? Does it refer merely to a kind of abiding fame before the life of the polity as it might chance to last down the ages? Does it leave itself open to questioning both from the city and from revelation?

So central are these questions to political theory that they must be seen in their true context. Continuity appears in intellectual history in connection with the issue of immortality and the proper life of man, also including, as directly related, the classic questions of friendship and its destiny, of truth and its source. A philosopher's attitude toward immortality and the proper life of man—a phrase used here to mean the life that is unique to man in the universe, that which distinguishes man from other grades of being, that is, man's political life—directly influences his theory of, and hence his practice in, the city. The denial of personal immortality, so that it is nothing more than abiding and exemplary reputation in the city, has not been a trivial issue in political philosophy. A logical consequence has been the doctrine that this life is all that is open to man, so that he should employ all his energies to make it "truly human," a position that lies at the heart of the difference between classical Greek and Roman theory (see below, Chapter 3).

Questions concerning immortality, in *The Apology* and *The Republic* of Plato, for example, do not concern the fully human or political life of man. For many, these questions seem to be merely pious, abstract issues, mindless hopes, analogous to games of "what if" speculating about that which will never be. Thus a radical humanism, itself rooted in post-Aristotelian political philosophy, has often affirmed that immortality is an alienation of properly human forces rather than a justification for their ultimate importance. When man concerns himself with immortality, in all the phases through which that concept has passed, including the notion of the resurrection of the body from revelation, he is said to neglect this world, his real "home." This neglect becomes the "reason" why the world is not as it "should" be, the basis for the "opposition" of politics to religion and contemplation. The eradication of philosophical and religious ideas about man's higher goals, then, becomes, in this view, the necessary "task" of living politics. Politics appears theoretically opposed to political reflection founded in or stimulated by revelation. A certain kind of political animus to revelation or speculative thought thus receives theoretical justification.

The denial of immortality does not, however, necessarily quiet the desires of men for personal completion and meaning, for their accurate understanding. Rather it has led, particularly in the modern era, to the construction of ideologies and doctrines that attempt as a substitute to give man—mankind generally, be it noted, and not just a particular individual—full autonomy in this life. Ideologies which replace religious belief or classical metaphysics almost invariably adopt methods and procedures which in practice prove incompatible with a normal human and political life for real human beings. Yet the alternatives to immortality are intelligible in the history of political philosophy. That is, we can "think" why they might seem "reasonable." The danger of ideological substitution is so vivid as to make Allan Bloom argue that the very purpose of *The Republic* was to warn men of the possibility that pure thought could destroy the real city.[2]

Such a result suggests a need to rethink and reinterpret Aristotle's distinction between the practical and the contemplative orders. Can we have a practical order without a contemplative order? If man is the highest being in the universe, political life must be his highest goal, as Aristotle remarked in VI *Ethics* (1141a20–22). Yet such a conclusion seems somehow to violate man's very dignity. For outside the political order apparently lie some truths for which men will even die rather than give them up, and the discovery of these truths seems to incite the most noble individuals of our kind. The pursuit of these higher things separates the serious from the frivolous. Indeed, the un-

---

2. Plato, *The Republic*, trans. with notes and an interpretative essay, by Allan Bloom (New York, 1968), "Interpretative Essay," 306–436. Hereafter, citations from *The Republic* will be cited from this edition as follows: Plato, *The Republic,* page number of the classical edition, page number of the Bloom translation.

willingness to die for anything, be it idea, person, or polity, is considered a characteristic not of civilization but of barbarism.

The notion that preservation of life is the highest good, for example, reduces all questions of principle to the lowest common denominator, that of survival at any cost. Thus if notions surrounding the idea of immortality are really "*in*human"—that is, if they are not proper to man, if they do not ground him in something beyond the civil order and how it is formed—then the political order can always force men into its own mold, not just physically, but also morally. This conclusion men have never been quite able to accept theoretically in its entirety, however often they may have been forced to live it in practice. The New Testament distinction between things belonging to Caesar and things belonging to God has served, in retrospect, as the classical locus in which this issue was further clarified (Matthew 22:22).

The advent of Christianity consequently brought with it a new type of problem relative to human life. Though it is a Greek not a Judaeo-Christian notion, Christian philosophy universally accepted the philosophical doctrine of immortality as made fully intelligible by faith. That is, immortality was not the creedal doctrine of the "resurrection of the body." But the philosophical doctrine did explain how this particular thesis was necessary and possible (that is, noncontradictory) if Christian doctrine itself was true. Immortality was not essentially incompatible with resurrection. Philosophy here was seen to be necessary to explain how revelation was not itself contrary to reason, which it would be if the doctrine of resurrection implied a "second creation" of a previously annihilated individual human being. Without a theory of immortality, philosophy would rightly conclude that the doctrine of the resurrection must mean the possibility of two distinct Platos, a theory which would deny the very point of individual resurrection in the first place. But did this concern for immortality not mean that the affairs of this world were at best temporary, even dangerous to the citizen-believer? Exclusive concern with the next life incited other problems.

For did not men, believers in immortality or resurrection, tend to neglect the energy and intelligence that seemed to be needed to construct the proper human city? And was this construction not what human life was about, its proper life? Christians found themselves tempted (and often forced) to accept unjust and inhuman social and economic orders on the ground that this life passes quickly anyhow, so little effort to change anything is called for. This attitude led to the challenging of the revelational position as incompatible with the world of real, suffering humanity, which presumably needs to have its evils changed, not just tolerated. Exclusive concern with the world, as a historical fact, however, has often led to world-weariness and boredom, so that the neglect was not remedied by the available alternatives to faith or philosophy.

Such unpleasant consequences therefore suggest that the relation between the two descriptions of immortality, mere abiding fame or permanent existence, along with the classical problems of friendship, the inadequacy of justice, and the final purpose of individual human beings in the context of political philosophy, should be reconsidered. The process involves identifying the sort of "reality" or "being" proper to individual humans and to the polity itself. Albert the Great's insight, which at first seems an anomaly, now appears to be one of tremendous, though unappreciated, significance. For Albert was trying to point out that the doctrine of immortality is not incompatible with the proper life of mortal man. On the contrary, the political life of man on this earth is very delicate, something which by its nature cannot be confused with man's concern for personal immortality or with any form historically taken by that desire, with the quest of philosophy as such for the highest things.

Unless some explanation for man's quest for personal transcendent meaning is found, no city will be allowed to do what can be done and ought to be done within it by the citizen's own political means, which are distinct from philosophical means. And politics, like philosophy, to be itself may require something more than itself, even revelation. Albert, in following Aristotle, saw clearly that man has two goals, one proper to the human being, a mortal creature, and one proper to the contemplative or supernatural order in which man can also somehow participate.

Thomas Aquinas, Albert's most famous pupil, established the relation between these two aspects of a single, complete human life, itself intelligently open to reason wherever found. He was particularly concerned with those questions which in fact arise in the exercise of human intelligence and in the fullness of the city. Historically, the development of the classical tradition in political theory has in large part been a constant effort to clarify these two different drives in man. Particular effort has been devoted to preserving the legitimacy of both the city and the highest aims of man as such, so that they will not seem to be in fatal opposition to each other.

Consequently, it is useful to trace and distinguish the development of these ideas as they reveal themselves in Western thought. It is particularly important to recognize that modern European speculative political theory, as contrasted at least until recently with American political practices, has more frequently attempted to combine both the metaphysical drives associated with immortality and the proper political life as such into one common life of this earth. The concept of culture or civilization, as contrasted with political philosophy, has come to suggest certain social "entities" in which the complete range of practical, artistic, and theoretical life can be lived. This concept has often tended to replace personal immortality as the only locus of abidingness that is conceivable.

In this context, political philosophy has become of central importance, not merely because political philosophy is required if philosophy is to be at all legitimately permitted in the city, but because the alternatives to philosophy and religion, as themselves valid explanations of what man in fact is, have tended to take political form, for which indeed there is a philosophical reason. It is a question not merely of some possible theoretical alternative but also of the very notion that a theoretical alternative is possible to a city whose political form is presupposed to nothing but itself. How is it, in other words, that we are not required to accept whatever constitution we live under as "the best"? Or again, why do we not always have to change our own constitution to what is proposed as a better or best system in thought? What, finally, is the import of our search for the best life?

PLATO

The central issue in political theory, what I will call its "foundation," centers on the question of whether politics, both as an intellectual discipline and as a way of active human life, solves the problems of man's ultimate destiny, problems that unavoidably arise in any individual human's serious self-reflection concerning his own life, or that of his family or of his city. If politics, on one hand, can solve these questions, as many political philosophers since Hobbes seem to have believed, then the political system will itself provide answers to the questions raised by the ideas of God, immortality, man's nature and destiny, friendship, the distinction between good and evil, virtue, and particularly courage. If, on the other hand, politics does not answer these questions, then politics can look to its own proper sphere, to questions and actions with which it can properly deal, while not forbidding the others as necessarily illegitimate or threatening. This proper sphere of politics is not the ultimate one, although it may well depend upon a definite theoretical basis to do what it can do.

In such a context, Aristotle remains central in political philosophy. And it was in connection with these issues that the commentaries of the medievals such as Albert and particularly Thomas gain in importance in political philosophy, the reason why our contemporary problem with political philosophy is not merely a rethinking of "modern" theory in light of the classics of Thucydides, Plato, Aristotle, or Cicero. But that problem demands a rethinking also in terms of medieval theory, which includes an orderly discussion of answers given to the classical questions, on the basis of the questions formulated by philosophy but encompassing an openness to any intelligibility which is itself "reasonable," that is, capable of being understood.

For in Aristotle, as well as in Albert and Thomas, the primary issues of political theory concerned the relation of the theoretic order to the practical, the effect of immortality, the meaning of the natural, and the task of man as man, 'hominis in quantum homo est,'" as Albert phrased the problem in his commentary on the *De anima* of Aristotle.³ Practical politics will take on its characteristic aspects from the answers given to these theoretic issues. For this reason, answers to ultimate questions must always, in some degree, form the foundations of political theory as well as the character of practical life. How this position works itself out in political philosophy remains the burden of this discussion.

Aristotle's political theory rested upon his correction of Plato's concepts of the place and nature of scientific knowledge and the nature of the passions. Plato held, according to Aristotle, that concepts such as justice, man, truth, and dog were "forms" whose true reality existed not in particular states or individuals but rather in separate, perfect entities:

> Socrates, however, was busying himself about ethical matters and neglecting the world of nature as a whole but seeking the universal in these ethical matters, and fixed thought for the first time on definitions; Plato accepted his teaching, but held that the problem applied not to sensible things but to entities of another kind—for this reason, that the common definition could not be a definition of any sensible thing, as they were always changing. Things of this other sort, then, he called Ideas, and sensible things, he said, were all named after these, and in virtue of their relation to these; for the many existed by participation in the Ideas that have the same name as they.⁴

Individuals, then, participated in these forms in only an imperfect manner; something "higher" existed than the single member of a form or class.

Theoretic science for Plato depended upon direct insight into the nature and stability of these separate forms, the highest of which, the Good, was so pure and overwhelming that man could only contemplate it.

---

3. Albert the Great, *De anima*, Lib. I, t. 1, c. 1, p. 118.
4. Aristotle, *Metaphysics*, I, 6, 987b1, *The Basic Works of Aristotle*, ed. Richard McKeon (New York, 1941), 701. Hereafter, references to Aristotle will be as follows: Aristotle, *Work*, book number, chapter number, Bekker number, page number of the McKeon edition.

"A god doubtless knows if it happens to be true. At all events, this is the way the phenomena look to me: in the knowable the last thing to be seen, and that with considerable effort, is the *idea* of the Good; but once seen, it must be concluded that this is in fact the cause of all that is right and fair in everything—in the visible it gave birth to light and its sovereign; in the intelligible, itself sovereign, it provided truth and intelligence—and that the man who is going to act prudently in private or public must see it."[5]

Matter and sensation impeded the mind's ability to penetrate to the "really real," to the form, because they were always changing.

Moreover, a man was passive with respect to these forms; they were given to, not made by, him. Man was free by submitting to the order of forms.

"In order that such a man also be ruled by something similar to what rules the best man, don't we say that he must be the slave of that best man who has the divine rule in himself? It's not that we suppose the slave must be ruled to his own detriment, as Thrasymachus supposed about the ruled; but that it's better for all to be ruled by what is divine and prudent, especially when one has it as his own within himself; but, if not, set over one from outside, so that insofar as possible all will be alike and friends, piloted by the same thing. . . ."

"Yes, by the dog," I said, "he will in his own city, very much so. However, perhaps he won't in his fatherland unless some divine chance coincidently comes to pass."

"I understand," he said. "You mean he will in the city whose foundation we have now gone through, the one that has its place in speeches, since I don't suppose it exists anywhere on earth."

"But in heaven," I said, "perhaps, a pattern is laid up for the man who wants to see and found a city within himself on the basis of what he sees. It doesn't make any difference whether it is or will be somewhere. For he would mind the things of this city alone, and of no other."[6]

---

5. Plato, *The Republic,* 517b–c, p. 196.
6. *Ibid.,* 590d, 592a–b, pp. 273–75.

Already here, of course, there appears the classical statement about ultimate truth, its "location," and its relation to the actual city. This theme will be found in Augustine, and its resolution is the fundamental contribution of medieval theory. Likewise, the rejection of this position, both as seen in Plato, who did not find the first city anywhere but in his argument, and in Augustine, who distinguished the City of God and the city of man, constitutes the underlying theme of peculiarly modern political philosophy, which, in one way or another, has sought to deny the validity of the classical and Christian positions with regard to the location of the best city.

In Plato, then, political theory at its highest resulted from a knowledge of the speculative order. The mass of men who lived by their senses were incapable of seeing the true order of reality in the separate forms; hence they could not "see" their own true good. *The Republic*, of course, was not a book unconcerned about the highest good of those who were not able to contemplate the Good directly. Their good was seen in the highest good by the philosopher-ruler. The "elitism" so often attributed to Plato had, in its justification, a rigorous concern for the objective, particular good of each member of the best polity. But it is important to note here that revelation later addressed itself especially to this side of *The Republic*, that is, to the final status of those who were individually humans but not philosophers. But it did so concerning not the political status of each citizen but his ultimate status before the Good, whatever his historical polity might be. It is important to observe that the problem is already posed in Plato: the problem of the highest end of each human individual in his particularity, not merely that of the status of the best polity itself.

In *The Republic*, there was thus a need for an individual or philosopher, or a group of men unencumbered by the passions or by economic constraints, who would be able to see the individual good of each person in the best polity. Freed from ordinary cares, these men could penetrate to the order of the real as seen in the Good and in the separate forms. These guardians, following their vision, could then establish a true and perfect political regime based on the order of reality itself, that is, on the order of the separate forms in which the good of each individual existed. The philosophical status of such forms therefore became a primary issue for political philosophy. Plato said in the *Statesman:* "We must train ourselves to give and to understand a *rational* account of every existing thing. For the existents, which are of highest value and chief importance, are demonstrable only by reason and not by any other means. All our present discussions have the aim of training us to apprehend them. For purposes of practice, however, it is easier in every case to work on lesser rather than on greater objects."[7] The true king, then, was one who could see the true order of reality and base his rule on it. His initial capacity to do so, in Plato, did not depend on, but was not impossible in, any existing city. The daimon that guided Socrates did not come from Athens itself, though Socrates was indeed a citizen of that city.

The Platonic theory of separate forms, together with its correlative implications in political theory, also involved a theory of knowledge which is pertinent both to subsequent discussions in Aristotle and to later political philosophy. Plato's main concern always revolved around the instability of sensible things and sense knowledge.[8] The long discussion about knowledge in the *Theaetetus* dealt with the effect of constant change on knowledge.

> *Theaetetus.* "Indeed, Socrates, I cannot answer; my own notion is, that these, unlike objects of sense, have no separate organ, but that the mind, by a power of its own, contemplates the universals in all things."
>
> *Socrates.* "You are a beauty, Theaetetus, and not ugly, as Theodorus was saying; for he who utters the beautiful is himself beautiful and good. And besides being beautiful, you have done me a kindness in releasing me from a very long discussion, if you are clear that the soul views some things by herself and others through the bodily organs. For that was my opinion, and I wanted you to agree with me."[9]

---

7. Plato, *Statesman*, trans. J. B. Skemp (New York, 1957), 50.
8. Plato, *The Republic*, 502–21, pp. 181–200.
9. Plato, *Theaetetus*, 185, trans. B. Jowett (Oxford, 1931), IV, 246.

Statement of the Problem

Plato had what might be called a "purity metaphysics." Things were not mixed in their true essences. They were only what they were. Virtue was only virtue.[10] Justice was only justice. Plato wanted to grasp virtue by itself, not virtue plus justice or courage, for the mixture would make virtue something else.

The implications of this approach are far-reaching. Knowledge meant for Plato discursive knowledge. Yet discursive knowledge could never, as the parable of the syllables in the *Theaetetus* showed, yield the thing to be known, to which the intellectual appetite tends or directs the individual. Discursive knowledge always resulted in a compound, not a simple essence.[11] Knowledge proved to be relational; it did not touch the true reality. But as a result, the ultimate constituents of reality were unknown. How could the known be drawn from a combination of the unknown? And yet, if it could not and cannot, if man must conjecture as to the reality of the constituent elements, does he know anything? Can there be a metaphysics in any sense? The only avenue that was open to Plato was that of intuition, or vision. Man must simply see the ultimate realities with the mind. Thus the knowledge of the Good in *The Republic* seems to be Plato's greatest attempt to cope with the consequence of this initial position.[12] The divine part of man, freed from the uncertainties of sensation and change, simply gazed upon its object and saw there the true order of reality, in the changeless forms.

In Plato, then, the objects of knowledge are already intelligible. They need not be "made" intelligible by some theory of abstraction or agent intellect because they are already separated from matter. "What is that which always is and has no becoming; and what is that which is always becoming and has never any being? That which is apprehended by reflection and reason always is, and is the same; that, on the other hand, which is conceived by opinion with the help of sensation and

---

10. *Ibid.*, 201–202, IV, 268–69. See also Plato, *Timaeus*, 27–28, trans. R. G. Bury (Cambridge, Mass., 1952), 47–53.
11. Plato, *Timaeus*, 27–28.
12. Plato, *The Republic*, 517–19, pp. 195–98.

without reason, is in a process of becoming and perishing but never really is."[13] The effect of this theory of knowledge is that the mind plays no active part in knowledge. It merely separates itself as much as possible from matter so that it can direct its gaze at the true realities. "And while we live, we shall come nearest to knowledge, if we have no communication or intercourse with the body beyond what is absolutely necessary, and if we are not defiled with its nature."[14] This experience of the true realities cannot be achieved by discursive knowledge; it is ineffable.

As a result, realities such as particular men, horses, and trees are of little import, since they constantly change. They are not the proper objects of our attention. According to the *Phaedo:*

> "Do absolute equality, absolute beauty, and every other absolute existence, admit of any change at all? Or does absolute existence in each case, being essentially uniform, remain the same and unchanging, and never in any case admit of any sort or kind of change whatsoever?"
>
> "It must remain the same and unchanging, Socrates," said Cebes.
>
> "And what of the many beautiful things, such as men, and horses, and garments, and the like, and of all which bears the name of ideas, whether equal, or beautiful or anything else? Do they remain the same or is it exactly the opposite with them? In short, do they never remain the same at all, either in themselves or in their relations?"
>
> "These things," said Cebes, "never remain the same."[15]

Thus, somehow this Platonic argument has let slip through its very fingers, as it were, the only realities that are immediately and initially experienced, about which we are ultimately interested. Man is to look for "man-in-himself," not for Socrates, Plato, or Mary, for whom he most seems to care. He is to gaze upon the state-in-itself, the state-writ-large of *The Republic,* not a state made up first of real human beings.[16]

---

13. Plato, *Timaeus,* 27–28, pp. 47–53. See also Plato, *Phaedo,* 78–79, trans. F. J. Church (New York, 1951), 27–28.
14. Plato, *Phaedo,* 67, p. 12.
15. *Ibid.,* 78–79, p. 28.
16. Plato, *The Republic,* 369–83, pp. 45–61.

Socrates in *The Republic* holds not that the private good of each individual is not known or that it is of no account in the polity which he is building in speech. The very nature of the Good is such that it includes the particular good of each individual human being, though this good seems somehow apart from the being whose real good it is. However, since this city in speech does not attain existence, even if it is the only city in which this private good can be stated, it follows that in all existing cities, the ultimate private good of each individual is not reached. From this account, then, the question of the status of each individual member of the polity in his or her particularity is already posed.

Otherwise stated, if the private good of each particular human being is reached in no particular polity, is it impossible as a result to answer this question, arising legitimately from political philosophy? Or should we try to put into existence some polity which can not only look to the good of each individual in his particularity but can also elevate each person so that he has the objective capacities of the philosopher-king? Political philosophy has inherited this question from Plato and has in one sense never moved very far from it. Yet, is it possible to discuss the "best" polity without involving directly, as a political project, its attainment, conceived as the highest end of man as such? In other words, can the classical discussion of good and bad regimes, which can be formed in practice, be carried out as an enterprise for determining the kind of happiness achievable by mortals living in this world, so that it does not include, but does not deny, the issue of another sort of happiness more fundamental to man's purpose? The central task of political philosophy is to answer this question and to answer it authoritatively, that is, in reason.

SENSORY AND THEORETIC KNOWLEDGE IN ARISTOTLE

Aristotle accepted Plato's idea that the forms were discovered or given by nature, but Aristotle located them in things themselves, not in separate forms.[17] As a consequence, Aristotle was willing to admit the

17. Aristotle, *Metaphysics*, VII, 8, 1033b19–34a8, pp. 794–95.

importance of sense knowledge as a bridge to reality. The senses now acquired their own legitimate task in knowledge. Unless they functioned, the human mind could not know. Aristotle continued to assert the primacy of reason rather than the senses. The rule of the intellect over the senses was not, however, "despotic," as in Plato, but "political," because the senses had their own legitimacy in knowledge.[18] Reason naturally ruled over the senses, but the senses must be ruled as powers which have their natural and legitimate functions. The Aristotelian state, then, could admit to its citizenship even men who lived by experience and sense knowledge—ordinary people—for they too had some direct access to the true order of things. Plato did not concede this point because for him true knowledge was not derived from the senses, from an intelligibility grounded in matter, even though matter itself did not create its own limited intelligibility.

But even though Aristotle recognized the need for and validity of sensory knowledge as a conduit to reality, he still remained at one with Plato in admitting the primacy of theoretical knowledge, the knowledge that "cannot be other that it is."[19] Man was not the highest being for Aristotle. Man did not cause himself or all that could be or be known. Since there were realities man could know but which he did not make, the political order could not be the highest order, for it could be otherwise. The political order was under man's free control, but presupposed the existence and being of man himself. And man did not make himself man. Aristotle describes his context:

> It follows that the wise man must not only know what follows from the first principles, but must also possess the truth about the first principles. Therefore, wisdom must be intuitive reason combined with scientific knowledge—scientific knowledge of the highest objects, which has received, as it were, its proper completion.
>
> Of the highest objects, we say, for it would be strange to think that the art of politics, or practical wisdom, is the best knowledge, since man is not the best thing in the world. . . .

---

18. Aristotle, *De anima*, III, 7, 431a1–b19, pp. 593–95; *Politics*, I, 4, 1254b1–36, pp. 1132–33, VII, 14, 1333a17–b11, pp. 1297–98.
19. Aristotle, *Posterior Analytics*, I, 1, 71b15, p. 111.

> Practical wisdom, on the other hand, is concerned with things human and things about which it is possible to deliberate, for we say this is above all the work of the man of practical reason, to deliberate well, but no one deliberates about things invariable, nor about things which have not an end.[20]

The political authority, therefore, could not presume to be the criterion of the theoretic order.

Man was free from the political order, then, in all things that pertained to the theoretic sciences. Mathematical, philosophical, and moral truths were consequently valid independent of the political society, though they might need a politcal order which allows them to be thought about. Man was free because he knew, in his individual being, truths that were beyond the political realm. As Charles N. R. McCoy asked, "Can we fail to be startled by the oversights of the histories of political thought when we consider that it was Aristotle who, reputed to have submerged the individual to the *polis,* insisted on a wisdom for man higher than that of the state; and that among the Romans, reputed to have engendered a doctrine of salvaging the individual man, political science and prudence came to hold the highest place?"[21] The legitimate polity was one built on these truths that existed independently of its structure, although not necessarily alien to it, except when the political structure presumed specifically to deny them in its laws. To make man the highest being—that is, the being obliged to no order but his own—therefore logically enslaved man to the actual political order or to the proposed order to be brought into existence by gradual or revolutionary means, but one with no further criterion of the good but itself.

Since Aristotle had admitted the validity of sense knowledge as a necessary means through which man must grasp the nature and meaning of the theoretic order, which man discovers but does not make, he denied that the objects of the senses were mere reflections or images of

---

20. Aristotle, *Nicomachean Ethics,* VI, 7, 1141a18–23 to 1141b8–12, p. 1028.
21. Charles N. R. McCoy, "The Turning Point in Political Philosophy," *American Political Science Review,* XLVI (September, 1950), 684.

true reality. They were themselves realities, substances, even though they were not the complete causes of what they were. Aristotle hierarchized the objects of sensible reality according to the degree to which each manifested activity.[22] This hierarchy arose from observation and from the analysis of data supplied by the senses and was not deducted from a theoretic order of separate, logical forms. Aristotelian theory was able to recognize the activity of man in forming the political community as the highest type of activity naturally open to a being containing matter in its essence. This was the highest good because it produced a good of the highest quality and extent, the common good, and because it was the highest and most direct spiritual influence on matter as such, existing within the very human body. Thus, if men were the highest beings in reality, politics would be the highest good.[23] In one very real sense, specifically "modern" political philosophy is an effort to carry out this project, already foreseen in some way in Aristotle, of what it means to "make" man the highest being, when this being is presupposed to no order not under his control.

But because Aristotle himself recognized the primacy of the theoretic sciences, a recognition based on the view that the multiplicity of existing beings is not in fact and could not even in imagination be brought into being by human art, he maintained that politics was a proper and necessary activity of man, though not the highest or the best. Man was free only if he recognized his dependence on the theoretic order, even though Aristotle, long before, say, Marx, acknowledged man's continual temptation to free himself from this dependence. "Evidently, we do not seek it [metaphysics]," Aristotle remarked, "for the sake of any other advantage but as the man is free, we say, who exists for his own sake and not for another's, so we pursue this as the only free science, for it alone exists for its own sake. Hence also the possession of it might justly be regarded as beyond human power; for in

---

22. Aristotle, *De anima*, II, 5, 416b32–418a6, pp. 564–67. See also Aristotle, *Posterior Analytics*, II, 19, 100a4–9, p. 185.
23. Aristotle, *Nicomachean Ethics*, VI, 7, 1141a16–25, p. 1028.

Statement of the Problem

many ways human nature is in bondage, so that according to Simonides, 'God alone can have this privilege,' and it is unfitting that man should not be content to seek the knowledge that is suited to him."[24] "What man is" and "What politics are" are facts of the theoretic order, which man finds but does not make. Man's political life, then, is an activity with ends fixed by nature but with means chosen by will and the experience of what man is and does. This argument of course asserts that reason indicates a cause of being higher than human intelligence, so that it is reasonable for man to be and to remain man.

In this respect, therefore, art differs from politics. The artist is free to establish his ends and goals. The politician creates only the means, since the ends are fixed by whatever established the theoretic order, though these same ends are to be understood as "reasonable" and are therefore not "imposed" on man.[25] Aristotle thus placed the theoretic sciences over the practical sciences in order to acknowledge the relation of truth to both. Within the practical sciences, he distinguished art from morals and politics because the ends of morals and politics are fixed by nature. Freedom, then, is not an absolute in Aristotle in the sense that man can construe the moral and political worlds wholly as he wishes, wholly as an artist can deal with his matter. In many areas, man can indeed do as he wills in the sense of "possibility" but not in the sense of "ought," in the sense of his understanding of what he is. Man is to understand what he is. He is freely to recognize this fact which he discovers as a truth best for him and the risk it involves. At this point, revelation likewise addresses man's intelligence, itself already having reached the question about the status of his being, its autonomy or its having been given. This reflection, at its best, reaches the suspicion that man's being as such is better than man could propose for himself. This is the metaphysical root about the precise nature of specifically "modern" political philosophy.

24. Aristotle, *Metaphysics*, I, 2, 982b28–32, p. 692. See Thomas Aquinas, *Summa contra Gentiles* (Rome, 1934), I, 5, pp. 4–5. See also Charles N. R. McCoy, "Ludwig Feuerbach and the Formation of the Marxist Revolutionary Idea," *Laval Théologique et Philosophique*, VII, No. 2 (1951), 219–20.

25. Aristotle, *Nicomachean Ethics*, II, 4, 1105a27–b4, p. 956, VI, 4, 1140a1–23, pp. 1025–26.

Behind this conclusion of Aristotle's lay a whole metaphysics and theory of knowledge with a vital place in our understanding of the foundation of political philosophy and how it developed. Real things for Aristotle were not the ideas or forms of man or animal but Socrates and Fido. Even here, though, it must be recognized that Aristotle always retained something of the truth of the Platonic view. For if he made the forms too much implicated in and individuated by matter, it would be difficult to admit anything like a common species or to admit any difference between kinds of things in reality. One step more would have placed Aristotle in nominalism, and that step was actually taken in the later medieval era. Too, Aristotle always needed an individual around to bear the forms. For this reason, perhaps, he was inclined to hold that there was no creation but an eternity of individuals. Aristotle was certainly not illogical in holding this view, but again here, revelation proposed a different, and again not illogical, sort of answer to problems he understood well enough. The individual, in Aristotle, thus seems to be something to ground forms more than a unique supposit, though Aristotle did not hesitate to recognize the centrality of each existing being.

Aristotle recognized a common notion of undifferentiated being that first falls in the intellect. His example of how all children first call every man "father" was meant to illustrate this point. But this undifferentiated type of being was not held by Aristotle to be more "real" than the men themselves.[26] If, however, we reverse the primacy of the real order over the logical order, then the abstractions of logic—man, dog, and substance—will acquire more "reality" than the substantial entities we experience through the senses. Ultimately, Plato seemed to have been bringing about such a reversal. For this reason, he could find more reality in man-in-himself, a separate form, than in Socrates and Callias.[27]

---

26. Aristotle, *Categories*, V, 2a11–18, p. 9, V, 2a33–b1, p. 9; *De interpretatione*, VII, 17a38–40, p. 453; *Posterior Analytics*, II, 19, 100a9–11, p. 185.

27. See Charles N. R. McCoy, "The Logical and the Real in Political Theory: Plato, Aristotle, and Marx," *American Political Science Review*, XLVIII (December, 1954), 1054–61.

For Aristotle, there are three types of "unlimited" realities. Two of them belong to the real order, and one to the logical order. In the real order, the Unmoved Mover is unlimited in the positive sense. That is, it possesses all perfections and requires nothing. Prime matter, on the other hand, equally belongs to the real order, but it does not have any positive perfection of its own.[28] It is pure potency opposed to the pure actuality of the Prime Mover. In the logical order, the common notion of being, that undifferentiated predicate which can be attached to all that is, likewise contains no differentiation. Much of later Western political philosophy will center on these three "realities," the kind of being we ought to attribute to the state and to the person. Consequently, it is well at this point to indicate how they fit into Aristotelian thought.

Aristotle maintained the autonomy of lesser social groups in political society. He did not absorb them into the state because, for him, the state was not a pure separate form which was only itself. Rather it was a community of actually living individuals, families, and villages. The order of the common good, in Plato, resulted from an intuition regarding the true reality on the part of the philosopher-king or the guardians. The dynamism behind this view to some degree explained Plato's endeavor to eradicate the actual entities such as the family and the village in his ideal Republic, since they interfered with the perfect unity of the ideal state. The unity desired was one of unanimity or sameness, as Aristotle pointed out.[29] This unity tended to take for its model logical being, not real being.

For Aristotle, the notion of the political task derived from his theory regarding the relation of the speculative orders and the practical. To say so is not to maintain that Aristotle "deduced" politics from some a priori presupposition but to indicate Aristotle's ultimate insight into its meaning and validity. Aristotle placed the contemplative life over the practical life, but he also held that the political life was itself a worthwhile life, though not the highest. Plato, in *The Laws*,

28. Aristotle, *Metaphysics*, VII, 3, 1029a19–26, p. 785.
29. Aristotle, *Politics*, II, 2, 126a10–b15, pp. 1146–47.

had also maintained that the vision of the Good was the highest end for man, but it somehow blinded him to a full appreciation of the more mundane tasks. Aristotle stayed primarily in the real order, not the logical, so that, for Aristotle, the First Mover, as final cause, extended to things in their differences, which, to be sure, was what the philosopher-king saw in the Good. The common good was not conceived after the manner of the logical or common notion of being as we know it in intellection, a notion which absorbs all distinctions. Rather the conception of the common good extends to the real order in its differences. Natural distinctions were formed by whatever formed the real order itself, to which the human intellect and human action were open, but were not formative of it in the first place.[30] Furthermore, the polity itself was not some abstraction or mental construct but concerned real, active relations among substantially existing human beings and what they touch with their activities.

The problem of political philosophy, again, is to understand itself, its own intellectual limits, without denying philosophy to the political philosopher himself. But each of these words is important. Political philosophy is "limited" in the sense that it is not itself a total explanation of reality. In other words, political philosophy is open to that which explains reality more fully than itself even in order to explain itself. But furthermore, politics, the actions of men in community in this world, though they do not form some sort of "super-being," are themselves real, themselves worthy of existence and study. Political philosophy to be itself, then, will have to know philosophy and to know what is addressed to human reason.

The human being who is by nature political, as Aristotle maintained, is a whole. It is not as though the questions addressed by the philosopher or presented to reason by revelation are somehow completely alien to the ordinary politician or citizen. There is in fact no theoretic reason why the politician cannot also be one who contemplates, however difficult it is in practice to have the time and energy

---

30. Aristotle, *Metaphysics,* XII, 10, 1075a1–23, pp. 885–86.

to do so, however much individual capacities for contemplation do objectively differ. The division of labor of which Plato spoke in *The Republic,* however necessary, was not intended to suggest that the knowledge of what each individual is in the Good was not really *his* knowledge or not really *his* good. That is to say, philosophy touched every member of the polity.

For Aristotle too, the metaphysician was not some other sort of being, not human at all, even though the knowledge of ultimate reality was difficult to attain, because, in its clarity, it approached the 'divine'. But without this effort to know what could be known, which is the natural tendency of the human mind in any case, politics can easily become a substitute intelligence which claims power and authority to explain *all that is*. The problem of political philosophy, then, is both to see how this latter claim has arisen and worked itself out in the history of political philosophy and to see how politics, by limiting itself to what it legitimately is, fulfills its own purposes and protects what is not itself. The crucial role of political philosophy in particular in intellectual history is that it is necessary to provide a careful, reasoned rationale for allowing politics to do what politics can do. At the same time, political philosophy does not deny to the other realities to which man is open—the same man who lives in the city—their claims on his intelligence about the meaning of everything, of *all that is*.

2
ARISTOTELIAN POLITICAL THEORY: IMMORTALITY AND HAPPINESS

Political philosophy has certain basic foundations without which politics tends to become a metaphysics, an all-embracing grasp and construction of *what is*. For Aristotle, politics, as it is actually lived, is not metaphysics, though it normally requires an orientation from the theoretic sciences to retain its relative autonomy. In the history of philosophy, a progressive denial of certain basic elements in Aristotle's theory (especially the function of the First Mover in nature, the relation between the logical and real orders, and the natural distinction in things) has been the main cause of the modern tendency to place all theoretic conclusions under some political or social authority which needs no correction from the theoretic sciences.

Aristotle's remark that, if man were the highest being, politics would be the highest science (*Ethics,* 1141a20–22), seems in retrospect a sort of map of modern intellectual history. For there is a widespread belief, implicit or explicit, that man is the highest being or that there is nothing higher than he is, by which he himself is addressed, either in nature or in revelation. What is decided by or put into effect by politics *is* the highest reality as such, in spite of nature. And to prove this point, nature must be actively overcome and replaced by man presupposed only to himself.

As a result, the political theory of the modern era has attempted to replace Aristotle's metaphysical analysis of the common good of the universe as a good penetrating to all creatures in their very being and distinctiveness to be legitimately what they are. In its stead modern theory offers this logical analysis, which sees primary being as the common being of predication which absorbs all distinction. Indeed, this modern adaptation of the logical idea of being has considered all natural distinction, even heredity and talent, as an "alienation" imposed upon men from outside themselves. This is the basis for the modern attack on classic natural law and order, with the shift in emphasis from law to "human rights," themselves presupposed to nothing but man's own self-definition. Man's reality must be taken not from the highest faculties but from the lowest instincts, which are to be formed into a new being which only includes ends exclusively fashioned by man from his own resources.

For this reason, too, Aristotle's notion that the ends in ethics and politics are to be compared to mathematical axioms, not final causes in nature, is very important. "For virtue and vice respectively preserve and destroy the first principle, and in actions the final cause is the first principle, as the hypotheses are in mathematics; neither in that case is it argument that teaches the first principles, nor is it so here."[1] For if the ends of man's being are to be discovered as given, then ethical and political truth consists in discovering what man is, not in what he makes himself to be, presupposed to no idea of himself in which there is already indicated his own real good. If he has no purpose or end, then the opposite of any value or dignity in mankind is itself equally thinkable and possible. The "reconstruction" of man, in this latter thesis, becomes almost a moral and intellectual imperative.

Within Aristotle's ethical and political discussions, the question of the nature of human happiness arose. Socrates had already demonstrated that immortality could lead to calmness in the face of death by the *polis* as well as provide grounds for judgments about its errors. Likewise, attention to truth itself brought up the question of whether anyone interested in truth could survive in any actual city. Socrates' death formed both Plato and Plato's pupil, Aristotle. Aristotle said once that he left Athens because he did not want it to be guilty of the death of Socrates a second time. The relation of the Greek teaching on immortality to polity, likewise, must be seen as an aspect of the problem of human happiness, treated by both *The Republic* and *The Ethics*.

The question is not merely obscure or esoteric. Later revolutionary

---

1. Aristotle, *Nicomachean Ethics*, VII, 8, 1151a15–18, p. 1050. See also *Physics*, II, 9, 200a15–25, p. 252.

political theories, in their philosophical comprehension, were direct intellectual results of the denial of a personal immortality in political and metaphysical theory. The denial of individual immortality has almost invariably given rise to an alternative collective "immortality," to which the individual is subordinated as part to whole. The individual becomes merely a memory or a monument of a glory within the *polis,* not an abiding entity also for its own sake. These latter two ideas—fame and individual abidingness—need not necessarily be contradictory, of course, though they often appear to be. Understanding the implications of this relationship is one of the major tasks in elaborating the foundations of political philosophy.

The relationship between the denial of immortality and revolutionary theory, moreover, pertains in its intelligibility to a confusion between the logical and the real orders. For later philosophy was to conceive primary being after the being of common predication (see below, Chapter 7). This notion of being tended to absorb all distinctions into itself so that "is" could be said indiscriminately, without attending to the differing forms that analogously activate the actual beings of reality. When being is conceived in this manner, any distinction in perfection or natural (or supernatural) gift will be felt as imposed from without by an essentially nonreal or nonhuman force. When the function of the First Mover in nature is denied to be the cause in some sense of the distinction of things whose ends are intended to be this or that, the natural distinctions lose their objective meaning, itself hypothetical to the workings of an intelligence but not human intelligence. The dynamic of this abstract, logical being is found to be against the actual distinctions and substances discovered to be given (and to be good) in existence.

What man is, then, was regarded as a challenge to man's own autonomy. Translated into the framework of political theory, the task of politics came to mean the attempt, not to make men "good," as Aristotle held, but rather to impel man to "refashion" himself. This refashioning was independent of the need to recognize, by the valid use of this individual intelligence, something outside his own control and making but something still addressed to him as good, indeed as his particular good, the good of his very existence, open to what he is not.

Ernst Cassirer observed that "one of the principal aims of Darwin's work was to free modern thought from this illusion of final causes."[2] This "illusion of final causes" is, of course, as Cassirer indicated, deeply rooted in Aristotle, for whom "evolution" was not apart from final causes in nature.[3] For Aristotle, the lower forms needed to be understood in terms of the higher, whereas modern theory purports to deal with change in terms of chance, as if something literally came from nothing. This latter position undermined the natural forms and the action of the First Mover in nature. All became one. "The human soul," Aristotle had said, "is in a way all existing things."[4] Reality, however, conceived on the model of logical being, tended to merge into a oneness that did not bear any definite separation or distinction in things. "The theory of evolution had destroyed the arbitrary limits between the different forms of organic life. There are no separate species; there is just one continuous and uninterrupted stream of life."[5] Man's claim to uniqueness in the universe, his identity as the *political* being, was thus jeopardized. He was merely another organism, higher perhaps than the others but not essentially different. He was therefore free to refashion all in his own image because no limits existed.

The basis of the Aristotelian view was teleology. That is, form or essence has a purpose in being the way it is. But if nature cannot support this teleology, where did it come from? "The teleological character of human life is projected upon the whole realm of natural phenomena." Ideas of God, immortality, order, and purpose are myths or projections of human desires and experiences. In particular, no natural purpose or stability made human nature as it is. It is intrinsically malleable. But through language, history, and science, man could gradu-

---

2. Ernst Cassirer, *An Essay on Man* (Garden City, N.Y., 1944), 36.
3. See Etienne Gilson, *God and Philosophy* (New Haven, 1941), Chap. 4. See also Leo Strauss, "Progress or Return? The Contemporary Crisis in Western Civilization," *Modern Judaism*, I (1981), 17–45.
4. Aristotle, *De anima*, III, 8, 431b21–22, p. 595.
5. Cassirer, *An Essay on Man*, 38.

ally make himself to be what he was and wanted to be. "Know thyself" came to mean a type of social knowledge which did not depend on an extrinsic cause. "Man is no longer considered as a simple substance which exists in itself and is to be known by itself."[6]

Man can pass along his own experience by language, myth, and history. Thus he can perpetuate his individual life as the animals cannot. "The various modes of this expression constitute a new sphere. They have a life of their own, a sort of eternity by which they survive man's individual and ephemeral existence." Seen from this aspect, man does survive. But this survival has two aspects—the scientific content of his thought and his artistic or personal expression. Shakespeare and Goethe leave what was uniquely theirs. But "in the objective content of science, these individual features are forgotten and effaced, for one of the principal aims of scientific thought is the elimination of our personal and anthropomorphic elements."[7]

Consequently, man's major task in life is to free himself from alien doctrines and myths which restrict and confine him, so that by experiment, science, and language he can construct his own world freed from any need of a maker outside himself. "Human culture taken as a whole may be described as the process of man's progressive self-liberation. Language, art, religion, science, are various phases in the process. In all of these man discovers and proves a new power—the power to build up a world of his own, an 'ideal' world."[8] Such has been the goal and result of the effort to replace the Prime Mover in nature by man as the cause of natural distinctions.

HUMAN AND DIVINE ACTIVITY

Cassirer's analysis placed Aristotle's theories in a new light. For Aristotle, man's final task was not "self-liberation," not exclusively the construction of his own world, however much politics was legitimate. Nor was the teleology of nature merely an anthropomorphic construc-

6. *Ibid.*, 35, 279.
7. *Ibid.*, 281, 285–86.
8. *Ibid.*, p. 286. See also Karl Popper, *The Unended Quest* (London, 1979).

tion.⁹ Things did happen always or for the most part in the same way in nature. The natural species were not all the same. Similarity of anatomical or behavioral patterns did not automatically fuse all species into one so that in time one became the other. The distinction of substances reflected the perfection, not a defect, of nature. The higher forms were not merely reducible to their lower elements. Things manifested a real existential difference.

Moreover, man occupied a unique place in the cosmos. He was the only creature able to vary his artifacts. He was not bound to one pattern. He could understand universally. Furthermore, he was connected with all of physical reality because each material thing could stimulate him to knowledge as well as contribute to the sustenance of his physical being. Indeed, without a particular physical thing, he could not begin to think at all. Without physical objects, he could not know. And what he knew was not just himself. Somehow he was a "microcosmos." In him the physical, vegetative, animal, and rational activities seemed to coalesce and attain their meaning, which did not consist simply in collapsing all things into each other. Man did not impose intelligibility on things; they imposed it on him. Yet he had a power to receive them in a higher mode. By knowing reality he changed, not it, but only himself to a higher grade of perfection. The order and regularity of nature were simply there. They were not merely projections of man's own finalizing tendencies, which originated in this desire to make or explain. For Aristotle, then, all of nature betrayed finality. In a famous passage he wrote:

> The acts in which it [the nutritive soul] manifests itself are reproduction and the use of food—reproduction, I say, because for any living thing that has reached its normal development and which is unmutilated and whose mode of generation is not spontaneous, the most natural act is the reproduction of another like itself, an animal producing an animal, a plant a plant, in order that, as far as its nature allows, it

9. See E. F. Schumacher, *A Guide for the Perplexed* (New York, 1977); Stanley Jaki, *The Road of Science and the Ways to God* (Chicago, 1978); Raymond Dennehy, *Reason and Dignity* (Lanham, Md., 1981).

may partake in the eternal and divine. This is the goal towards which all things strive, that for the sake of which they do whatsoever their nature renders possible. . . . Since then no living thing is able to partake in what is eternal and divine by uninterrupted continuance (for nothing perishable can forever remain one and the same), it tries to achieve that end in the only way possible to it, and success is possible in varying degrees, so it remains not indeed as the self-same individual but continues its existence in something like itself—not numerically, but specifically one.[10]

What is to be noted, consequently, is that already here Aristotle has at least raised the question about the possibility of participation in the divine in some sense while still remaining human as well as the question of the numerical continuity of each individual. At the natural level he apparently saw no solutions. And this finality was itself an imitation of and a tendency toward the extrinsic common good of the universe. Aristotle was very existential here. He saw in nature natural tendencies which operate apart from man. Aristotle, too, saw a tendency to imitate and reach the Final Good in all of nature because all of nature's existence is hypothetical. That is, each being is as it is for a reason that lies outside the being itself. By itself, it need not be. Consequently, everything imitates the divine after the only manner open to it. This doctrine of the *De anima* forms the very basis of Aristotelian ethics and politics. Man is no exception to the law of nature. Reproduction of man by man on its physical side is an endeavor to imitate the divine, insofar as possible. It is a form of immortality. But man also has another way to imitate the divine. Man's nature allows more than the animal's.

In Aristotle's view, two specific types of life are open to man, the life of contemplation and the life of action. These two types of life are both imitations of the divine and are related as means to end. But the life of activity is more than simply a tool for Aristotle. Both lives reflect the same reality in differing ways. Politics, the active life, possesses its own dignity and legitimacy because it does reflect something

---

10. Aristotle, *De anima*, II, 4, 415a25–b8, p. 561.

of ultimate reality. Of these two types of life, one is "properly" human, the life of politics. Politics is the one type of life that is unique to existing human beings. It is something above the animals and below the separated substances. Even the family for Aristotle still retained much of its animal origin and is not the properly human life, though it is necessary for human life, so that it needs to be protected for what it is. "In the first place," Aristotle wrote, "there must be a union of those who cannot exist without each other; namely, of male and female, that the race may continue and this is a union which is formed, not of deliberate purpose, but because, in common with other animals and with plants, mankind have a natural desire to leave behind them an image of themselves."[11]

But although man has his own unique activity, proper to him, it is still Aristotle's consistent doctrine that, although politics is man's proper life, the highest life open to him is the contemplative life. This life is in a way beyond his capacities and in any case is proper to only part of man, the rational soul, which, however, remains, for Aristotle, the form of the body.[12] This conclusion rests on the following three doctrines of Aristotle: 1) all beings strive to perpetuate themselves as much as possible, according to their own peculiar mode or grade of reality; 2) even though man's highest act is contemplative, his peculiar activity, that which distinguishes him from all the rest of reality, is politics; 3) the placing of an "order of parts" in the universe is a function of the First Mover which is not primarily contemplative and is therefore not peculiarly His. The First Mover's primary activity is to "think himself." Therefore, if man in contemplation imitates that activity of the First Mover, which is peculiarly His and not man's, then the only activity of the First Mover in the universe that man can imitate, which will correspond to man's own peculiar nature, will be the ordering of that life which is singularly man's, the political life.[13]

11. Aristotle, *Politics*, I, 2, 1252a26–31, pp. 1127–28.
12. Aristotle, *Nicomachean Ethics*, VI, 13, 1145a8–12, p. 1036, X, 7, 1177b26–78a8, p. 1105; *Metaphysics*, I, 2, 982b28–83a11, pp. 692–93.
13. (1) See Aristotle, *Politics*, I, 2, 1252a26–31, pp. 1127–28; *De anima*, II, 4, 415a25–b8, p. 561; (2) *Nichomachean Ethics*, X, 7, 1177b26–78b7, pp. 1105–1106; (3) *Metaphysics*, XII,

Political life therefore imitates the First Mover in the line of the First Mover's placing hypothetical necessity and order in nature. "Bonum est diffusivum sui"—good is diffusive of itself, after the manner of a final cause. That is, the good of one thing, even the First Mover, does not take away the possibility of other goods imitative or reflective of it but good in themselves. What is good does not necessarily exist except that good of the First Mover, which is itself. Finiteness does not exhaust substance.

Although this imitation of putting order in things is a great good and includes the order of society, which is the proper good that belongs to the being man in his free actions, it is not the highest good even for man. The highest human good for Aristotle is to be found in the internal life of God, in Thought thinking on itself.

> And thought thinks on itself because it shares the nature of the object of thought; for it becomes an object of thought in coming into contact with the thinking its objects, so that thought and object of thought are the same. For that which is capable of receiving the object of thought, i.e., the essence, is thought. Therefore, the possession rather than the receptivity is the divine element which thought seems to contain, and the act of contemplation is what is most pleasant and best.
>
> If, then, God is always in that good state in which we sometimes are, this compels our wonder; and if in a better state this compels us yet more. And God is in that better state. And life also belongs to God; for the actuality of thought is life, and God is that actuality; and God's self-dependent actuality is life most good and eternal. We say, therefore, that God is a living being, eternal, most good, so that life and duration, continuous and eternal being belong to God; for this is God.[14]

This most famous passage in Aristotle is the foundation for his notion that man's contemplative life is also primary for him. Man is to "wonder" because of the fullness and completeness of God, full substance

---

10, 1075a12–23, pp. 885–86, XII, 7, 1072b13–29, p. 880; *Nicomachean Ethics*, X, 7, 1177b26–78b7, pp. 1105–1106.

14. Aristotle, *Metaphysics*, XII, 7, 1072b19–29, p. 880.

and being, as well as the fullness of the cosmos itself. "Therefore the activity of God, which surpasses all others in blessedness, must be contemplative; and of human activities, therefore, that which is most akin to this must be most of the nature of happiness."[15]

The contemplative life, then, is superior because it imitates, in its own way, the divine after the manner of the divine's own self-activity, which is union with thinking itself.[16] For this reason the notion of unity as a relation to an actuality prevented Aristotle from ever falling into a logicizing which would absorb the being that contemplates the divine into the divine itself, which is the perennial temptation of Platonism and neo-Platonism. "Unity has many senses (as many as 'is' has), but the most proper and fundamental sense of both is the relation of an actuality to that of which it is the actuality."[17]

Contemplation is thus a perfect appreciation of *what is,* both in man and in God. Contemplation in man can achieve only the limited perfection due to a being whose good is not to become itself God. Both logically and actually, contemplation comes before making or creating or doing, without denying the worth of any of these because substance lies before the activity of substances. Thus for Aristotle the goal of human endeavor is not "self-liberation" and self-construction of reality. Reality is, in its most complete sense, *given,* though Aristotle did hold that there is a great task of liberation and construction open for man in morals, art, and politics.[18] But this contention "adds" not to Aristotle's divinity but rather to the happiness of those who contemplate *what is,* that is, rational creatures.

Aristotle was constantly concerned, then, to preserve man's capacity to leave himself open to the highest things, even though these seemed

---

15. Aristotle, *Nicomachean Ethics,* X, 8, 1178b22–23, p. 1107. See also VI, 13, 1145a7–12, p. 1035.
16. This is another point at which philosophy and revelation meet in the context of political philosophy. That is, what is the nature of the internal life of the First Mover or God? Is it as "solitary" as it appears, and how does philosophy think on it? See James V. Schall, "The Trinity: God Is Not Alone," in *Redeeming the Time* (New York, 1968), Chap. 3.
17. Aristotle, *De anima,* II, 1, 412b8–9, p. 555.
18. "We can contemplate our neighbors better than ourselves and their actions better than our own" (Aristotle, *Nicomachean Ethics,* IX, 9, 1169b34–35, p. 1089).

most difficult to attain. He believed that this difficulty should result not in despair but rather in some hope of learning a higher wisdom. In this sense, he left man open to receive, with a metaphysical openness in the highest things which could not be replaced by politics, however legitimate politics remained for Aristotle. In Book X of *The Ethics,* thus, Aristotle acknowledged the greatness of military and political actions but ranked them lower than the activity of reason, which was self-sufficient, and the location of "the complete happiness of man" if he is given a full life.

> But such a life would be too high for man; for it is not in so far as he is man that he will live so, but insofar as something divine is present in him; and by so much as this is superior to our composite nature is its activity superior to that which is the exercise of the other kind of virtue. If reason is divine, then, in comparison with man, the life according to it is divine in comparison with human life. But we must not follow those who advise us, being men, to think of human things, and, being mortal, of mortal things, but must, so far as we can, make ourselves immortal, and strain every nerve to live in accordance with the best thing in us; for even if it be small in bulk, much more does it in power and worth surpass everything. This would seem, too, to be each man himself, since it is the authoritative and better part of him. It would be strange, then, if he were to choose not the life of his self but that of something else. And what we said before [1169b33; 1176b26] will apply now; that which is proper to each thing is by nature best and most pleasant for each thing; for men, therefore, the life according to reason is best and pleasantest, since reason more than anything else is man. This life therefore is also the happiest.[19]

The program outlined here by Aristotle is the ultimate basis for the defense of the human against the philosophical, political, or religious movements that would radically change it, and would make it, as Aristotle understood, into something less noble and elevating.

---

19. *Ibid.,* X, 7, 1177b16–78a8, p. 1105. Again it is worth noting that the notion that reason is "man," the philosophical position, constitutes the exact point at which revelation is addressed to human intelligence, which can understand that individual man includes more than reason.

HAPPINESS

If man's highest activity is contemplation, the activity of the best in him, then, and if all of man's actions, in some sense, imitate the Divine Activity, the central place of the meaning of happiness in Aristotle's ethical and political theory will be readily understood. "Everything that we choose," Aristotle observed, "we choose for the sake of something else—except happiness, which is an end."[20] What is the full content and condition of happiness in Aristotle? Aristotle's discussion of happiness is found primarily in the first and tenth books of *The Ethics*. This fact has been unfortunate in a certain sense, since there is a tendency to believe as a result that the discussion of happiness is more or less irrelevant to *The Politics*, however much the tenth book is directly a transition to *The Politics*. But this view fails to take into account the way in which Aristotle related happiness to politics. To see this point more clearly, then, the elements that constitute Aristotle's definition of happiness must be drawn out.

Aristotle began his discussion with the empirically based observation that all art, inquiry, and action strive for some good but that there is a difference between goods. Some are for themselves, some for others. If everything is done for an end, and if there can be no infinite regress, since that would deny a first and therefore a present, some good must be the chief good and must have the greatest influence on us. The close connection between this final good and politics was immediately noted by Aristotle. Politics uses all other sciences, rhetoric, and strategy. Therefore, "since politics uses the rest of the sciences, and since, again, it legislates what we are to do and what we are to abstain from, the end of this science must include those of the others so that this end must be the good for man."[21] And it is more "god-

---

20. Aristotle, *Nicomachean Ethics*, X, 6, 1176b30–32, p. 1103.
21. *Ibid.*, I, 1, 1094a1–24, p. 935; I, 2, 1094b5, p. 936. See also I, 7, 1097a24–35, p. 941. We should recall, however, that for Aristotle mathematics and metaphysics are, as such, beyond the order of politics, which derives its final causes from nature, fixed there in relation to the First Mover, not by man. That is, as Aristotle said, man does not make himself man: "For . . . political science does not make men, but takes them from nature" (Aristotle, *Politics*, I, 10, 1258a21–22, p. 1140).

like" to attain this good for a group or for a state than for oneself, since this is the imitation of the First Mover in its relation to the "order of parts" in the universe.[22]

But Aristotle did not say that politics is the highest good. Rather, it is concerned with the "highest of all goods achievable by action."[23] Contemplation is beyond action and is the end of action. Action, in fact, can itself be contemplated because it is the act of an existing substance. From this context of action, Aristotle proceeded to identify several elements of the definition of happiness by excluding various types of life as the adequate context of happiness. Thus, money making is thought by some to be happiness but lacks the notion of finality. Money is always for the sake of something else, though there is a kind of infinity to money making, since it portends the means of fulfilling all one's desires.[24] This latter quality leads some to confuse money making with happiness.

Others, however, hold pleasures to be happiness. But pleasure as such, while good, is always something that accompanies activity and acquires its goodness or badness from the type of activity performed. However, pleasure, like contemplation, does have the character of being for itself, of being an end. As a result many confuse it with true happiness, but this attribute suggests why happiness and pleasure may be confused.[25]

Happiness, then, has the character of being for an end, the highest end. It is also self-sufficient, needing nothing else, since it would otherwise be insecure. "Happiness, then, is something final and self-sufficient, and is the end of action." Moreover, Aristotle insisted that the action be that which makes man unique. "Presumably, however, to say that happiness is the chief good seems a platitude," Aristotle wrote,

---

22. Aristotle, *Nicomachean Ethics*, I, 2, 1094b7–10, p. 936; *Metaphysics*, XII, 10, 1075a12–23, pp. 885–86.
23. Aristotle, *Nicomachean Ethics*, I, 4, 1095a15–16, p. 937.
24. *Ibid.*, I, 5, 1096a5–10, p. 939.
25. *Ibid.*, I, 5, 1095b14–22, p. 938, X, 2–5, 1172b9–76a29, pp. 1094–1102.

and a clearer account of what it is, is still desired. This might perhaps be given, if we would first ascertain the function of man. For just as a flute-player, a sculptor, or any artist, and, in general, for all things that have a function or activity, the good and the 'well' is thought to reside in the function, so would it seem to be for man, if he has a function. Have the carpenter, then, and the tanner certain functions or activities, and has man none? Is he born without a function? Or as eye, hand, foot, and in general each of the parts evidently has a function, may one lay it down that man similarly has a function apart from all of these?

Animals and plants are not said to be happy. The life of the mind is man's highest activity. The rational principle itself, however, is divided in the sense that one part obeys reason (the senses) and the other part rules. "There remains, then, an active life of the element that has a rational principle; of this, one part has such a principle in the sense of being obedient to one, the other in the sense of possessing one and exercising thought."[26] The ruling principle is, of course, the higher. To these qualities, Aristotle added "in a complete life" to avoid saying that happiness is only for a short time or by chance.[27]

The virtue of courage, moreover, addressed the problem of how a short life might reach the highest good by not sacrificing particular goods to keep to life at whatever cost. Aristotle rejected the life of pleasure as happiness, since pleasure is common to both man and animals, whereas happiness refers to the proper good of man. The civic or public life is held to be a true good, but it is itself subordinate to the contemplative life. Happiness, then, is the activity of a man for the highest, self-sufficient, and final end in a complete life.

Aristotle used the analogy of the lyre player and the good lyre player to bring out the *genus* and *differentia* of the definition. Just as the proper function of lyre playing and the good playing of the lyre are in the same kind of activity, so the proper function of man and his good functioning are in the same activity. The function of a thing is

26. *Ibid.*, I, 7, 1097b21–34; 1098a2–5, p. 942.
27. *Ibid.*, I, 7–9, 1098a18–1100a4, pp. 943–46.

what makes it unique, what it is, its form. Man's form is rational animal. Therefore, the genus of the definition of happiness is: activity of the soul according to reason. The differentia has two aspects. The first is that which good adds to simple activity. The second lies in the desire that this good activity be continuous. These, then, are the essential elements in Aristotle's definition.

However, this definition contains several obscurities over which later political theory will be greatly perplexed. First of all, Aristotle's discussion is confusing. It is never quite clear whether he is discussing happiness that is open to mortal man in this life or, in addition, happiness in an absolute sense. In other words, is "continuous" life really "continuous"? This element in political philosophy is important, since Aristotle seemed to limit his political life as such to goals attainable in this life. On the other hand, his definition demanded a final, self-sufficient, and complete life. Yet the fact that death seems to end all in this life indicated the practical necessity of modifying or interpreting the elements of happiness to fit the demands of mortal men. Besides, death ends this life; it does not complete it.[28] Consequently, Aristotle introduced his qualification "in a complete life," with a sufficiency of material goods and friends, to modify the absoluteness of his definition so that it could fit the conditions of human mortality.

Nevertheless, it would be an error to maintain that the Aristotelian notion of happiness is necessarily limited solely to the conditions open to this life, for that definition would ignore the whole discussion of the contemplative life as such and its primacy. Aristotle always maintained that the contemplative life was, in a way, beyond human nature but was still to be striven for. The answer to this very real difficulty seems to be evident in the argument previously noted, namely, that Aristotle distinguished between the proper human life, the life of the individual supposit, the man who is to die, Socrates or Plato, and the life of the highest part of man, the rational part. This distinction in Aristotle did not imply that two "separate" human beings existed in

28. *Ibid.*, I, 10, 1100a10–1101a20, pp. 946–49.

the same body. Aristotle's idea of happiness was not exactly the same for both, for the composite and for the intellectual soul. One sort of happiness was properly human, occurring in this life and involving a sufficiency of goods, friends, and fortune. The political life (analogous to the family and the individual to himself), which seeks to imitate the divine by placing order in the multitude, is the highest expression of this type of happiness.[29]

However, another higher type of happiness, a life not properly human but divine, the contemplative life, was proper to only part of man, to the soul. Compared with such a life politics was "unleisurely." "Now, the soul of man is divided into two parts, one of which has a rational principle in itself, and the other, not having a rational principle in itself, is able to obey such a principle. And we call a man in any way good because he has the virtues of these two parts."[30] Because Aristotle recognized that both the speculative and practical virtues were in man, he understood that the life of the moral virtues was good, proper to man as he is in this life, and at the same time that it contributes to contemplation, by which man partakes of the divine. Man was a whole, in this sense.

> But in a secondary degree, the life in accordance with the other kind of virtue is happy, for the activities in accordance with this befit our human estate [that is, the moral and political virtues]. Just and brave acts, and other virtuous acts we do in relation to each other, observing our respective duties with regard to contracts and services and all manner of actions and with regard to passions; and all of these seem to be typically human. Some of them seem even to arise from the body, and virtue of character to be in many ways bound up with the passions. Practical wisdom, too, is linked to virtue of character, and this to practical wisdom, since the principles of practical wisdom are in accordance with the moral virtues and rightness in morals in accordance with practical wisdom. Being connected with the passions also, the

---

29. *Ibid.*, I, 2, 1094b7–10, p. 936.
30. Aristotle, *Politics*, VII, 14, 1333a17–19, p. 1297. See also *Nicomachean Ethics*, X, 7, 1177a19–b25, pp. 1104–1105.

moral virtues must belong to our composite nature; and the virtues of our composite nature are human; so, therefore, are the life and the happiness which correspond to these. The excellence of the reason is a thing apart.

Thus Aristotle's discussion of happiness can admit to some sense that politics and moral virtues are the highest good in "our human estate," in "our composite nature," while at the same time admitting that contemplation, "wonder," is the highest activity open to man as such. Politics, then, and all of the values of being human are among the things which are ends, and by being ends, at the same time are means to higher ends. The happiness of the city is a beginning, "whose end is relative to further ends."[31]

This twofold position of Aristotle is of considerable significance in understanding what has happened in political philosophy, particularly in relation to revelation. For essentially, if the things of the theoretic order are given to, not made by man, and if they are the highest, then man will not look to politics for the fulfillment of his ultimate desire to be united to the Highest Good, however defined. In politics he will look for the limited good, no doubt itself reflective of a higher order, of a civil order which allows the pursuit and recognition of the theoretic order but which limits itself to a type of happiness attainable in this life as its immediate and legitimate purpose.

For this reason Aristotle rejected as the good to be attained by politics the "Idea" of the good, as Plato saw it, even if, *per impossibile*, in Aristotle's view, there were such a thing. "And similarly with regard to the Idea; even if there is some one good which is universally predicable of goods or is capable of separate and independent existence, clearly it would not be achieved or attained by man; but we are now seeking something attainable."[32] Again here, however, evidently nothing can prevent intelligence from being addressed by intelligence if this turned out to be a fact of some sort. Nor, apparently, can any-

---

31. Aristotle, *Nicomachean Ethics*, X, 8, 1178a8–22, p. 1106. See also *Politics*, VII, 15, p. 1300.
32. Aristotle, *Nicomachean Ethics*, I, 6, 1096b33–34, p. 940.

thing prevent the actions of the moral virtues, in their serious relation to the polity, from being also pertinent to the connection between the individual and the First Mover. That is, the contemplative end was not meant to abolish the value of the moral virtues exercised in familial or public life, the orderly interrelation of all good things.

Unless, then, these two drives in man—the drive to imitate the First Mover by making a suitable order of this life (in the self, in the family, and in the polity) and the drive to union with the First Mover in an unceasing state—are adequately distinguished and accounted for, man will attempt to revolt by employing means suitable to politics, the more familiar reality to him, to achieve his ultimate desire for unity and full knowledge. This will generally take the form of an imposition of man-made norms into the public order as man's exclusive good. It is to the credit of Aristotelian theory that it provides, even yet, for these two desires without corrupting or destroying them, usually one by the other. The application of this position can therefore prevent both the "politicizing" of the theoretic order and the "spiritualization" of the political order in its own autonomy and legitimacy. Both orders in their distinctness are needed and interrelated ones.

IMMORTALITY

Yet the thesis that happiness can be understood in two senses in Aristotle is not established until a foundation for a belief that contemplative life might actually be continual and unceasing could be found in Aristotle. This, of course, is the question of immortality. And if there is no provision for it in Aristotle in any sense, then indeed nature produces a desire that is "in vain," for Aristotle himself recognized the effect of death on the happiness attainable in this life.[33] Consequently, if there is to be any kind of secure happiness, it must not be conceived in terms of the political autarchy and the happiness of man in this life—that is, of man individuated by matter, of the mortal man.

The polity, of course, has a kind of permanence of its own which

---

33. *Ibid.*, I, 10, 1101a20, p. 948. "Nature never makes anything without a purpose and never leaves out what is necessary" (Aristotle, *De anima*, I, 1, 402a10–11, p. 535).

may last through many generations of men, but this kind of happiness and permanence does not apply to the individual as such, even though great deeds and great words attain a kind of political immortality as long as the *polis* itself endures. Rather, we must examine further the rational or highest part of man which Aristotle thought to be the most divine element in him. Yet this examination must not fail to take into account that, for Aristotle, man was a particular being, body and soul, one being or substance, not two.

"To attain any assured knowledge about the soul," Aristotle frankly affirmed, "is one of the most difficult things in the world."[34] But the task is not hopeless. The soul in its activity, especially in its highest activity, thought, can be known. Thought for Aristotle began in sensation, upon contact with the real things in the world. Without this contact, man could not know.[35] The soul, therefore, revealed a certain natural hierarchy based on reality which placed reason as its highest faculty.[36] The rational element in man was the natural ruler over both the body and the appetites. "And therefore we must study the man who is in the most perfect state both of body and soul," Aristotle wrote,

> for in him we shall see the true relation of the two; although in bad or corrupted natures the body will often appear to rule over the soul, because they are in an evil and unnatural condition. At all events we may firstly observe in living creatures both a despotical and a constitutional rule; for the soul rules the body with a despotical rule, whereas the intellect rules the appetites with a constitutional and royal rule. And it is clear that the rule of the soul over the body, and of the mind and the rational element over the passionate, is natural and expedient; whereas the equality of the two or the rule of the inferior is always unnatural.[37]

In other words, the highest faculty in man is the ruler, and its highest operation is man's noblest. But in addition, the activities of man inso-

---

34. Aristotle, *De anima*, I, 1, 402a10–11, p. 535.
35. *Ibid.*, III, 7, 431b3–9, p. 595.
36. Aristotle, *Politics*, VII, 15, 1334b14–16, p. 1300.
37. *Ibid.*, I, 5, 1254a38–b8, p. 1132. See also VII, 14, 1333a17–1334a11, p. 1297–99.

far as he is connected with sensation and body are proper to man. The body and senses have a legitimacy and function which cannot be ignored or neglected.

Thus when Aristotle said that these powers are ruled with either a despotical or a "constitutional and royal" rule, he was saying something different with respect to the nature of the body and sensations. Body is ruled despotically. It cannot resist. But although the senses are disordered if they rule the intellect or even if they are "equal" to it, they are nevertheless ruled as subjects having their own proper power of resistance which cannot be destroyed by the intellect. They are ruled as being guided through their own proper objects.

In man, knowledge begins in sensation and ends in thought. But Aristotle consistently held that the ultimate and prior cause of the things in nature which first caused man to know (the objects of thought and love are unmoved movers) themselves were based on intelligence—and this even on the assumption that "the heavens are due to spontaneity." For "intelligence and nature will be prior because of this All and of many things in it besides."[38] The soul of man, moreover, was related to this initial mind through sensation and external objects in the world, hence the dictum "the soul is in a way all existing things."[39] The mind of man was open to the "order of parts" in the universe. This order was related to the final causality of the First Mover, for whom the ends of nature were hypothetical, though they were stable principles for other rational creatures.

Consequently, through this "order of parts," the mind could arise progressively to the First Mover. This inherent faculty in man not only distinguished him from the animals but also enabled him to stand outside his own instincts and habits and to overrule them should reason so judge.[40] Aristotle could then speak of a function for man, the human function, the activity of politics and the moral virtues as

---

38. Aristotle, *Physics*, II, 6, 198a12, p. 247.
39. Aristotle, *De anima*, III, 8, 431b21, p. 595.
40. Aristotle, *Politics*, VII, 13, 1332a39–b8, p. 1296. See *Nicomachean Ethics*, X, 9, 1179b20–30, p. 1109.

well as the function of the highest part, the rational soul, which was ordained to the theoretic order.[41] Reason, then, is always "the best thing in us."

What is the status of this mind or reason or highest faculty of the soul in Aristotle? Is it perishable? The textual answer is not definitive, as any slight knowledge of the effort that Western, Jewish, and Arabian philosophy has spent on the problem will testify. In any case, if we are willing to accept Aristotle's discussion of the happiness of the contemplative life as our guide—that is, an activity of the soul that is self-sufficient, final, lasting, for its own sake, and of the highest unchanging object—one can make a reasonable case for the immortality of the highest part of the soul, at least on the basis of Aristotle's own premises. This part is not connected with matter; it lies beyond sensation and the political life. Furthermore, without this element in Aristotle—that is, immortality of the rational soul—his whole metaphysical, psychological, and ethical structure would logically collapse, since it would undermine the finality of man and thereby that of *what is*. Again, Aristotle himself only provides the arguments from which this conclusion might reasonably be drawn, something that Aquinas was later to do.

Yet finality is the very foundation of Aristotle's whole philosophy, metaphysics, psychology, and ethics. It is too much to assume that Aristotle of all men would in practice deny his own first principles. But Aristotle's idea of immortality is certainly not by the same token the Christian one of personal resurrection of the body, the reunion of body and soul. Aristotle's notion of immortality in man is similar to, and probably modeled on, the type of activity and immortality of the separate substances, which are unmoved movers in this system, but whose substance is still potential and therefore subject to the First Mover for what it is, though the character of this subjection in Aristotle did not imply or exclude the possibility of creation. Aristotle simply said, "But we must examine whether any form also survives

---

41. Aristotle, *Nicomachean Ethics*, VI, 12, 1144a10, p. 1034. See X, 8, 1177a17–32, p. 1108.

afterwards. For in some cases, there is nothing to prevent this; e.g., the soul may be of this sort—not all soul but the reason; for presumably it is impossible that all soul should survive."[42]

The point is that the impact of Christianity on political theory centers on the revelational solution to Aristotle's problem of immortality and whether this solution could hold its own against the modern ideological alternatives to it. Likewise, post-Aristotelian Greek and Roman philosophy, as well as most modern philosophy which takes its rise from the revival of Stoic, Epicurean, and Cynic philosophy in the sixteenth and seventeenth centuries, also finds its impact on political theory at this juncture. Some souls, for Aristotle, simply perish; certainly animal and vegetable ones do so. Must this category include the human soul in principle?

Aristotle argued for the necessity of intelligence behind nature. He based his argument both on observed regularity and on a psychological analysis of human knowledge, which revealed that "actual knowledge is identical with its object." But since, "in the individual, potential knowledge [man comes to know] is in time prior to actual knowledge," Aristotle concluded that "in the universe as a whole it is not prior even in time. Mind is not at one time knowing and at another not. When mind is apart from its present conditions, it appears as most what it is and nothing more: this alone is immortal and eternal."[43] In this argument Aristotle has combined the knowledge principle with his analysis of nature, which always acts in the same way or does so for the most part. The intelligence that rules within the universe is a kind of "substitute intelligence" in nature, as Aquinas later called it.[44] But if nature revealed this intelligence to the human mind and if, from an analysis of human knowledge, knowledge was identified with its object, then the knowledge in the universe clearly was

---

42. Aristotle, *Metaphysics*, XII, 3, 1070a24–27, p. 874.
43. Aristotle, *De anima*, III, 5, 430a20–25, p. 592. See also III, 7, 431a1–7, p. 593.
44. "Nature is nothing else but a reason put in things by a certain art, namely the divine one, by which things are moved to a determined end." (my translation of Thomas Aquinas, *De physico*, ed. A. Pirotta [Naples, 1953], Bk. II, 1, 14, p. 121).

prior to the knowledge in man. For this reason man is open to what is not himself even in nature.

In the beginning man's knowledge was likewise potential, so that man too was primarily a receiver, not a maker of knowledge. Therefore the knowledge of the First Mover was first. Another possible interpretation of the above passage is, of course, that all is mind, a position that will be taken up in later philosophy. But this interpretation does not fit the context. For Aristotle is clearly maintaining that what was potential knowledge in time (*i.e.*, the reason of man), when separated from that which causes this potentiality of knowledge (*i.e.*, the body), comes to be actual knowledge. It is then identified with its object in knowledge and is therefore eternal. Thus as a logical consequence either the soul itself disappears or it has its own being, but the soul does not become the First Mover itself, though it is a limited first mover in its own order, an originator of real actions.

The importance of the analysis in Aristotle seems clear, since later philosophies had to overcome this doctrine that "actual knowledge is identical with its object" if they were to make man independent of God, even of the final causes in nature. When Marx, concluding the Hobbesian tradition, came to believe that a man knows only what he makes, that the sum of his labor is the sum of what he knows, he could then conclude that man knows only himself, that the "object" of knowledge is not something outside of man but man himself. This view completely reverses the Aristotelian position. There is no "contemplation" left in this sense, no wonder about what is not the self or the collective being reduced to the self.

Aristotle's main doctrine with respect to the mind is that, contrary to sensation, it is separable from the body.[45] "We have no evidence as yet about mind or the power to think," Aristotle remarked. "It seems to be a widely different kind of soul, differing as what is eternal from what is perishable; it alone is capable of existence in isolation from all other psychic powers. All the other parts of the soul, it is evident from what we have said, are, in spite of certain statements to the contrary,

---

45. Aristotle, *Metaphysics*, XII, 3, 1070a24–27, p. 874; *De anima*, II, 4, 429a31–b4, p. 590.

incapable of separate existence, though, of course, distinguishable by definition."[46] Aristotle, then, conceived at least the possibility of separation of body and soul. Actually, this possibility is established by Aristotle's recognition of universal knowledge. "The objects that excite the sensory powers to activity, the seen, the heard, etc., are outside. The ground of this difference is that what actual sensation apprehends is individuals, while what knowledge apprehends is universal, and these are in a sense within the soul. That is why a man can exercise his knowledge when he wishes, but his sensation does not depend upon himself—a sensible object must be there."[47] The possibility of this universal knowledge involves the doctrine of what later became known as the agent and possible intellects.

The textual sources of this theory show why Aristotle could regard the separability of the rational soul as at least a theoretical possibility. "And in fact mind as we have described it," he wrote, "is what it is by virtue of becoming all things, while there is another which is what it is by virtue of making all things: this is a sort of positive state like light; for in a sense light makes potential colors into actual colors. Mind in this sense of it is separable, impassible, unmixed, since it is in its essential nature activity (for always the active is superior to the passive factor, the originating force to the matter which it forms)."[48] Both Avicenna and Averroes held on the basis of this passage that either the agent or the potential intellect was a single power separable and separate from the individual man. But this separation resulted in no abiding individuality. Christian philosophers, on the other hand, especially Albert the Great and Thomas Aquinas, recognized here an implicit destruction of the unity of the human supposit and, in the case of the separate intellect, a denial of personal integrity and immortality as well.[49]

We should note here, however, simply that Aristotle, in recogniz-

---

46. Aristotle, *De anima*, II, 2, 413b24–29, p. 558. See Josef Pieper, *Death and Immortality*, trans. R. and C. Winston (New York, 1969).
47. Aristotle, *De anima*, II, 5, 417b20–25, p. 566.
48. *Ibid.*, III, 5, 430a14–19, p. 592.
49. See Etienne Gilson, *A History of Christian Philosophy in the Middle Ages* (New York, 1955), 197–205.

ing such powers in man in order to explain the way man does know and the content of his knowledge, was drawing the logical conclusion from his dictum that, "if there is anything that has no contrary, then it knows itself and is actually and possesses independent existence." That the rational soul has no contrary can be seen from Aristotle's observation that, "since everything is a possible object of thought, mind in order, as Anaxagoras says, to dominate, that is, to know, must be pure from all admixture."[50]

From such analyses, then, we can conclude that Aristotle did at least provide a basis for thinking the soul capable of existing separately from the body, so that when so separated it could know uninterruptedly and could be identified with the highest object of knowledge, the First Mover, though without becoming the substance of the First Mover itself. Aristotle was no pantheist. Happiness could therefore be at least possible in an unceasing and uninterrupted form, but this happiness was not of the whole man, body and soul, but only of the rational power. Even if this soul seemed capable of somehow perishing on other grounds or would become a separate substance, the principles of Aristotle hold.

The only happiness open to the complete man in Aristotle was the limited happiness of political life and the moral virtues. Thus the Aristotelian solution left a certain dissatisfaction and incompleteness in man. The rise of post-Aristotelian philosophy, as well as the particular impact of Christian revelation, derives much of its impetus from such dissatisfaction, a condition with both metaphysical and political implications. These must be understood if we are to understand how they relate to the foundations of political philosophy.

50. Aristotle, *De anima*, III, 6, 430b24–25, p. 593, III, 4, 429a18–19, pp. 589–90.

3

FROM THE STOICS TO AUGUSTINE: PRACTICAL PHILOSOPHY, NEO-PLATONISM, AND REVELATION

Political philosophy is intelligible to itself primarily as philosophy, not as history, even though the status of history is a major philosophical problem directly related to the limits of politics. The understanding of post-Aristotelian philosophy, in its relation to Plato and Aristotle, as well as to modern political theory, has been a widely discussed problem of considerable subtlety.[1] Briefly stated, late Greek and Roman philosophy already contained a shift from the primacy of theoretical knowledge to practical knowledge, that is, to ethics and politics, a reversal of the classical hierarchy.

Many earlier writers, such as Sabine, the Carlyles, and Tarn, had argued that modern political philosophy was rooted in the post-Aristotelian philosophies of withdrawal from politics and protest against the theoretical order, against Aristotle's notion of devotion to the highest things even if such devotion proved difficult. Modern political philosophy was held, even by Marx, who wrote his thesis on Epicurus and Democritus, to find its origins here where the "consciousness of the self" became the grounds of the central alienation of man from himself.[2] To restore man to himself became in some sense the intelligible link of political philosophy separated from classical theory and revelation. The natural and social distinctions which were

---

1. "In the history of political philosophy, the death of Aristotle in 322 marks the close of an era, as the life of his greatest pupil [Alexander], who died a year before him, marks the beginning of a new era" (George Sabine, *A History of Political Theory* [rev. ed.; New York, 1953], 141). See also A. J. Carlyle and R. W. Carlyle, *A History of Mediaeval Political Thought in the West* (London, 1950), I, 2; Whitney J. Oates, "General Introduction," in *The Stoic and Epicurean Philosophers*, ed. Whitney J. Oates (New York, 1940), xxiv; W. W. Tarn, *Hellenistic Civilization* (3rd ed. rev.; London, 1952), 327–28.
2. Karl Marx, "La différence de la philosophie de la nature chez Démocrite et chez Epicure," *Oeuvres philosophiques*, trans. J. Moliter (Paris, 1937), I, 2–4.

normal to the classics, themselves originating outside man, were to be actively replaced by man. In this theory of political philosophy, then, Christian revelation in particular was not seen to be unique except in its later contribution in separating the individual from the state in the early modern period, where it functioned as a step in the state's gaining complete autonomy over the ethical and metaphysical orders.[3]

These post-Aristotelian philosophies—Epicureanism, Stoicism, and Cynicism—contained within them strong elements of universalism, brotherhood, and virtue, which at first sight seemed to form also the major political components of Christianity rather than anything distinct in Christianity itself or in the classical philosophers. The life of the polity, in which the classics had found the human strivings of man to be necessarily expressed, became an impediment. Philosophy became only moral philosophy, often because of the uncertainties of the speculative order, a point that will also be important for philosophy addressed by revelation. First philosophy was not metaphysics, as with Aristotle, but politics, as often with Cicero. However, this choice presented an intellectual problem of great moment, one whose dimensions are even yet not adequately appreciated. For Aristotle, man's highest act was contemplation of the things that could not be otherwise. This category included the structure of man himself and the ends of the moral order, which were in nature by virtue of hypothetical necessity, that is, which did not depend on man to establish their limits. Man did not make himself man but, being man from nature, was to become good man in the *polis*. This was Aristotle's consistent doctrine.

With the Epicureans and the Stoics, the idea began to germinate that ethics and politics were superior to the confusions of the speculative order. Peace was attained by a form of moderation and self-control, which had most peculiar theoretical implications. These propositions held that man was not affected by what went on in the cosmos, that there was no passage from the practical to the speculative orders, no unity of the whole. Aristotle had held that ethics and poli-

---

3. Carlyle and Carlyle, *A History of Mediaeval Political Thought in the West*, I, 82.

tics were the *proper* life of man, to be sure, but not his *highest* or best life, so that the practical order was preparatory to contemplation. He did not deny value or relative autonomy to the practical order. In the post-Aristotelian philosophers, man himself became the theoretic center. The intellectual implications of this position were far-reaching, since they constituted the foundations of the speculative effort to identify man with *what is*. The human order came to be transformable into metaphysics itself. The effect of this reasoning is, again, to make politics into a kind of metaphysics of a very odd sort.

The early German historian Eduard Zeller had already hinted at the direction and dimension of the problem.

> What could be expected in such an age but that philosophy would take a decidedly practical turn, if indeed it were studied at all? And yet, such were the political antecedents of the Stoic and Epicurean systems of philosophy. An age like this did not require theoretical knowledge.... No other course seemed open for the best-intentioned, as matters then stood, but to withdraw entirely within themselves, to entrench themselves behind the safe barrier of their own inner life, and, ignoring the troubles raging without, to make happiness dependent on their own inward state alone.[4]

The significance of this passage should not be missed. For if there is a serious reason to question the too easily made assumption that Christianity merely absorbed Stoic thought, so that there is no break in political philosophy between Aristotle and the moderns, it lies here. The endeavor to make men's "happiness depend upon their own inward state alone" is really the issue that radically separates Christian and Aristotelian thought from that of the post-Aristotelians. Unavoidably, this endeavor soon ceases to be merely "practical" and becomes theoretical.

However much the Christian philosopher or Aristotle might agree that disordered passions, politics, or even God can disturb men, he would never agree that the solution to this uneasiness consisted in a

---

4. Eduard Zeller, *Stoics, Epicureans, and Skeptics*, trans. Oswald J. Reichel (London, 1890), 16–17.

complete withdrawal into the self alone, presupposed to nothing but itself. Ernst Cassirer grasped the significance of this point: "Nevertheless, there always remains one point on which the antagonism between the Christian and the Stoic ideals proves irreconcilable. The asserted absolute independence of man, which in Stoic theory was regarded as man's fundamental virtue, is turned in the Christian theory into his fundamental vice and error. . . . The struggle between these two conflicting views has lasted for many centuries, and to the beginning of the modern era—at the time of the Renaissance and in the seventeenth century—we still feel its strength."[5] Insofar as post-Aristotelian theory adhered to the principle of the autonomy of man, then, it remained in direct opposition to Christian theory, even on such points as brotherhood, equality, law, and unity, which appeared on the surface to be so similar but whose intellectual comprehension revealed quite a different basis.

Failure to grasp this dissimilarity between post-Aristotelian and Christian thought has been a constant cause of confusion in the history of political philosophy. Whether it upholds a quasi-pantheistic doctrine, which makes man's reason identical with the divine intellect, as in Stoicism, or relegates the gods to a sphere completely outside human life and the world itself, as with the Epicureans, or simply maintains with Pyrrho that "we can know nothing about the nature of things: hence the right attitude toward them is to withhold judgment: the necessary result of suspending judgment is imperturbability," these doctrines fundamentally agreed, in opposition to Plato, Aristotle, and Judaeo-Christian revelation, in their placement of man at the absolute center of their reality theory.[6] Because of this "freedom of thought," presupposed to no given order or relation to a First Mover or God, Christian revelation could not, in the first analysis, base itself on post-Aristotelian philosophy. Failure to recognize this fact has led many

---

5. Cassirer, *An Essay on Man*, 24.
6. Zeller, *Stoics, Epicureans, and Skeptics*, 492, 457. See also John Hallowell, *Main Currents in Modern Political Thought* (New York, 1950), 16; Cyril Bailey, *The Greek Atomists and Epicurus* (Oxford, 1957), 426; John M. Rist (ed.), *The Stoics* (Berkeley, 1977); James M. Nichols, *Epicurean Political Philosophy* (Ithaca, 1976).

scholars to overlook the true impact of revelation on political philosophy, indeed to overlook the nature of political philosophy itself.[7]

For this reason, too, the revelational relationship to Plato and Aristotle remains alive and vital. The philosophical questions lie here, whereas the answers are contained both in revelation as addressed to these already existing questions in their own terms and in the subsequent history of political philosophy. The answers need new formulation in the light of new experience and new political results. In the direction that political philosophy took and the experiences it accumulated, there was need for an intelligible explanation of the occurrence and recurrence of certain things. There was, likewise, need to explain why purely philosophic answers were inadequate.

The Epicurean idea of withdrawal from the polis was that the simple relation of man to man would become the foundation of that notion of contentment which does not allow itself to be bothered by problems of personal, political, or theoretical life. Its basis, in other words, is the rejection of any real relation of order between the human mind, will, and physical presence in the world with some right order of things, which man knew but did not make. Zeller wrote, "Both [Epicureans and the Stoics] have renounced the political character of the old propriety of conduct, and diverting their attention from public life, seek to find the basis for universal morality in *the simple relation of man to man*."[8] The Stoic notion of apathy, moreover, bound up as it was with Stoic physics, was a sort of noble claim of the human mind to be the absolute master of reality. The notion of suffering or pain, whatever its source, was a sign not of sacrifice, as it was to become in revelation, but of pride, of the denial that anything higher could happen than what the human mind acknowledged. Indeed, through its notion of physics and intelligence, Stoicism was able to suggest how the absolute freedom of ethics, presupposed to no higher order, was able to identify itself with a deterministic cosmos but in a fashion that left the human mind master of itself. "Zeno enunciated the Stoic con-

---

7. Michel Spanneut, *Le Stoïcisme des pères de l'église* (Paris, 1957). See also James V. Schall, "Post-Aristotelian Philosophy and Political Theory," *Cithara*, III (November, 1963), 56–79.

8. Zeller, *Stoics, Epicureans, and Skeptics*, 478. Italics added.

cept of a divine reason imminent in nature and in the wise man," Margaret Reesor wrote. "According to the principle, the laws which govern the universe and the laws which govern human society on earth are alike universal and moral, and the reason which is exercised by man is essentially of the same quality as the reason which governs the world."[9] No gulf between the divine and human intellect existed, so that the latter could begin to conceive itself as the former.

For philosophical purposes in this regard, perhaps Cicero is the most important and in some ways most neglected political philosopher. In Cicero, the speculative sciences became subordinate to the practical ones, although in a most noble and powerful fashion. "All these professions [mathematics, law, dialectics] are occupied with the search after truth; but to be drawn by study away from active life is contrary to moral duty. For the whole glory of virtue is in activity."[10] Cicero made the idea of serving the state the supreme virtue. "And service is better than mere theoretical knowledge, for the study and knowledge of the universe would somehow be lame and defective, were no practical results to follow. Such results, moreover, are best seen in the safe-guarding of human interests. It is essential, then, to human society; and it should, therefore, be ranked above speculative knowledge."[11]

Cicero's position, then, taken along with his suggestion that the best theoretical state actually has (or had) historical existence, left no doubt about the priority of practical to theoretical science. Philosophy was not denied, but it was what man did in exile or old age, when he could not actively participate in the polity. This view reversed the Aristotelian position. The result was that all later philosophy in any way starting from his analysis likewise started from this theoretical posi-

---

9. Margaret E. Reesor, *The Political Theory of the Old and Middle Stoa* (New York, 1951), 9. "They [the Stoics] wish to find the reason for the existence and for the nature of this individual in the intimacy of the body itself and no longer in a cause acting from the outside on a previously given matter, such as participation in the Idea (Plato) or the tendency to achieve an end (Aristotle)" (my translation of Emile Bréhier, *Chrysippe et l'ancien Stoïcisme* [Paris, 1951], 108). See S. Sambursky, *The Physics of the Stoics* (London, 1959), 115.

10. Cicero, *De officiis*, trans. Walter Miller (London, 1921), I, 19, p. 21.

11. *Ibid.*, I, 43, pp. 153, 157.

tion about the relation of the practical and the theoretical sciences. One of the major functions of political philosophy is to understand what this consequence meant.

Cicero's notion of service further illustrated this point. At first sight, service can easily be compared to the Christian concept of charity. But what did service mean in this Roman context? The Cosmic City for the Stoic, which included all rational beings, had a moral purpose tending to the good of the whole cosmos. Whatever happened to anyone in this universe, even suffering and evil, nevertheless achieved the good of this City. Man's virtue was to conform himself to what had to be. "The thing that really matters depends on you, and on no one but you."[12] The Cosmic City already exists; its material dynamism works for the good of the whole, which is likewise man's good. As a result, man could serve others in this City, but he could not really love them because his service was a detached service that recognized the continuing achievement of the good of the Cosmic City no matter what happened there.

The Stoic ideal of service seems to have been an ideal of detachment and noninvolvement. "The [Stoic] Wise Man was not to *concern* himself with his brethren—that is the point—he was only to serve them," Edwyn Bevan wrote in a famous study. "Benevolence he was to have, as much of it as you can conceive; but there was one thing he must not have, and that was love. Here too, if that inner tranquility and freedom of his was to be kept safe through everything . . . , he must engage in action without desire."[13] The Stoic ideal was designed to enable man to participate in all reality no matter what the external conditions of his life. He must guide others, but he is indifferent to success.[14] For the very nature of the Cosmic City in which man is to participate is that it is already successful, already achieving the greater good.[15] From this viewpoint, the Ciceronian notion of service

---

12. Gilbert Murray, *The Stoic Philosophy* (New York, 1915), 31.
13. Edwyn Bevan, *Stoics and Skeptics* (Oxford, 1913), 66.
14. See Bréhier, *Chrysippe et l'ancien Stoïcisme*, 213–15; Reesor, *The Political Theory of the Old and Middle Stoa*, 11, N. 5.
15. Bréhier, *Chrysippe et l'ancien Stoïcisme*, 263.

is not the same as Aristotle's view of politics, which had at least this merit, that it gave man a true and independent task to perform. Cicero's famous notion of a common universal law of reason seems at first sight quite similar to that of Aristotle, who also made reason the highest faculty.[16]

But for Aristotle, in radical contrast to Stoicism, the order of the universe, as it led to the First Mover, was not the same order that man could make by his own reason. The fact that man possessed reason and that the First Mover also moved by love and intelligence did not mean that these faculties were so identical that whoever participated in one also participated directly in the other, as Cicero and Stoicism in general seem to have believed. Aristotle rather held: "For law is order, and good law is good order; but a very great multitude cannot be orderly: to introduce order into the unlimited is the work of a divine power— of such power as holds together the universe."[17] There was not merely a univocal notion of reason in the universe. Aristotle had no pantheistic tendencies. Aristotle's god was apart from nature, including human nature. That is, he was the primary "cause" of the distinction of things, not a part of things themselves, for if the First Mover were another finite "thing," the transcendence of the First Mover would be jeopardized.

The philosophic import of this difference enables one to see just why Stoic philosophy tended to define such things as law or equality or brotherhood in terms of withdrawal or abstraction from concrete situations. This concept seems to be what Cicero had in mind when he described a common human nature as something withdrawn from the additions of custom, habit, choice, and accident, which accrue to existing persons.[18] The law is within. It needs no interpreter but oneself, because the law of reason is common to man and God. The idea that Cicero appeared to have had in mind when he spoke of the natural

---

16. See Cicero, *De re publica* and *De legibus*, trans. Clinton Walker Keys (Cambridge, Mass., 1948); *De legibus*, I, 7, 22, p. 321. (Hereafter citations from this Loeb edition will take the form just shown, with the last number indicating the page number in the edition.)

17. Aristotle, *Politics*, VII, 4, 1326a28, p. 1283.

18. See the famous definition of law in Cicero, *De re publica*, III, 23, 34, pp. 211–13.

law, a community of reason and equality, seems to have been a concept based on the logical abstraction of man as yet undifferentiated by any additions. This is not the existentially distinct, unique nature fully and necessarily individuated in a human supposit, for whom Aristotelian politics existed.

On this logical nature, then, and not on the ontological one of real beings, Cicero based his doctrine of equality, brotherhood, and society. "We must realize," he wrote, "also that we are invested by nature with two characters, as it were: one of these is the universal, arising from the fact of our being all alike endowed with reason and with that superiority which lifts us above the brute. From this all morality and propriety are derived, and upon it depends the rational method of ascertaining our duty. The other character is to be assigned to individuals in particular."[19] For this reason the Stoic philosophy of withdrawal can become communal. What is different is left out; what is abstracted is common and therefore equal. The "human" is more real than Socrates, Plato, or Mary. But the type of community that results is by no means Aristotelian, or geared as much to individuals in their uniqueness as to what they have in common.

The implications of post-Aristotelian philosophy are profound. Its tendency eliminated the First Mover as a cause of the distinction of things. This change led to a concept of nature and its autonomy which Marx would place at the center of later theory. But Marx was not alone in doing so. The analysis of scholars like Sabine and Carlyle also used this idea of a common, abstract human nature as the basis for interpreting modern democratic theory. The much-discussed "break" that arose with post-Aristotelian theory was a departure not so much in the sense of something new as in the sense of a reversal of basic Aristotelian positions in the direction, for the most part, of errors which Aristotle attempted to correct in Plato. But the post-Aristotelian system, contrary to both Plato and Aristotle, transformed the contemplative order into a dynamic, concrete system which elevated concepts and exigencies of the practical life into the highest positions while at

19. Cicero, *De officiis*, I, 30, pp. 107, 109.

the same time subordinating concrete uniqueness to logical abstractedness. Man came to hold the center of attention not merely in practice, but in theory as well. Aristotle's dictum that, if man were the highest being, politics would be the highest science was on the way to becoming true.

Moreover, Christianity was born into a Stoic intellectual world. In many ways, Christianity appeared to possess several postulates in common with Stoicism, from which it did borrow a great deal in the area of philosophy. But Christianity, faced with the self-sufficiency of the individual that was characteristic of the post-Aristotelian system, ultimately found itself turning to Plato and Aristotle for sounder theoretical bases in explaining what it was about even to itself.[20] Plato and Aristotle recognized the primacy of the theoretic order, the order which man could know but did not make. Thus in the long history of the West, Aristotle in particular seems to have gained more and more prominence in Christian theory because his human substance was incarnate, existentially unique, and identifiable. It was something that could be touched and loved, something that could be respected as a person not because of its abstract commonness with others, something not to be denied, of course, but because of its very uniqueness in the being it is.

This will also be the issue to confront, that of the nature of the person, when the question arises as to whether revelation has itself in certain areas tended to embrace "the modern project" (Leo Strauss's phrase), to reject the guidance of classical philosophy. The underlying doctrine of the post-Aristotelians was based on an abstract nature and man, the same in Athens, Rome, and throughout the world. And for all its genius, Christian revelation could not determine how to baptize an abstraction. Fundamentally for this reason the impact of Christian revelation on political theory seems rather to have been found in its

---

20. See also the reflections of Augustine, who admired the Stoics on many points but who could not agree with them on the basic point of happiness and its means. See St. Augustine, *The City of God*, in the *Basic Writings of St. Augustine*, ed. Whitney J. Oates (New York, 1948), Bk. XIX, Chap. 4, Vol. II, p. 476. (Hereafter the Oates edition of Augustine will be cited as *Basic Writings, Augustine*. Citations from the *City of God* will include book and chapter number of the *City of God* and volume and page number of this edition.)

relationship to questions of immortality, happiness, friendship, and society as these questions arose in the ancient world in Plato and Aristotle, rather than as a mere elaboration of post-Aristotelian positions, as many scholars would have it.

Post-Aristotelian philosophy is therefore of major importance in the history of political theory. Without an understanding of this period's implications, the main significance both of Aristotle, who comes earlier, and of Plotinus and Augustine, who come later, can easily be missed. Aristotle's distinction between the theoretic and practical orders was sound, but his solution to the nature of the theoretic order left men insecure. The post-Aristotelians sought to alleviate this insecurity, which was caused both by the chaos of the times and by the nature of the problem itself. They did so by absorbing all the cosmos into a moral city of the universe centered on man and his practical participation in the City of Reason. This view was itself somehow related to Plato's formulation of the problem of the best regime in theory and in existence.

Plotinus and Augustine vigorously objected to this man- or reason-centered universe, arguing that it was unreal and incapable of meeting man's ultimate desires. They would again uphold the primacy of the contemplative order though unfortunately not always in a manner sufficiently protective of the practical life of the city. Consequently, it is significant that modern philosophy—which has gradually sought to replace God with man, nature with function, and the speculative life with the practical—again turned, as Marx observed, to the philosophy of the post-Aristotelians. The sometimes obscure ideas and relationships of speculative thinkers such as Plotinus could form the background of a version of humanism and political philosophy which allowed nothing but what man permitted to enter. Ideas, in this sense, remain prior to politics.

The post-Aristotelian philosophies, however, grew from a disillusionment with classic contemplative theory. The Cynics and Skeptics had gone about the Greek and Roman world showing that the solutions of the philosophers were fruitless. Men simply could not decide the answers to the questions of the philosophers, so why bother about them? Aristotle had said that even the little we might know about the speculative order was worth a whole lifetime, but even he felt that this little was for only a few. The atmosphere contributed to a concentration on things that could be achieved in this world. The spread and consolidation of the Roman Empire, furthermore, occasioned the new type of philosophy, particularly Stoicism, which would account for the overall unity and union of men of different races and creeds, however questionable certain philosophic explanations might prove to be. During the often peaceful years of the Empire, the moral stature of the people did not continue at the high level that such writers as Cicero and Tacitus had identified in the Roman Republic.

The alternative open to the emperors, however, was not the Republic as Cicero has praised it. Christianity was clearly gaining strength from the spiritual vacuum caused by the decline of the gods of the city-state, though the new religion ought not to be explained totally or even primarily in such terms. But before Christianity finally became established, "Aurelian began and Diocletian completed the introduction of a new system of Oriental absolutism; and Aurelian made an Oriental cult the religion of the Empire, and bade his subjects regard him as the earthly vicar and emanation of the "'Unconquered Sun'."[21] This attempt to deify the imperial state further disillusioned men about the politics of this world. As a result, there arose a general philosophical turning away from the realities of political life as it was being lived.

PLOTINUS

There were in a sense two reactions to the situation. One was Christianity. The other, philosophical, was best represented by Plotinus. The first was, in addition to a doctrine and a moral practice, an external society with a visible structure. The philosophy of Plotinus, however, never succeeded in becoming a society. Plotinus was not really in-

---

21. Sir Ernest Barker, "The Roman Conception of Empire," in *Church, State, and Education*, ed. Ernest Barker (Ann Arbor, 1957), 20. See also Christopher Dawson, *The Making of Europe* (New York, 1957), 25–41.

terested in practical life, which had seemed to be unworthy of the philosopher. Augustine, who knew his Plato mainly through neo-Platonism, shared the belief that the practical order was not stable or worthy of man except insofar as it was necessary to continue in the important tasks of life. The philosophical meaning of the era of the late Roman Empire was that the post-Aristotelian alternative had reached an impasse, that the contemplative order did need to be reasserted.

It is important, however, to consider how the impasse was understood. To do so we must briefly consider Plotinus because of the efforts he made in the speculative order. Reaffirmation of the contemplative indicated that certain shifts away from Aristotle, within the thinking of the post-Aristotelians, needed to be stressed.[22] The transformation of Plato by Plotinus made the universe a necessary one in which all things proceeded in an orderly fashion from the One. "The total scheme may be summarized in the illustration of the Good as center, the Intellectual-Principle as an unmoving circle, the Soul as a circle in motion, its moving being its aspiration: the Intellectual-Principle possesses and has ever embraced that which is beyond being; the soul must seek it still."[23] However contemplative this statement may sound, it does not easily preserve any distinction between the One and that which comes from the One. Once the active life is seen as a necessary emanation from the One through a series of progressions or emanations, what remains is an idealism with no roots in a political life with some autonomy of its own. Political life is deprived of its variety and freedom, however much the latter are apparently accounted for. The One cannot change; neither can what comes forth from the One.

The effect of Plotinus's effort to unite reason and mysticism no doubt directly deprived the individual of any real autonomy or destiny. The soul merged into the Mind, and this into the One. "But our

22. See Thomas Whittaker, *The Neo-Platonists* (Cambridge, 1928), 92–93.
23. Plotinus, *Enneads,* trans. Stephen Mackenna (Boston, n.d.), IV, 4, p. 16. See A. H. Armstrong, *Plotinus* (London, 1952); James V. Schall, "Plotinus and Political Philosophy," *Gregorianum,* LXVI (1985), 687–707.

concern is not merely to be sinless," Plotinus protested, "but to be God."[24] The active life could have no real virtue or merit, since it proceeded necessarily. The Stoic effort to identify the reason with what happens in history became here the effort of the mind not merely to dominate what happens but to be what happens.[25] Change in this system lacks potency, so that all the ethical and political powers and virtues disappear.

The cost in Plotinus of a philosophic reaffirmation of the contemplative was the world itself, which disappeared into the One. But if what comes from the One necessarily proceeds, the fact is that the One has no form or essence, so that reality is deprived of any fixed order. What at first sight appears to be absolute necessity proves to be a strange sort of absolute freedom in which the external world can be anything. Plotinus lies in the background of the effort to resolve the difference between the One and the world by including all reality within a single, ongoing system not itself different from or outside what is open to the human intelligence. Man is to be related no longer as receiver to giver, either of the world or of knowledge, but as a direct participator in being itself, not as what is received, but as what is being formed.

AUGUSTINE

In the history of political philosophy, it is instructive to contrast Augustine and Plotinus in their respective endeavors to reestablish the primacy of the contemplative order. As a result of his Christian faith, Augustine saw that the doctrines of the Incarnation, immortality, redemption, resurrection, and the Church necessarily demanded, in their intellectual formulations, that the One, God, be kept distinct from the many, yet not so distinct that God could not come into the world. The One for Plotinus was simply the One. Consequently, as Bréhier noted, "the very idea of salvation, which implies a mediator

---

24. Plotinus, *Enneads*, I, 2, p. 6.
25. *Ibid.*, I, 5, p. 10.

sent by God to man, is foreign to him [Plotinus]."[26] Because of its ideas of the Incarnation and immortality in particular, Christianity remained human.

The "humanity" of the Romans, which did not subordinate the practical to the speculative intellect, was replaced by a Christian humanism that did recognize the givenness of man. God, then, became man. Individual men could become, in the revelational view, immortal. "In its emphasis on the resurrection of the body," Joseph Katz wrote, "Christianity again showed a 'humanistic' outlook quite different from that of the neoplatonists. The life of the transfigured soul is described in bold strokes in the last chapter of the *City of God*. . . . The community of souls takes the place of the earthly community. Such a communion, however, does not imply the separation of individuals but their complete togetherness."[27] Christianity can have a revelation, grace, a resurrection, notions which were impossible to Plotinus because the One could not descend in Plotinus's system or reach anything but the One itself.

Augustine, following the Greek fathers, was the first philosopher-theologian in the West to see how the rather abstract conceptions of Greek thinking on God could be transformed into the living, personal, loving reality that the Christian God is described to be. "The first epoch-making contact between Greek philosophical speculation and Christian religious belief took place, when, already a convert to Christianity, the young Augustine began to read the works of some neo-Platonists, particularly the *Enneads* of Plotinus."[28] And the essence of the difficulty for Augustine was to determine "how to express the God of Christianity in terms borrowed from the philosophy of Plotinus."[29] Despite the inherent complexity of this effort, or perhaps

---

26. Emile Bréhier, *The Philosophy of Plotinus*, trans. Joseph Thomas (Chicago, 1958), 114.
27. Joseph Katz, *Plotinus' Search for the Good* (New York, 1950), 99. See also Etienne Gilson, "God and Christian Philosophy," in *A Gilson Reader*, ed. Anton C. Pegis (Garden City, N.Y., 1957), 201.
28. Gilson, *ibid.*, 195. See also F. Cayré, *Initiation à la philosophie de Saint Augustin* (Paris, 1947), 76; Christopher Dawson, "Saint Augustine and His Age," in *Saint Augustine*, ed. M. C. D'Arcy (New York, 1957), 49–77.
29. Gilson, *A Gilson Reader*, 196.

because of it, Augustine was able to show how an Incarnate God could emerge into human history in terms intelligible to and dependent on Greek philosophy, even though the event that caused this thinking did not arise in the Greek intellectual world itself, even though it appeared within the confines of Alexander's conquests. That is to say, there was a real link between revelation and the work of the philosophers, a real need for a polity in which this work could continue and be deepened.

The historical and philosophical importance of *The City of God* is beyond discussion. But its importance in political philosophy cannot be recognized until we understand that *The City of God* represented an attempt to reaffirm the primacy of the contemplative order in terms based essentially on the implications of Christian revelation but still expressed within the scope of genuine philosophy. "The Christian . . . ," Dawson noted, "possessed no philosophy of society or politics, but he had a theory of history."[30] The politics of this world, the early Christian felt, seemed fleeting, probably corrupting. As a result, there emerged a "social dualism" which is "one of the most striking characteristics of early Christianity. Indeed, it is characteristic of Christianity in general; for the idea of two societies and the twofold citizenship is found nowhere else in the same form."[31]

Augustine, to be sure, must be seen in that aspect of Platonic theory which concerned itself with the location of the ideal state. Augustine did not disagree with Plato that this endeavor was not a necessary part of the intellectual experience. As a Christian philosopher, Augustine admitted the legitimacy of the enterprise and located the ultimate answer to a valid philosophical question arising from philosophy in revelation. But this answer required philosophical reflection on this very revelational data before what it was about in terms of

---

30. Dawson, "Saint Augustine and His Age," 45. See also Herbert Deane, *The Political and Social Ideas of St. Augustine* (New York, 1956); John East, "The Political Relevance of St. Augustine," *Modern Age*, XVI (Spring, 1972), 167–81; James V. Schall, "St. Augustine and Christian Political Theory," in *The Politics of Heaven and Hell*, 39–66.

31. Dawson, "Saint Augustine and His Age," 48. Leo Strauss made much the same point in his "Jerusalem and Athens," in *Studies in Platonic Political Philosophy*, ed. Thomas L. Pangle (Chicago, 1983), 147–73.

philosophic questions could be grasped. Once this point had been settled, Augustine could look upon politics as relatively unimportant or, if politics was important, as in no wise the location of the highest good.

Paradoxically, the attempt to show how the contemplative order was a world or society consisting of a creating God, who is at once One and Triune yet who descended into human history to call those who love Him, to a certain degree ran a danger parallel to that in Plotinus. Efforts to expound upon the proper understanding of the contemplative or revelational order displayed a tendency to downgrade or even to exclude the relative autonomy and legitimacy of the practical order, wherein politics was lived. Consequently, even though the early Church's initial theoretical struggles were in great part efforts to uphold the legitimacy of marriage, family, and other aspects of a normal human life, still Hannah Arendt was probably correct in noting that the immediate effect of the Christian doctrines of good works, humility, and personal immortality tended to subvert the legitimacy of the *vita activa* in its Aristotelian and political sense.[32] The millenarist tradition to which, in common with the whole African church, St. Augustine was not wholly immune, simply eliminated any effort to improve the temporal city.[33] As later theology and political philosophy would show, it is but a short step from this pessimistic view to efforts to relocate the ideal kingdom in this world.

The tradition in Christian history of subsuming the natural order into the supernatural, an enterprise precisely "heretical" in orthodox terms, has been aptly called by H. X. Arquillière "l'Augustinisme politique."[34] This position reversed the practically oriented, post-Aristotelian tradition toward the contemplative. At the same time, it outlined the task that political philosophy would have after *The City of God*, that is, to regain the legitimacy of the practical order while still retaining the primacy of the theoretic order. This political Augustinianism was not, of course, the fully developed phenomenon that it

---

32. Hannah Arendt, *The Human Condition* (Garden City, N.Y., 1959), 15–17, 55–59.
33. Dawson, "Saint Augustine and His Age," 67.
34. H. X. Arquillière, *L'Augustinisme politique* (Paris, 1934), 4.

became in later medieval philosophy.[35] Augustine's main concern, however much he did in fact know about it, was not with the practical life, which was fully capable of defending itself in his own era.

"What is the important and fundamental thing in Augustine's political theory?" Michael Foster asked. "It lies, I think, in his doctrine that no man owes an absolute allegiance to any earthly society."[36] Augustine's desire for the Eternal City often inclined him, however accurate his descriptions of the Earthly City were, to a kind of indifference to civil society, or at least a realism that did not promise what it could not deliver.

"For, as far as this life of mortals is concerned, which is spent and ended in a few days, what does it matter under whose government a dying man lives, if they who govern do not force him to impiety and iniquity?"[37] Augustine's constant concern was with man's ultimate goal, but this was a goal the desire and quest for which did arise in the philosopher, in Augustine himself. Even the punishment of the innocent was to remind men that they were here for another than political purposes. Augustine wrote in *The City of God*:

> But what is blameworthy is, that they who themselves revolt from the conduct of the wicked, and live in quite another fashion, yet spare those faults in other men which they ought to reprehend and wean them from; and spare them because they fear to give offense, lest they should injure their interests in those things which good men may innocently and legitimately use—though they use them more greedily than become persons who are strangers in this world, and profess the hope of a heavenly country. . . . Accordingly, this seems to me to be one principal reason why the good are chastized along with the wicked, when God is pleased to visit with temporal punishments the profligate manners of a community. They are punished together, not because they have spent an equally corrupt life, but because the good as well as the wicked, though not equally with them, love this present

---

35. See Charles H. McIlwain, *Growth of Political Thought in the West* (New York, 1932), 154–60. See also Arquillière, *L'Augustinisme politique*, 44.
36. Michael Foster, *Masters of Political Thought* (Boston, 1941), I, 224.
37. St. Augustine, *The City of God*, Bk. V, Chap. 17, in *Basic Writings, Augustine*, II, 78.

life; while they ought to hold it cheap, that the wicked, being admonished and reformed by their example, might lay hold of life eternal.[38] Augustine is always mindful of what life transcends the city.

At first sight, for Augustine, the state is an evil, solely the result of sin. Indeed, this point, one not unlike the end of Aristotle's *Ethics,* has some foundation. In Book IV of *The City of God,* for example, Augustine asked, in a famous passage, mindful of Cicero, "Justice being taken away, then, what are kingdoms but great robberies? For what are robberies themselves, but little kingdoms?"[39] Rome, for Augustine, was not a true state because there was no justice in it.[40] The pagan states were therefore not models of natural law but bands of brigands. So also was any state in which the worship of the true God was not allowed, a worship which justice would demand. Augustine did often exalt justice and wise rule. He seemed to feel, however, like Plato, that most actual states were foredoomed to poor rule. Augustine admitted that full human life was a social life, yet it was difficult to measure the anguishes of man. "If, then, home, the natural refuge from the ills of life, is itself not safe, what shall we say of the city, which, as it is larger, is so much the more filled with lawsuits civil and criminal, and it is never free from fear, if sometimes from the actual outbreak, of disturbing and blood insurrections and civil wars?"[41] In the case of international affairs, Augustine saw an unending stream of strife and conflict.

Behind this realistic analysis, Augustine found that both the individual and society arose from a tainted source. He wrote, then, "for as in the individual the truth of the Apostle's statement is discerned, 'That is not first which is spiritual, but that which is natural, and afterwards that which is spiritual' [I Cor. 15:46], whence it comes to pass that each man, being derived from a condemned stock, is first of all born of Adam evil and carnal, and becomes good and spiritual only

---

38. *Ibid.,* Bk. I, Chap. 9, II, 13–14.
39. *Ibid.,* Bk. IV, Chap. 4, II, 51–52.
40. *Ibid.,* Bk. II, Chap. 21, II, 46.
41. *Ibid.,* Bk. XIX, Chap 5, II, 478. See also Bk. V, Chap. 24, II, 89, Bk. XV, Chap. 4, II, 278, Bk. XVIII, Chap. 22, II, 425; Bk. XIX, Chap. 7, 481.

afterward, when he is grafted into Christ by regeneration: so was it with the human race as a whole."[42] Thus although "no one is evil by nature, but whoever is evil is evil by choice," the human race is still a *massa damnata,* since as a race or people, it does not and cannot attain the lofty desires of human nature.

Augustine felt that the glory of Rome was all the glory which the Romans would get for their admitted but limited virtues, so "there is no reason why they should complain against the justice of the supreme and true God—they have received their reward."[43] The best Augustine could say about the state was that its earthly peace could be of use to the elect.[44] Augustine examined the historical states he did know in terms of their actual records. He held that the historical states worshiped false gods. And because of the false worship, these states degraded human worth. "For he lives ill who does not believe well concerning God."[45] The Augustinian tradition emphasized the de facto corruption and degradation that history records in states as a proof of the need for grace, even for the natural to be natural or, in politics, even that the state be just. Chesterton once summed up this frame of mind when he remarked that "the only objection to natural religion is that it somehow always becomes unnatural."[46] Augustine would have agreed that this was the actual record of human experience for which some account must be given. And that account ought to be both philosophical and open to revelation as itself intelligible in the light of the philosophic problem and responsive to it.

The essential importance of *The City of God* is its effort to Christianize the whole theoretic order as that order had been conceived in Greek philosophy. And this "Christianization" of the theoretic order means basically the personalization of the First Mover, or the One, or the Good, so that man's relationship with the objects of the con-

42. *Ibid.,* Bk. XV, Chap. 1, II, 275–76. See also Bk. XIV, Chap. 6, II, 246.
43. *Ibid.,* Bk. V, Chap. 15, II, 77.
44. *Ibid.,* Bk. XIX, Chap. 26, II, 505. See Norman Baynes, *The Political Ideas of St. Augustine's 'De civitate Dei'* (London, 1949), 14.
45. St. Augustine, *The City of God,* Bk. V, Chap. 10, II, 69.
46. G. K. Chesterton, *Orthodoxy* (New York, 1909), 140.

templative order became more intimate and tangible to human beings. Indeed, ultimately, almost as if to recognize the human dimensions of the problem, in this faith God became man. If one wishes to state this idea in Aristotelian terms, it is that man's ultimate desire for complete, perfect happiness was to be fulfilled in a manner that did not imply some abstract form or recipient other than the one experiencing the actual desire. Aristotle was correct in postulating the desire itself and its metaphysical realism.

But this accomplishment was to be carried out not by politics, nor by intellectual contemplation alone, not even by the philosophic contemplation of the soul separated from the body, but rather in the resurrection of the human person into a society of men, angels, and God, into what Augustine called "the City of God."[47] For this reason we could well reflect that "here then we have two incredibles—to wit, the resurrection of our body to eternity, and that the world should believe so incredible a thing."[48] This was something that no philosophic thinker had dared to suggest. But those who failed to enter the Heavenly City were also members of another city, the City of Man, Babylon. Augustine's commitment to freedom is, in this sense, radical and absolute. There is no ultimate solution to the problems present in the universe except through human understanding and will, however much these do not constitute by themselves what this happiness is when attained.

The City of God, then, is not the Church, nor is the city of man the state. The two eternal cities take their prime philosophical significance from the fact that they are Christian solutions to the

---

47. "Sacred Scripture gives the name 'gods' more expressly to men than to the immortal and blessed angles (with whom we have been promised equality after the resurrection) because the perfection of the angels is such that in the weakness of our faith we might be tempted to choose one of them as our god, whereas the temptation to make men into a god is easily overcome" (St. Augustine, *The City of God*, Bk. IX, Chap. 23; translation here from *The City of God*, ed. Vernon J. Bourke [Garden City, N.Y., 1958], 183–84). Hereafter, Bourke's translation will be cited as *The City of God*, Bourke. See also Thomas Aquinas, *Summa contra Gentiles*, Bk. I, Chap. 5.

48. St. Augustine, *The City of God*, in *Basic Writings, Augustine*, Bk. XXII, Chap. 5, II, 613.

Aristotelian-Platonic problem of the good, or ultimate happiness. And for this reason, Augustine saw clearly that he must reject and replace the whole Stoic tradition which claimed to find happiness in this life. Augustine wrote with some force:

> I am at a loss to understand how the stoic philosophers can presume to say that these are no ills, though at the same time they allow the wise man to commit suicide and pass out of this life if they become so grievous that they cannot or ought not to endure them. But such is the stupid pride of these men who fancy that the supreme good can be found in this life, and that they can become happy by their own resources, that their wise man, or at least the man whom they fancifully depict as such, is always happy, even though he become blind, deaf, dumb, mutilated, racked with pains, or suffer any conceivable calamity such as may compel him to make away with himself; and they are not ashamed to call the life which is beset with these evils happy. O happy life, which seeks the aid of death to end it![49]

The essential meaning of Christianity in political philosophy, therefore, is the definition of man's good and eternal goal as lying outside the political order, indeed, outside this life as such. The true significance of *The City of God* consists in Augustine's realization that those actual desires for personal happiness which Plato, Aristotle, Cicero, and Plotinus so well recorded are to achieve completion in another life and in another society, but they pertain to the actual persons found in existing polities. The goal of the civil state was the temporal peace, not the heavenly city.

"In that city all the citizens shall be immortal, men now for the first time enjoying what the holy angels have never lost. And this shall be accomplished by God, the most almighty Founder of the city."[50] This passage contains what is perhaps the core of the contrast between Christian-classic and modern liberal and totalitarian political theories. Christian revelation held that immortality and happiness complete man's particular desires, themselves discovered as given in

---

49. *Ibid.*, Bk. XIX, Chap. 4, II, 476–77.
50. *Ibid.*, Bk. XXII, Chap. 1, II, 609.

nature and reflectively known to exist in each human individual. Politics, however good, did not achieve this end and could not be made to do so, however proper it is to acknowledge an earthly peace.

This view likewise held that God, not man, could accomplish these ends. The accomplishment is not an illusion or figment of the imagination. Philosophy could not anticipate or rationally exclude revelational answers to questions posed in political philosophy. Augustine did not deal with a "myth," however defined, which would have made revelational explanation either psychologically subjective or reflective of some future earthly condition as a mere continuation of this life. Augustine's effort in *The City of God* was to describe the extent and content of the eternal society to which man can belong. Man's task, the one that took priority over all else, was to join this eternal society. The political life, man's earthly task, paled in meaning before this primary obligation and destiny, though political life did not rule out a reflection of the order in the mind. Good and evil regimes were not simply arbitrary in their distinctions. "What I want to bring out," Augustine observed, "is that, although we depend on the true and truly holy Divinity for such things as are needed to support our weakness in this present life, nevertheless, we should not seek and worship God for the sake of the passing cloud of this mortal life, but for the sake of that happy life which cannot be other than everlasting."[51] And ultimately, man's own personal choice determines God's judgment of him. "He judges, too, not only in the mass, condemning the race of devils and the race of men to be miserable on account of the original sin of these races, but He also judges the voluntary and personal acts of individuals."[52]

In following this line of thought, Augustine reintroduced the idea of finality into nature and extended the concept to include human history as such, which no longer seemed cyclic or endless. Augustine explained.

---

51. St. Augustine, *The City of God, Bourke,* Bk. VII, Preface, 135.
52. St. Augustine, *The City of God,* in *Basic Writings, Augustine,* Bk. XX, Chap. 1, II, 509.

At this point, I must mention various operations of the one true God. It was because of these that the pagan philosophers, who were making a serious effort to interpret the indecent and immoral mysteries, made for themselves so many false gods. First, then, it is the God we worship who constituted, for each of the natures He created, an origin and purpose of its being and pioneers of action. He holds in His hands the causes of things, knowing them all and connecting them all. It is He who is the source of all energy in seeds, and He who put rational souls, or spirits, into living beings He selected, and He gave us the gifts of speech and language. The God we worship chose certain spirits and gave them the power of foresight, and through them He makes prophecies. To others He gave the gift of healing. He controls the beginnings, progress, and endings of wars, when they are needed for the punishment or reformation of mankind.[53]

Augustine transformed Aristotle's idea that nature has only hypothetical necessity, and therefore requires the action of the First Mover to establish its limits, into the Judaeo-Christian scheme, which maintained that nature is the product of a creating God. On that very account, then, nature is open to intellect and ordering.

Thus Augustine saw in nature a finality and a stability placed there by the creator, a finality that cannot fully be grasped apart from the Creator but a finality in some sense intelligible. In this context, Augustine believed that he saw the true meaning of Plato and Plotinus. "For those who are praised as having most closely followed Plato, who are justly preferred to all the other philosophers of the Gentiles, and who are said to have manifested the greatest acuteness in understanding him, do perhaps entertain such an idea of God as to admit that in Him are to be found the cause of existence, the ultimate reason for the understanding, and the end in referring to which the whole life is to be regulated."[54] In this way Augustine resolved the relation of the classics to Christianity.

Though we probably have less difficulty in imagining Augustine's own particular personality than that of almost any other man in the

---

53. St. Augustine, *The City of God, Bourke*, Bk. VII, Chap. 30, 139–40.
54. St. Augustine, *The City of God*, in *Basic Writings, Augustine*, Bk. VIII, Chap. 4, II, 105.

ancient world, perhaps his one great weakness in political philosophy was his use of a version of the Platonic and Plotinian definition of man as the basis for this intellectual system. Plato seemed to have held that the true man was a separate Idea, whereas tangible, changing men were only reflections of true man's glory.[55] "The other [the soul], the most honorable phase of our being," Plotinus said, "is what we think of as the true man."[56] Augustine's idea was similar: "Man, then, as viewed by his fellow man, is a rational soul with a mortal and earthly body in its service."[57] Thus as Gilson pointed out, Augustine was an inheritor of the Platonic tradition that the soul is a substance joined to a body which is also a substance.[58]

Augustine of course avoided the idea that man was two substances joined to a unity which is another substance or a sort of accidental unity of two incompatible things. But Augustine undoubtedly had great difficulty once he accepted the Platonic tradition on this point. Indeed, a Platonist, as opposed to an Aristotelian, must always have great difficulty with the Incarnation, whether it be the incarnation of soul to body or the Word made flesh. For Aristotle, man is body and soul; one is incomplete without the other. They do not form "two" different "things." For Plato, the soul tended to be man, hence the great temptation of Platonizing Christianity was always to declare the body of Christ to be a mere illusion and the motherhood of Mary an equivocation.[59]

The metaphysical implications of Augustine's emphasis on the soul are of great importance in political philosophy in particular. Politics, if it is to attain legitimacy, must see in man more than an immortal soul. The task of the earthly city must be important as such, something that is related both to the city itself and to the City of God. But if the soul is emphasized, even while recognizing the union of body

55. Plato, *Alcibiades*, trans. W. R. N. Lamb (London, 1927), I, 129C–130E, pp. 197–201.
56. Plotinus, *Enneads*, IV, 4, p. 18.
57. St. Augustine, *The Morals of the Catholic Church*, in *Basic Writings, Augustine*, Bk. I, Chap. 27, I, 344.
58. Etienne Gilson, *Introduction á l'ètude de Saint Augustin* (Paris, 1943), 57–58.
59. See Philip Hughes, *A History of the Church* (New York, 1952), I, 74–77, 117–20, 230–63.

and soul, as Augustine (and sometimes Plato) did, still the main task, if not the only task, will concern the soul's effort to achieve beatitude. The body will be seen largely as an impediment. Perfection will be seen as a release from the body rather than a completion of its real existence and tendencies. The life of politics, which Aristotle felt to be man's unique task, will be avoided except insofar as it is needed to achieve the heavenly city. There will be lacking that cosmic scheme of interrelated finalities discovered in Aristotelian biology, physics, psychology, metaphysics, ethics, and politics, that constant progress from lower things to higher things in which the higher things are not merely aspects of the lower things, the passions. For Aristotle, the contemplative life was beyond politics, but not apart from it. Man needed political life not only for itself but even for the contemplative life.

Augustine's metaphysics, on the other hand, as Gilson noted, did not start from or concentrate on things as such. True, Augustine, like Thomas Aquinas and Aristotle, did not start with God, as the ontologists or Spinoza did later. The creature was not "deduced" from God; God was reached at the end of a rational argumentation that began with creatures. Augustine's distinct approach was through that being which he used to ascend the scale. "The *primum cognitum* of St. Augustine is not God; it is man within the universe, and, within the universe and this man, the experience of a true judgment."[60] Augustine's starting point, then, was Augustine's own initial grasp of his spiritual, immortal soul, a soul which was directly an image of the Trinity, of the teaching, that is, that within the godhead there is not sterile aloneness but a community of relationships. Self-reflection for Augustine revealed more than just the self of Augustine, a "more" not arrived at arbitrarily but based in a known argument, which Augustine followed and proposed to all who read him. "And we indeed recognize in ourselves the image of God," Augustine wrote, "that is, of the supreme Trinity, an image which, though it be not equal to God, or rather, though it be very far removed from Him—being nei-

---

60. Etienne Gilson, "The Future of Augustinian Metaphysics," in *A Gilson Reader,* 97.

ther co-eternal, nor, to say all in a word, consubstantial with Him—is yet nearer to Him in nature than any other of His works, and is destined to be yet restored, that it may bear a still closer resemblance. For we both are, and know that we are, and delight in our being, and in our knowledge of it."[61]

Augustine's metaphysical analysis, consequently, began not with a thought or an idea as such, as with Descartes, but with a true knowledge of his own soul, with its own knowledge and love. "For if I am deceived, I am," Augustine wrote in a most famous passage. "For he who is not, cannot be deceived; and if I am deceived, by this same token, I am. And since I am if I am deceived, how am I deceived in believing that I am? For it is certain that I am if I am deceived. . . . Further, as there is no one who does not wish to be happy, so there is no one who does not wish to be. For how can he be happy, if he is nothing?"[62] Augustine did begin in the real order. Indeed, as Gilson indicated, Augustine began in both the natural and supernatural orders. That is, he did not postulate that reality would only contain in theory what the human mind could anticipate, by its own imaginings or method, what was in fact in it.

"For Augustine . . . , the initial *sum* [I am] contains the supernatural order as given in his experience and his being, as well as the natural order into which the supernatural is inserted." Consequently, "the supernatural order by which he had access to the truth was for him always an integral part of his philosophical inquiry."[63] This was conceived to be not somehow an alienation but merely a response to what was there in Augustine's complete experience, the denial of which would be a philosophical betrayal as well as a theological fault.

The key word in Augustine's philosophical analysis was *truth*. For

---

61. St. Augustine, *The City of God*, in *Basic Writings, Augustine*, Bk. XI, Chap. 26, II, 168. The book of Augustine on the Trinity is in fact a basic treatise on the nature of community as well as a revelational reflection on what the Good or First Mover must mean. For this treatise, see *Basic Writings, Augustine*, II, 667–878. See also Charles Norris Cochrane, *Christianity and Classical Culture* (London, 1977), Pt. 3.
62. St. Augustine, *The City of God*, in *Basic Writings, Augustine*, Bk. XI, Chap. 26, II, 168.
63. Gilson, "The Future of Augustinian Metaphysics," 98.

him, truth could not be changing; it was eternal. As he put it in his *Soliloquies,* "*Reason.* Thou are sure that thou are minded to know the soul, and God? *Augustine.* That is all my desire. *R.* Nothing more? *A.* Nothing at all. *R.* What, do you not wish to comprehend Truth? *A.* As if I could know these things except through her. *R.* Therefore, she first is to be known through whom these things can be known."[64] Augustine realized that he did not by himself possess or establish the truth, that truth was unchangeable, yet that "nothing is true, except those things which are immortal."[65] This led Augustine directly to God as the cause of truth. "The course recommended by St. Augustine—and herein lies his personal contribution to the treasure of tradition—is the path to God, leading through this particular creature which is man, and in man, thought, and in thought, truth."[66] This internality, this seeming independence of things as such, can, though it need not necessarily, support a metaphysical attitude, which can take a different path to God than the one through the things and obligations of this world, but may remain one rooted in being because it is guided by a really existing man in reflection on what he is.

In conclusion, for Augustine as for Plotinus, an emphasis on and justification for the theoretic order are discovered which tended to absorb the practical order or at least to deemphasize it. Plotinus, it seems, occurs also in political philosophy because he represented, as did Augustine, a prime example of the reversal of the trend to exalt the practical life, a trend which was so characteristic of post-Aristotelian philosophy. But Augustine could not accept the Plotinian system insofar as it excluded the possibility of God's descent into history or insofar as it proposed that man's ultimate happiness was to merge into the One in indistinction rather than the personal immortality of the whole individual of the revelational teaching.[67]

---

64. St. Augustine, *Soliloquies,* in *Basic Writings, Augustine,* Bk. I, Chap. 27, I, 274. See Gilson, *Introduction á l'ètude de Saint Augustin,* 102.
65. St. Augustine, *Soliloquies,* in *Basic Writings, Augustine,* Bk. I, Chap. 29, I, 275.
66. Gilson, "The Future of Augustinian Metaphysics," 102.
67. "But the doctrine of the incarnation of the Word, the essential point of Christianity, he [St. Augustine] did not discover it in the *Enneads: I did not read it there*" (my translation of Paul Henry, *Plotin et l'Occident* [Louvain, 1934], 143).

The overall effect of Plotinus and Augustine in political philosophy is that they represent the perennial need of man to recognize the primacy of the contemplative order, so that man can be all that he is. Indeed, they also stand for man's need to have some authentic description of this order, however little directly it can be known. They likewise stand as witnesses to the inability of politics to be the proper and unique means for man to achieve his ultimate goals. Yet the very success of their systems carried with them their own particular dangers. For in both Plotinus and the movement later named "political Augustinianism," a definite tendency existed so to absorb and minimize the politics of this world that man was left with only the contemplative itself understood in opposition to the full being of man. Plotinus in particular also set the stage for the intellectual effort which was so to identify thought and being that it was at least intelligible to seek by the human mind alone the freedom of the One or the divinity.

The history of political philosophy for the next thousand years was the history of the consequences of these positions, together with the beginnings of a more proper appreciation of the political. The political realism of Augustine, in particular, has remained an active current in political philosophy, something directly in the line of Plato's and Aristotle's descriptions of the decline of states and their revolutions.[68] Whenever this clearer realization of what does happen in politics disappears, thoughts of actually creating a perfect republic on this earth, a heavenly city, immediately arise. As Ernest Fortin has written, "with or without its revolutions, the political life is incapable of exhausting the full range of human possibilities or satisfying completely man's longing for wholeness. When all is said and done, there is, according to Augustine, only one life which deserves to be called blessed, the future life, in which alone the true knowledge of God is to be found (*Retract.*, I, 2)."[69]

In conclusion, then, Augustine stands as the central figure in po-

---

68. See Reinhold Niebuhr, "Augustine's Political Realism," *Perspectives in Political Philosophy*, ed. J. Downton (New York, 1971), 243–57.
69. Ernest L. Fortin, *Political Idealism and Christianity in the Thought of St. Augustine* (Villanova, Pa., 1972), 35.

litical philosophy when it comes to the necessity, as it always must, of denying that the ultimate spiritual enterprise is to be achieved in some existing city. In the end, there is nothing wrong with a political philosophy in which questions arise to which political philosophy itself cannot give the full answer. This is merely another sign of the full unity of the human being. And it is too, after all, why Aristotle wrote both a book of *Politics* and a book of *Metaphysics,* why Augustine himself wrote of the City of Man and of the City of God. The complete political philosopher needs to be also someone who has considered revelation and philosophy itself as addressed to his own discipline and reflection.

4

THOMAS AQUINAS AND THE
PROPER LIFE OF MAN

"To strive for any end that cannot be secured is futile," Thomas Aquinas wrote in his *Summa contra Gentiles*.[1] The place of Thomas Aquinas in the history of political philosophy can be considered in various ways. He can be seen as a commentator on Augustine and especially on Aristotle but still as someone who deviated from both on various fundamental points. He can also be seen as a theologian whose main emphases are therefore irrelevant or unknowable to political philosophy. He can be seen as valuably summarizing medieval thinking, as a thinker whose "system" is out of date but served its time well.

Again, he can be seen as a formulator of a certain strand of religious, particularly Roman Catholic "ideology," to be compared perhaps favorably or unfavorably with other ideologies but having no more grounding than any of the others which have appeared before or after his time. Aquinas can be regarded, finally, however, as the prime example of that "perennial philosophy" whose principles abide and recur whenever men think accurately and truthfully about reality. In this latter sense his contribution seems best understood in the ongoing argument that is political philosophy.

To understand Thomas Aquinas apart from the whole unity he proposed is, no doubt, "futile." But more fundamentally, Aquinas addressed himself to the questions of what appeared to be natural "futility" but ones that appeared necessarily from correct thinking about human existence. He ascertained that a number of valid observations and positions, clearly formulated in the classical authors and sharpened in the medieval writers, suggested that the fullness of natural desires could not be adequately met in human reason by itself. Yet

1. Thomas Aquinas, *Summa contra Gentiles*, III, 44, I, N. 58.

even Aristotle held that a natural desire could not be "in vain." So how was it possible to reconcile what was "natural" with what seemed "futile"?

In the present context, then, political philosophy especially, even for its own abstract clarification of itself, rarely considers how these questions were answered in Aquinas. "Alexander [of Aphrodisias] and Averroes alike," Aquinas wrote in his *Summa contra Gentiles*, "recognized that man's ultimate happiness does not lie in knowledge acquired by scientific means, but in continuous conjunctions with an unearthly substance. Yet, as Aristotle was aware, there seems no other way open at present save the scientific, and so the happiness in our power is qualified and not complete. This goes to show how great minds have been hemmed in. We shall be free of these straights, however, if we suppose that the human soul is immortal and that men can reach perfect happiness after this life."[2] What is to be argued, consequently, following the account of these points in Aristotle and Augustine, is that only when this futility is understood will the full unity of political philosophy be grasped. "Modern" political philosophy and experience can be understood best when they are seen as developments of or deviations from these theoretical positions found in Aquinas as he related them to the classics, particularly Aristotle.

In this sense even though Aquinas is widely admired, he is a much more central figure in political philosophy than he is normally considered. To understand and present this approach clearly, unique as it is, we must assume, for the sake of argument, the unity of reason and revelation which Aquinas proposed. We need presuppose not theoretical or religious agreement but rather the lively intelligence that can grasp what is argued, from whatever source, if it is presented in an intelligible fashion. At this point, however, it is not necessary for political philosophy itself to enter into the question of the truth of revelation, something it is incapable of doing in any case, except when its claims contradict reason.

2. *Ibid.*, III, 48, I, N. 91.

Political philosophy, however, cannot be something totally indifferent to the claims of revelation on it, since both sources of knowledge propose their truths to all men as men. Political philosophy can and must, however, understand what revelation presents as responses to the questions which political philosophy genuinely and constantly proposes to itself from its own sources. This part of the historic record is open to intelligence in terms of at least understanding what is being articulated.

Thus political philosophy is capable of reflection on those forms of hope or striving that curiously appear in political experience for which there seem to be no adequate responses in reason itself. Aquinas wrote: "Philosophical truths cannot be opposed to the truths of faith; they fall short indeed, yet they also admit common analogies; and some, moreover, are foreshadowings, for nature is the preface to grace."[3] Is there, then, something "in vain," something disordered in the very heart of reality itself, since certainly the initial questions in the classics are legitimately posed in human experience and understanding but apparently have no natural answers? Are political philosophy and revelation simply divergent worlds with no crossings even in the individual in which they reside?

No doubt the most memorable example of these instances, not necessarily by itself presupposing revelation, occurred in Book X of *The Republic* of Plato, when the admitted inability of any actual polity to reward all good and punish all evil is addressed in its clarity. The proposal that the soul is immortal, so that these unsettled questions will be resolved beyond this life, derives from Socrates' realization that, in this life, not all evil will in fact be punished nor all good rewarded. Socrates knew, furthermore, that doing evil was wrong or evil, but he was not sure that death was evil. In other words, the striving for pure justice, which the young men in *The Republic* insisted upon hearing praised in its purity, leads to a philosophical question about how its problematic is resolved, without which the striving is in vain. But if

---

3. Thomas Aquinas, *Opusculum* XVI, Expositio, *De Trinitate*, ii, 3, I, N. 80.

justice is pursued relentlessly to accomplish its ends, it becomes itself revolutionary to any public order by seeking an impossible end.

Moreover, this philosophical solution found already in *The Republic* is itself unsatisfactory since, as Aristotle would subsequently show, the essence of man, of the individual, is not to be as soul alone but as a substantial unity of soul and body in one being related as act to potency. Aquinas put it in this way: "To appreciate existing human nature, we must reckon with the particular physique and mentality of Peter and Martin."[4] Again, this either presents us with a "futile" problem, which is the inability of the individual human to reach actual happiness for his particular whole self, or it is suggestive of a solution which fits in with the argument. That is, such a goal is desired and possible but not on the basis of political experience alone or in this life. The essential uniqueness of Peter and Martin—of Socrates, Plato, or Mary—then, is a fact that implies the abidingness of each, a question to which the theology of resurrection responds directly, as Aquinas argued, in terms of what is formulated in ethical reflections about exactly who wants to be happy. The rewarding of justice and the punishing of injustice, moreover, require that the person rewarded and punished be the particular one responsible for the act of justice or injustice in the first place.

But—and here modern political philosophy enters the discussion—a denial of the soul's uniqueness, the individual's particular existence, or ultimate destiny, incipient answers to which were placed in existence in political philosophy also by revelation, reduced the individual to the "species" man, the abstract form wherein the particular Peter or Martin disappeared in a commonness of essence. This abstraction, in turn, elevated politics to the highest of the sciences because its real limits were no longer operative. To understand the logic of these premises is, in a basic sense, the meaning of political philosophy taken as an abiding argument transcending time, which is open to any thinking mind, whenever it happens to confront the

4. Thomas Aquinas, *Summa theologiae* (Turin, 1948), I, 119, 1.

problem in its proper terms. That is, if we regard each unique human existent in his particular form, in Peter or Martin, Socrates, Plato, or Mary, in whom the actual desire for happiness exists and for whom the question of meaning arises, then no form of politics can provide what the existing Peter or Martin actually desires.

Political philosophy, however, is required for the existence of philosophy itself. And without a being capable of "philosophizing," of thinking about *what is,* there can be no "revelation," no communication of truths not capable of being arrived at by human intelligence but which respond to real questions in Peter, Martin, Socrates, Plato, and Mary. Political philosophy, according to the classics, raises the question of the Good and how man is related to it, beginning with his own individual good, in the fullest sense, in the course of his single life, within a family and a polity.

Political philosophy wanted to know, then, which of all the choices open to men are the better ones for this end and why. These choices dealt, first, with what men are as men, nourished as men in the household, and second, with what they were as good men, in the polity. Men were "given" their being as men. That is, they did not make themselves men, but they did make themselves good or bad men. There was a weight, a responsibility, therefore, in the very self-discovery that men were men. This was the "burden" of openness, of the possibility that men living under their own control might relate themselves properly and freely to the order of things that do exist, including themselves and their understanding of *what is.*

In the "Prologue" of his commentary on the *Politics* of Aristotle, Thomas Aquinas wrote: "Politics, among the other practical sciences, is more fundamental and 'architectonic' than all others, because it considers the ultimate and perfect good in human affairs. And because of this, the Philosopher [Aristotle] says at the end of the Tenth Book of the *Ethics,* that the philosophy which deals with human affairs is perfected by politics."[5] Politics is here called, in the specialized vo-

---

5. Thomas Aquinas, *In octo libros politicorum Aristotelis expositio* (Quebec, 1940), 6.

cabulary of Aristotle, a "practical science," the highest of the practical sciences, of intelligence directed to action in existing formed matter.

Practical sciences, we should recall, deal with those things which can be "otherwise," which need not be in this way or that but must be made (art) or chosen (ethics and politics) to be such and such. Politics, moreover, addresses itself unavoidably to the perfect good in human affairs. This category will include, as a consequence, not merely a reflection on the best but also a full consideration of all that is not the "perfect good" in human affairs. Though political philosophy is primarily concerned with action among human beings, it is likewise concerned with understanding such actions and with ordering them so that they can be understood. This understanding will never be perfect, since, as Aristotle warned, we should not expect more certitude than a subject matter can contain.[6] And since ethical and political matters deal with particular, singular actions, which must take circumstances into account, the multiplicity of elements will never be perfectly mastered, even though action still ought to and does take place in the singular circumstances of human life.

Political philosophy is not directly a "speculative" science, then, even though, in the classics, it raises questions that eventually lead to the truth of *what is,* of what is for its own sake. Political life pertains to the "highest practical science," the architectonic science, the one that orders all of other goals and actions to "this perfect good of human affairs." This perfect good was not, in Aristotle, as in the post-Aristotelians (Chapter 2), the highest good of all but the highest good open to man as man, although it was recognized that he was open to something higher as "divine." The peculiar status of man as containing all elements of reality within him (the microcosmos) meant that he shared in some sense in all the "lives" or qualities of all the grades of being. But because of this participation, man was unique. What no one else had was politics.

---

6. Aristotle, *Nicomachean Ethics,* I, 2, 1094b24–26, p. 935. "The same sort of certitude is not to be expected in all fields of scientific inquiry. The well-disciplined mind will not demand greater certitude than the subject will offer, nor be content with less" (Thomas Aquinas, Commentary, *Nicomachean Ethics,* I, 3, I, N. 31).

Philosophy itself inquires about what exists, about the causes and nature of present reality. Philosophy seeks a complete account of the whole. How is, the classic writers wondered, *what is,* reality itself, related to that good which is sought in one form or another by human beings in all their activities? Actual political societies in history and in the present could be described and classified by the sort of good or end they sought, by their priorities. This classification was rooted in the actions of human beings, in their reality, while it admitted wide existential variety, even within a common type. The action of a being, Aquinas would say, follows from the kind of a thing that it is. Political thought ordered in an intelligible manner the sorts of goods that were in fact sought in a regime by its members. These goods or ends are discovered in the chosen actions of the individuals who perform them. They are reflected in the laws and offices of particular polities, in what is legislated and enforced. The human intellectual capacity to transcend the particular action and polity by its understanding enabled men to compare and order, enabled them to think about the meaning of differing regimes.

Thus Plato's notion that the polity is "the individual writ large" had considerable truth if it was taken as a description of what most men choose in most polities rather than as a foundation for the idea, so dangerous in the history of political thought, that some quasi-substantial "being" more fundamental than the individual human being exists as "the polity." The meaning of part and whole in political theory, then, is one of its most important and difficult elements, because the "whole" of the polity is not higher in substance than the whole that is each individual human being.[7] The cycle of regimes found in Plato and Aristotle, together with the mixed regimes found in Polybius and Cicero, enabled classical political philosophy to ask about the good and about the deviant regimes, about how these were related to each other and to the best regimes, which were held to exist in the mind, in some future, or in God.

---

7. See J. Bochenski, *Philosophy—An Introduction* (New York, 1972), 101; Schall, *Politics of Heaven and Hell,* 235–52.

Augustine, of course, had noted that the actual regimes all contained some deviation from the good, so they could not be the location of the final human good in its highest sense. This statement did not mean, however, that the question of the location of the best regime was unimportant. But the question of the theoretic best regime and its relation to the good is legitimate and arises necessarily from lived politics itself. Action and thought are directly connected in this sense. Contemplation arises from the very "living well" that is the end of the polity. This lived politics, however, is futher confused and disordered when the question of the best actual regime becomes an ultimate explanation of all reality. How to keep these questions distinct has proved to be one of the most difficult issues in political philosophy itself. Yet no one doubts that the ultimate good ought, in some sense, to be related to the good regimes.

Modern political philosophy began with the denial of a connection between the best regime and the actual regimes, in Machiavelli and Hobbes. At first sight, this denial would appear to be simply what Augustine had recommended. But this "modern project" appears to undermine the unity of the human whole or to deny its highest reaches, its connection with ultimate reality. From this beginning, however, modern theory would come to argue that philosophical and religious questions were indifferent to the public order, that human good or happiness was purely a private matter, so that there was no connection between the truth of *what is* and the public order. Aristotle's practical and speculative sciences were simply torn asunder. The logical consequence was that speculative truth had no effect on the practical truth of living; rather, practical living independently found its own truth.

The end of modern political philosophy in this sense, then, is the ideological proposal to establish a new "public truth" and "order" presupposed to no theoretic foundation except the human will. The proposals to return to "classical" or "medieval" political theory are, in essence, endeavors to reaffirm the whole of the human being and experience, itself grounded in something more than what man merely chooses, presupposed to nothing but his own autonomous will. If political philosophy as such has an empirical level, it will most likely be found in the accurate description and classification of the regimes that are established in history by such views of the nature of reality and human reality.

In the classics, however, philosophy and actual politics could indeed come into conflict. *The Apology* of Plato is the perennial reminder of this point. The conflict happened when someone, the Philosopher, questioned the sort of order established by law or habit in a particular existing polity, even the best existing one of its time, as in the case of Athens. This action suggested that any individual, by virtue of his power of self-reflection on what exists in his city, had some access to a reality that was not totally enclosed by politics. The human reasoning power, which at its highest ought to be devoted to "divine" things, as Aristotle said, was possessed by each individual in all historical polities.

The mere possession of this power was not enough, however, to assure that the highest end would in fact be reached by each person having such a faculty, even when it was used properly. This suggested, if not an injustice, at least some kind of incompleteness or deviation in the right order of things to one another. How, in other words, was it possible to maintain some balance in all these various relationships between individuals and the First Mover, between practical and speculative intellect, between completeness and incompleteness?

The work of Thomas Aquinas is a harmonious consideration of these topics, against which classical questions are to be seen as legitimate problems with feasible solutions, not merely myths or artistic creations. Likewise, modern intellectual developments can be seen as deviations from or confirmations of Aquinas's endeavor to think philosophically about questions that were addressed to man by revelation but especially about questions which had roots somehow in the political order. Even when these revelational-philosophic answers have been rejected in modern theory, they are rejected not in their classic formulations alone but in their philosophical formulations hammered out under the influence of revelational questions. Here it is a matter less of the validity of revelational corpus of doctrine, though that should be argued in its proper place, than of its intelligibility and its relationship to questions of history and philosophy which have become the key issues in modern political philosophy.

Thomas Aquinas understood, then, that Aristotle's notion of human immortality, correct as far as it went yet incomplete, had to be clarified and justified more adequately in the context of each human's possession of a personal intellectual power. This faculty in each person did not require some outside faculty or power before each human being could understand. It was internally required before the questions posed at the end of *The Republic* and by Aristotle himself could be fully confronted. The consequence, which was considered a philosophical proposition, not revelation, was the existence of an immortal soul which possessed as such, by itself, a higher grade of being than was the life of any polity as a collectivity composed of human actions and relationships based in them. Aquinas, in fact, posited that each individual could reach to the common good of the universe itself, though surely not by himself nor by politics, yet by his own intellectual powers as given in his natural being. "For a thing is known inasmuch as it has come home to the knower," Aquinas held. "Whence Aristotle says (*De anima*, 429a19; 430a15) that the soul is potentially everything and is what it is by becoming all things. So it is possible for the perfection of the whole world to exist in one thing. Such is the fullness the soul may achieve. According to the philosophers, the entire system of the cosmos, complete with all its causes, may be delineated in the soul. This, they maintain, is the last end of man. We, however, set it in the vision of God, for, as Gregory remarks, for those who see him who sees everything, what is there they do not see?"[8]

The difference between classical and medieval theory is thus not to be decided by any necessary conflict between the demands of reason and those of revelation. Likewise, the difference between practical and speculative sciences should be seen as a matter not of permanent opposition but rather of subordinate, interrelated order. Revelation was

---

8. Thomas Aquinas, Disputations, II *De veritate*, 2, I, N. 1117. See also Thomas Aquinas, *Summa theologiae*, I–II, 21, 4, ad 3, I, N. 1111.

to be understood as an intelligence directed to philosophy, legitimate in its own order, to the philosophers, to real men and women. Indeed, revelation was primarily to be directed to each human person, even if he was not a philosopher. Also revelation was an intelligible suggestion, as it were, about the human good in particular, about the prudence of the politicians. Both philosophy and politics became more themselves as a result, more philosophical, more properly political. Some would see this as somehow "alienating" because it implied that man did not have full control over *what is,* particularly the power to define the essence of reality. This was merely the truth, of course, as men did not have this sort of power to establish the ends and nature of reality, particularly their own. But it was also in the nature of human power at least to be open to questions it could by itself formulate, so that it could recognize what was being suggested in terms of what it had already discovered by its own self-reflective activities.

Because of the admittedly delicate relations existing between philosophy and theology in any case, there can perhaps be too much caution in recognizing that revelation is capable of discussing itself in terms taken from philosophy and in terms addressed to it. These terms are intelligible to the philosopher because of what he learned in his own mind from his own experience and because there is an "intelligibility" to all points in authentic revelation. This intelligibility was to arise from the evidence drawn from contact with the world, which Aristotle said was the beginning of all human knowledge. But it was to continue by virtue of its own innate powers open to and included in *all that is.*

This self-description of revelation, worked out historically because of the need to resolve conflict and the need to explain authoritatively what this revelation means, is among the facts of intellectual history and an "actor," as it were, in political philosophy. The grounds and evidence for the truth of revelation are themselves common sense and philosophical reason, however much the human intellect may not be able by itself fully to grasp the life of the divine itself. But this human intelligence is rooted in being and can understand what is contradictory to its reality. Men cannot be addressed by the divine unless, in some sense, they are ontologically the sorts of beings capable of being so addressed. There is no direct "revelation" to rocks or toads. This is already the ultimate basis of man's unique dignity. Philosophy may not be adequate to resolve all the answers to questions that philosophy can properly formulate. On the other hand, it is possible to recognize that certain truths given in articulated revelation are indeed answers to questions properly formulated in philosophy in any city which allows men to think on *what is*.

Such answers, of course, will not, unless they are repetitions of truths the human intellect can know by itself, be rationally "compelling" by definition, since they are seen first by faith. The hypothesis that the human intellect can "understand" revelation fully means, equivalently, that man is himself divine. Yet this is exactly what the notion that revelation, which is beyond man's capacities but proposed to his intellect, was designed to deny. But if we reflect on the proposals of revelation seriously, they will be seen to relate to the questions asked by reason and experience. Likewise some things reached in reason will also be found to be revealed, so that the intelligence seems to correspond to revelation whenever it occurs. This tendency is, in fact, what particularly justifies man in his suspicion that many of his questions, which do not seem to have answers, which seem to be "in vain," can potentially be resolved. "There are two methods of argument, demonstrative and persuasive," Aquinas wrote. "Demonstrative, cogent, and intellectually convincing argument cannot lay hold of the truths of faith, though it may neutralize destructive criticism that would render faith untenable. Persuasive reasoning drawn from probabilities, however, does not weaken the merit of faith, for its implies no attempt to convert faith into sight by resolving what is believed into evident first principles."[9]

Human reason may be open to, but incomplete before, the reality it does not itself make. Intelligence may thus be broader than reason, so that reason may be made more complete in its own order by the

---

9. Thomas Aquinas, *Opusculum*, XVI, *De Trinitate*, ii, i, ad 5, I, N. 77. See also Thomas Aquinas, *Summa contra Gentiles*, I, 3.

facts and challenges of revelation presented to it. This possibility does not obviate a theory of faith to account for what finite reason may not see but requires such a theory. But the contrast or difference between faith and reason is not in consequence one of contradiction. Thomas Aquinas thus denied in principle the Averroistic "two truth" theories, which implied that a truth of reason and a truth of revelation, in full intellectual opposition, were possible. Aquinas wrote, then, that "this is tantamount to holding that belief can be about things whose contrary can be demonstrated. Since what can be so demonstrated is bound to be a necessary truth and its opposite false and impossible, the upshot would be that faith avows what is false and impossible. This is intolerable to our ears, for even God could not contrive such a situation."[10]

Faith was not, consequently, in Aquinas, some kind of myth or description designed to let the philosophers be about the "real" truth unbeknownst to the majorities in all polities, as if there were somehow two radically different types of human beings, the few philosophers and the vast majority of some lesser sorts. The reworking of ideas found initially in Aristotle established the intrinsic unity of the human knowing capacities. The implications of this unity for what a human being as such was, then, turned out to be the key to locating the proper place of politics and political philosophy, which Thomas Aquinas did.

AQUINAS AND MEDIEVAL POLITICAL PHILOSOPHY

The approximately eight hundred years between the death of Augustine (A.D. 430) and the death of Thomas Aquinas (A.D. 1274) are important in political philosophy because of the "raised expectations" that subsequently existed in the civil order as a result of revelation, expectations, rooted in revelation, which, however, seemed to be merely "natural," as Machiavelli complained.[11] These expectations, however, needed to be spelled out and articulated. Revelation in fact

---

10. Thomas Aquinas, *Opusculum* VI, *De unitate intellectus contra Averroistas*, I, N. 81.
11. See Strauss, *What Is Political Philosophy?* 41–44.

did not suggest or propose what might most obviously be expected of it in political philosophy, namely, that its purpose was the establishment of a sort of Platonic "best regime" as a properly successful political project in this world. This sort of revelation, if it had occurred, would presumably have validated revelation by a sort of political "proof."

Though this came to be the project of the Enlightenment and the ideological political theory in postmedieval times that was based on it—what Strauss will call "the modern project" and Voegelin "Gnosticism" (see below, Chapter 8)—this was not what Christianity proposed to men as the purpose of revelation, as the Crucifixion at the hands of the state and the theories of Augustine had clearly seen (Chapter 3). Indeed, the proper task of political philosophy is the clearer understanding of what can and what cannot be expected from political life, not expecting too little, not demanding too much, together with the consequences of pursuing either beyond its prudential limits, the limits of the practical sciences, the limits of moderation.

Nevertheless, Christian practice and speculation made it clear that citizens were expected to be "better" human beings because of the presence of revelation. This was not a purely "interior" religion with no visible contact with the external world of action, as Marsilius of Padua seemed to think it was.[12] The Christian revelation contained no theory of regime or civil office or citizenship, except to affirm that these questions were in themselves "Caesar's," that is, legitimate functions of reason and reflective of lived experience. These political issues were the areas of the practical sciences, of which Aristotle had spoken and whose voice again was heard through the Arab, Jewish, and Christian commentators in the thirteenth century.[13] Christianity was not a revelation about politics in its proper sphere. That is, it acknowledged that there were spheres of reality and human activity that were

---

12. See Leo Strauss, "Marsilius of Padua," *History of Political Philosophy,* ed. Leo Strauss and Joseph Cropsey (Chicago, 1972), 251–70.
13. See the discussion of the difference between Islam and Judaism in contrast to Christianity in Leo Strauss, *Persecution and the Art of Writing* (Glencoe, Ill., 1952), 19–21.

not political, without the need to deny that what was political was proper and had its own place.

But Christianity also held that the human being was a unified whole such that, if its essentially religious recommendations were practiced by large numbers of citizens (by one, indeed), the burden of rule, by classical standards, somehow, even in the worst regime, would be easier. The inner spiritual life of the human being, though it could not directly be reached by human law, as Aquinas held, still needed rectification even for the purposes of the human law itself.[14] Again, a "problem," the limits of human law, posed by experience and reason—namely, how to reach the inner life of man which guided his external acts—received an unexpected "answer" to it addressed by revelation. This answer directly related to the highest end and full nature of each individual but included the external and hence civil activities of the citizens. What men were admonished to do in ordering their inner lives had the public effect of concern and aid to all types of human beings in the direction that the philosophers knew to be virtue even in its highest reaches.

During the medieval era, classical thought was assimilated in such a way that philosophy, human reason as actively engaged in understanding *what is*, considered its own questions because it was prompted also by what happened from revelation, now more and more articulated with the help of philosophy. This revelation was looked upon not as a "theory" but as a series of facts, the capacity to receive which depended on the understanding of singulars as derived from Aristotle.[15] Thomas Aquinas's oft-repeated principle upon which he based his theory of the relation of revelation and reason, that grace builds on nature, involved not only the question of the status of nature and how

---

14. Thomas Aquinas, *Summa theologiae*, I–II, 91, 4.
15. Thomas Aquinas, *Summa contra Gentiles*, I, 63–64. See also Commentary, II *De anima*, Lect. 13, I, N. 659; Henri de Lubac, *The Sources of Revelation*, trans. Luke O'Neill (New York, 1968), 159–239; Josef Pieper, *Scholasticism* (New York, 1972); Josef Pieper, *The Silence of St. Thomas* (Chicago, 1957); Hans Urs von Balthasar, *A Theological Anthropology* (New York, 1967); Ralph McInerny, *St. Thomas Aquinas* (Notre Dame, 1982); G. K. Chesterton, *St. Thomas Aquinas* (New York, 1933).

it differed from convention but what is meant by "grace."[16] The question arose, then, as to why man was not "left alone" by this God. Why is not some "natural" or political happiness indeed sufficient for him?

What is central about the philosophical contribution of Thomas Aquinas is his ability to accept and reformulate the classical systems in such a fashion that they contributed directly and necessarily to the full comprehension of that in which human reality, in all its dimensions, consisted. This reformulation presupposed the unity over time of the philosophical questions that critical refection discerned to fall within the range of human intelligence. It also suggested that the source of intelligence itself does not exclude human intelligence as that appears in each individual—in Socrates, Plato, or Mary.

In the context of political philosophy from Augustine, however, this taking up again of the themes in Aristotle reopened the question of "the proper life of man." The reintroduction of Aristotle stressed the aspects of intelligence that were required for the kind of concrete revelation presented in history to be distinguishable from, but connected with, questions already evident and posed in human experience. If at least Christian revelation (Jewish and Muslim revelations were revelations of a Law) contained not a prescribed outline and establishment of a political order but rather a description of the destiny of each individual appearing in history, then politics must necessarily gain its legitimacy from nonrevelational sources, that is, from reason.[17] In effect, political thinking, valid in itself, needed to be placed within the order of human goods and achievements.

Political thinking, then, should be conceived not as a total explanation of all reality but only as an explanation of itself as an activity properly within human reality, not as a description of a transcendent city. By the same token, the other questions that did arise about the further meaning of political man had to find some sort of answers. But

---

16. See Henri de Lubac, *Nature and Grace* (San Francisco, 1984).
17. Strauss, *Persecution and the Art of Writing*, 18.

these answers ought not to make politics a tool to provide alternate answers to those posed by revelation or metaphysics. Politics, in knowing its own limits, could allow revelation to address each human being without fearing that the city would destroy or be dangerous to a politics that truly understood man and his limits. On the other hand, the denial to politics of the locus of ultimate issues did not mean that there was no real distinction of regimes based on an accurate study of being or that the polity itself was unimportant to man's ultimate end.

Here the heritage of Aristotle best served to define this legitimate area of the proper life of man. Aristotle had seen that politics was not the highest science of *what is*. Rather politics was the highest of the practical sciences that dealt with human actions insofar as they pertained to the life of man on earth, his coming to be, the family, education, and the activity of keeping alive and living well in a full life, ending, as a composite of body and soul, with death—the life that is "proper" to man as such. That is, politics distinguishes man in the universe from other sorts of beings. There was no question that politics was not legitimate to man.

Aristotle, of course, noted that a more divine or contemplative life was the activity of the rational faculty on the highest object, which attracted man as an end or final cause. But this First Mover did not seem itself related to or interested in the universe or particularly the individuals with intelligence within it. The key elements in revelation which guided Aquinas's understanding of Aristotle were the ideas of creation from the Old Testament, the ideas of Trinity, Incarnation, and grace from the New Testament.

A question needed to be asked: how were these events and teachings, which appeared at an identifiable historical moment, to be formulated in terms of human reason such that they were capable of being understood and believed? That is, how were they persuasive and still noncontradictory? In this sense, revelation came before reason, although reason in every case had at least wondered in the classics about the limits of the question as posed. Reason, in a sense, opened itself to the stimulus of revelation, because actual problems did exist and were posed, while the law and doctrine of revelation were seen as constituting at least conceivable answers to the same problems.

Christian revelation taught that the inner life of God was personal and triune, that the world was created by God from freedom, not necessity, that the variety of things in the world was good, including man, but each was different in being and goodness. Human beings possessed immortal souls directly created by God, but the primary promise to each human being was not immortality but the resurrection of the body, the abidingness of his unique individual wholeness—according to the terms of revelation. Each human being was free to choose or reject his destiny to participate in the inner life of God, which was the ultimate (nonpolitical) purpose of creation and the locus of happiness.[18]

Man, then, did not have the capacity to reach the goal for which he was created and redeemed without God's help, called "grace," but this help was offered to him in various historical interventions culminating in the Incarnation. The life of Christ was the definitive intervention of God to man and man to himself. Since Christ was born, lived, suffered, died, was buried, and rose again, this path was to be open likewise to each human person according to the order of redemption offered. The order of redemption was located in the Church, not in a polity. It was not political in essence. It was intelligible in itself and was offered as something intelligible to human beings, but not as something they could have figured out by themselves and brought into reality by their own efforts. This was the common teaching.

AQUINAS ON ARISTOTLE'S POLITICAL THOUGHT

Aquinas's commentaries on Aristotle, particularly those on the *Ethics* and the *Politics,* which are more directly pertinent to the argument here, manifest a close attention to how the Philosopher argued and to what he specifically concluded. Aquinas sought to be as faithful as possible to Aristotle, within the context of a philosophy of being, of

---

18. See Schall, *Redeeming the Time,* Chap. 3.

Aquinas and the Proper Life of Man

existence, which was Thomas's fundamental teaching about philosophy itself.[19] Rarely in the Aristotelian commentaries of Aquinas do we more than glimpse his further teachings about where Aquinas thinks the Philosopher's arguments might, as arguments, actually lead, even if the Philosopher (Aristotle) or any other philosopher may not have seen their logic and import. (To out-Aristotle Aristotle, as it were, does not have to be seen as a denial of the worth of Aristotle himself.) Yet these glimpses are precious and serve to set the stage for that unity of reason and revelation in what is intelligible in being. These glimpses also form the background of modern problems in political philosophy on which its overall intelligibility turns.

After discussing in his prologue to the commentary on the *Politics* the famous principle "art imitates nature," which serves to connect natural philosophy with ethical philosophy through the intellects which know both art and nature, Aquinas explained why political philosophy needed to be treated for the completion of philosophy itself.[20] "Now that kind of group called the city or state is a topic of reasoned judgment," so it was necessary for the completion of philosophy that the subject of politics be fully treated.[21] But this treatment located politics within philosophy as a "practical science," since human reason knows the polity as having not only something in it of the not "having-been-made" by itself or by man but also something which men can shape to be otherwise.[22]

Politics, then, is considered a practical science; its ends are formed by the final cause of nature, not by human art. Hence these likewise become first principles of action. They are as they are because of the structure of nature as made by mind, in this case, the divine mind.[23]

---

19. See Anton C. Pegis, *St. Thomas and Philosophy* (Milwaukee, 1964); Gilson, *God and Philosophy*.

20. Thomas Aquinas, Commentary, *The Politics*, I, 1, I, N. 1078. The Latin text is found in Thomas Aquinas, *In octo libros politicorum Aristotelis expositio*, Bk. I, Lect. 1, pp. 5–6.

21. Thomas Aquinas, Commentary, *The Politics*, I, 1, I, N. 1078.

22. See Thomas Aquinas, Commentary on *The Ethics*, *In decem libros ethicorum ad Nicomachum expositio* (Turin, 1934), N. 1431.

23. Thomas Aquinas, Commentary, *The Politics*, I, 1, I, N. 1078.

Thus what is made by the human practical intellect is, in a way, like the creaton of the shipbuilder who makes a ship (art). But the subject matter here in the practical, political sciences is human actions, not wood or steel. These human actions remain in the doers—actions like giving, choosing, consulting, willing, and such things that pertain to moral sciences.

Politics is the highest of the practical sciences with which the human intellect can deal. Politics considers "the last and perfect good in human affairs." These are the highest reaches to which matter as such can naturally extend in the universe, since it is matter directly infused by a spiritual power within a single whole substance. Thus political philosophy completes philosophy itself. It deals with specifically human affairs, so infused with intelligence in the human being, and remains in the existing doer but related also to other doers. It concerns what is proper to man in this world. Philosophy must consider all reality and must be open to it and not merely to politics. The human intellect is capable of knowing *all that is,* including human actions, but is not limited to them. It is thus a part of wisdom to know where human actions fit into the whole scope of reality.

But why did Aquinas think that there needed to be a special branch of practical philosophy over and above the *Ethics?* True, he followed Aristotle's view that man is by nature "a social and a political animal." There was a natural reason discovered by reflection, whose subject matter was human actions and the passions as related and guided by intellect. Some of these actions, particularly justice, required others for their very existence. Yet it is instructive here to note that Aquinas, again following Aristotle, emphasized coercion and power as basic elements in the formation and need of the polity. Augustine, as we have seen (Chapter 3), frankly held that the evil found in the world was due to "the Fall." That is, he gave a revelational reason for a problem found in, though not fully explained by, the normal experience of civil and personal life. Plato and Aristotle were no less frank than Augustine and Aquinas in admitting the problem itself.

However much we find Aristotle and Aquinas treating arguments that did not necessarily presuppose any "Fall" of man to justify the polity (see Chapter 1 of the *Politics* and Aquinas's commentary on it), still the main arguments in both *The Ethics* and Aquinas's commentaries do often recall this "Fallen" side of the argument.[24] Evil and disorder were givens, which only the blind did not see. This disorder does exist. There is need for public coercion to control it or remedy it, if possible, without which things will be considerably worse. There is a constant, recurring, factual recognition that most men, most of the time, will not be especially virtuous, though there is also a recognition that virtuous acts also have public consequences which must be accounted for. Thus law does need a coercive factor for the very possibility of even a minimum of virtue and order for most people. In this sense, neither Machiavelli nor Hobbes was more "realistic" than Aristotle or Aquinas, let alone Augustine.

In Book II of *The Politics* (1263b23), while commenting on Plato and Phaleas, Aristotle had remarked that evils arise not because goods are ill distributed but because of the perversity of human nature as such. Aquinas, without much additional comment, repeated this observation as follows: "Someone makes the accusation that the evils which now happen in cities, such as deceptions men make about contracts, or judgments about false testimony, or that the poor envy the rich, these are due to the fact that all this happens because possessions are not held in common. But if anyone rightly thinks about this, none of these things happens because possessions are not held in common but because of the evil in men."[25] Aquinas simply accepted this, not as a dogmatic statement about human nature, that it is in itself "evil," which would be contrary both to Aristotle and to the revelational tradition, but because this disorder is an observed fact which must be accounted for particularly in politics. This existence of disorder is likewise the most obvious reason for the need of law. And this "need" made revelation seem to be in fact a response to a politically experienced reality.

In the passage from Aquinas's commentary at the end of Book X of

---

24. See also Thomas Aquinas, *On Kingship to the King of Cyprus*, trans. Gerald B. Phelan (rev. ed.; Toronto, 1949); *Summa contra Gentiles*, III, 111, 158; IV, 54.

25. Thomas Aquinas, *In octo libros politicorum Aristotelis expositio*, II, 4, p. 69.

the *Ethics,* in which he was discussing why politics must be treated, the general topic of law and its relation to coercion was predominant. Noting with Aristotle that much of the violence in any given society in fact comes from young men, who are not yet willing or able to follow their own right reason or any good norm, Aquinas commented that we need laws not just for guidance or decision "but from the beginning, when we are young . . . namely when we are becoming men. But we also need them universally through the whole lives of men. For there are many more who are more obedient to necessity, that is, who are coerced, than who are attentive to speech and advice. And most obey the lash which they incur by way of damage or punishment rather than that they obey the honest good itself."[26]

Thus the institutional proposals to cure human evil (which can be mitigated somewhat by good habits and laws, something which enables the political philosopher to classify regimes in the first place) will never fully work because of this tendency to "evil" and the consequent need for the coercion of the law. We simply ought not to expect most people to act from noble motives, but we still need to guide and even coerce them to understand a more proper order. "It often happens in a polity that one or a few are found who are able to exceed others in virtue. But it is very difficult that many be found who arrive at perfect virtue."[27] Most, in fact, are guided by much less noble motives, which is one of the reasons why, in both Aristotle and Aquinas, much discussion is devoted to oligarchies and democracies, since most men most of the time will be found in these types of regime.

And what is the cause of this "evil," with which political life must deal as a question of fact and which the Philosopher simply acknowledges to exist? Political philosophy itself has no direct answer to this question except its capacity to acknowledge, on the basis of long evidence, that institutional arrangements, such as property redistribution or political refashioning, will not eliminate it or prevent it from reappearing. Both Aristotle and Plato thus stressed virtue as the first

---

26. Thomas Aquinas, *In decem libros ethicorum ad Nicomachum expositio,* N. 2150.
27. Thomas Aquinas, *In octo libros politicorum Aristotelis expositio,* III, 6, p. 141.

requirement. The cause of evil, however, lies somewhere within men, more basic than regimes or external laws or social arrangements. For this reason one of the principal endeavors of political philosophy itself is to keep this fact in mind and to account for it in terms of regimes and their deviations, not to hide it from view. This very fact leaves political philosophy open to several possible answers to problems it cannot itself fully account for.

What Aquinas wrote in his commentaries on Aristotle parallels the points he treated in the *Summa theologiae* about the necessity of divine law (I–II, 91, 4). This concern is precisely the insufficiency of human law as a fact to solve the disorder existing in political regimes. Human law can reach only to the exterior, so it cannot correct this interior evil from which external disorders flow. Thus the questions present in classical political philosophy do demand, for intellectual integrity, some response which will not deny either the evidence of evil or the need of some order in which it is put into place. And yet the answers found in political experience and theory do not fully work either to remove these evils or to explain their presence in men.

The revelational answer to this question, which Aquinas set down in his *Summa contra Gentiles,* a work addressed to the philosophers, then, was that, however normal it is in our experience, "the necessity of death is a defect in human nature, arising from sin."[28] And Aquinas went on, in the same article, to contrast the purpose of natural generation, which is to keep the species in being, with the resurrection of the body, which pertains directly to the end and happiness of each individual as such, Socrates, Peter, and Mary.

For Aristotle, however, the end of generation is explained (II *De generatione et corruptione,* X, 7, 336b) so that the things generated might participate in the "divine reality in some perpetuity. Much greater therefore is the action which tends to something perpetual. The resurrection is not ordained to the perpetuity of the species, since this is conserved by natural generation. Therefore, it is necessarily ordained

---

28. Thomas Aquinas, *Summa contra Gentiles,* IV, 82. See also Oscar Brown, *Natural Rectitude and Divine Law in Aquinas* (Toronto, 1981).

to the perpetuity of the individual. And this not only according to his soul, for this the soul had before resurrection. Man risen, then, lives perpetually."[29] Now in this context it is of some use to see that the escape from evil is not to be achieved politically or even philosophically. Nor is happiness to be directed finally to anything less than to each individual who possesses both the desire and the capacity for it. As we shall suggest, the lines of friendship, as they appear in Aristotle's *Ethics* and *Politics,* can be adequately understood only with this background. Individual human beings bear reality. They are not subsumed into some higher sort of being, political or otherwise. And yet by virtue of their will and intelligence, they live in community with all other rational beings, because each reaches that which is in fact sought by one's own intelligence itself, something in common with all other rational beings, who likewise in their own being achieve the same end and good.[30]

Throughout his commentaries, however, Aquinas noted that politics is concerned with *this* life, so that all the various individual lives in differing polities, whatever their form, do not achieve the full sort of happiness to which man (each man) is open by virtue of this contemplative intellect, to which the practical life, by being itself, is ordered. Aquinas is conscious of the fact that the inability of philosophers to account fully for all reality by their own intellectual powers is a cause of unrest in every polity and perhaps in every life, even a cause of skepticism. "What a pity if philosophers, who are expected to be the chief seekers and lovers of truth and to see as much of it as can be seen by man," Aquinas wrote in his commentary on the *Metaphysics,* "should decide, after all, that truth cannot be discovered."[31] Now, the "instruction" which Aristotle found in the law apart from its coercion, its teaching on temperance, and its recognition of the meaning of possessions is not by itself completely adequate for what it proposes, even though it is the highest explanation available to the philosopher.

29. Thomas Aquinas, *Summa contra Gentiles,* IV, 82.
30. *Ibid.,* III, 37.
31. Thomas Aquinas, Commentary, *Metaphysics,* IV, Lect. 12, I, N. 26.

The cautious manner in which Aquinas relates the political and speculative lives in Aristotle is instructive, since he is careful both to preserve the Philosopher's love for truth and to suggest that its highest manifestation, achieved through the peace of the political order, is itself limited by, but not closed to, some further "instruction." "The sort of happiness which someone intends to achieve by political life," Aquinas observed, "is other than the political life itself. For by political life, we seek another kind of life beyond it. This is speculative happiness, to which the whole political life seems to be ordered, since through the peace which is established and preserved through the political life, the capacity of contemplating the truth is given to men."[32]

Aquinas then noted that, since the political virtues have by their end the common good as their goal, they are ordered to things which are for their own sakes. There is not a full happiness in the operations of the moral virtues in this world.[33] The activities of the moral virtues are, to be sure, the highest acts of man as a composite, body and soul. But although the speculative activities are pursued for their own sakes, have no higher end, and fulfill the requirements of self-sufficiency and ease of acting, still, Aquinas concluded, "I say this only insofar as it is possible to men acting in this mortal life. In this life such things are not able to exist perfectly."[34]

This seems to be a remarkable passage in political philosophy, since it clarifies the highest activity that is possible, a fact that limits the civil order but does not deny its worth or necessity. At the same time, it recognizes that the human intellect will not, as a matter of fact, achieve full happiness in this life, either in any object presented to it or in any partial participation in the whole.[35] Earlier in Book I of the *Ethics,* Aquinas concluded with a clear expression of this point.

> Nothing prevents us from calling that man happy who acts according to virtue in a perfect way, who has a sufficiency of external goods to act

---

32. Thomas Aquinas, *In decem libros ethicorum ad Nicomachum expositio,* N. 2101.
33. *Ibid.,* N. 2102.
34. *Ibid.,* N. 2103.
35. Thomas Aquinas, *Summa contra Gentiles,* III, 39.

virtuously and not just in a short time, but in a perfect life, that is, for a long time. And this is sufficient indeed for this, that someone can be said to be happy in this life.

But if we wish to understand happiness as according to the highest happiness which can be, to this we must add to the concept of happiness that it will be lived through a complete life and that it will end, it will die, according as it is agreeable to reason. The reason why this needs to be added is that the future is unknown to us. To the concept of happiness since it is the final end, everything which is highest and perfect pertains. . . .

But since these things do not seem to obtain very often to the condition of happiness described, we must add that we call such men happy who in this life, subject to changeableness, cannot have perfect happiness. And since no natural desire is totally in vain, we can rightly judge that there is reserved to men a perfect happiness after this life.[36]

Thus far Aquinas has said nothing more than Plato or even Aristotle.

Yet Aquinas recognized as a philosopher that happiness is other than something inclusive of the whole life of man on earth and his intellectual power in act. But its exact content is impossible for the philosopher to establish. However, Aquinas's very argument implied that openness to a perfect life "after this life" is reasonable, both because no natural desire can be intrinsically in vain and because man must firmly see as much truth as is open to him, which, ultimately, seems to be all reality, the proper object of intellect as such.

In Book II of *The Politics,* while discussing the question of whether all laws need to be changed frequently, Aquinas remarked on the Aristotelian concept that "the world was from eternity." This passage brings up from the Old Testament, in Aquinas's own system, the question of creation from nothing. As Aristotle had noted, some historians saw that certain regions of the earth began to be inhabited only after a lengthy period of time, which seemed contrary to the idea of the eternity of the world. Aristotle proposed two solutions to this problem, that some flood or natural disaster had destroyed the earth but (1) that these areas later came to be inhabited because "men are

---

36. Thomas Aquinas, *In decem libros ethicorum ad Nicomachum expositio,* N. 200–202.

generated from the earth" spontaneously or (2) that not all men were destroyed and some simply moved back.

Of interest here is the argument used by Aquinas, who agreed with Aristotle that the ancients were no better or worse than the present generation. But Aquinas noted that "nature produces its effects from determinate principles through determinate means. Perfect animals would never have been generated except from their own seed, whence we do not believe that men can be naturally generated from the earth but only by divine power."[37] If we recall that, in the *Summa contra Gentiles,* Aquinas had argued that the human soul was generated not from "seed" but by a particular, specific act of creation from nothing, it is clear that Aquinas already has his arguments marshaled from Aristotle about where Aristotle's arguments themselves ought to lead.[38]

The import, of course, is that, both at the beginning and at the end of life, men who come to live in the city acquire their origins and ends from something beyond the polis, even beyond this life, but through something proper to it. Thus when he discussed the question of who is happy, with regard to Socrates' stress on the unity of the polity, Aquinas repeated with Aristotle that this happiness did not belong to the whole as if it did not devolve on each particular member of the human society.[39] In other words, the highest kind of happiness is something that is beyond this life and pertains to each human being but according to those faculties by which the highest things are possessed. Thus the highest things can be rejected by men. And this possibility is the root of all risk, and even drama, in the human enterprise—the risk even of the philosopher who despairs of the truth itself or who simply rejects it.

Aristotle had said, however, that temperance and moderation of possessions could resolve many of the problems that arise in most societies because of excessive human wants and desires. But he likewise recognized that there are still other causes of unrest in a society not reducible to either cause. For this problem, he thought, the only remedy was

37. Thomas Aquinas, *In octo libros politicorum Aristotelis expositio,* II, 12, p. 96.
38. Thomas Aquinas, *Summa contra Gentiles,* II, 86.
39. Thomas Aquinas, *In octo libros politicorum Aristotelis expositio,* II, 5, p. 74.

philosophy (*Politics*, 1267a11). On this point, obviously, Aquinas followed Aristotle to clarify the possible ultimate implications.

> It is necessary for the peace of a polity that a legislator think of remedies against these three causes of injury. To those who injure others so that they might have the bare necessities, a modicum of possessions suffices for a remedy and a proper occupation through which someone may acquire provisions needed for himself. For human nature is content with just a few things. But to those who are injured because of concupiscence for the delightful things, the remedy is temperance, by which a man is moderated in his desires.
>
> But against the third, namely, against those who are injured so that there be no sadness, their remedy is philosophy with regard to those who are able to appreciate the sort of joys which are without sadness, which makes men not to be sad in unfortunate circumstances.[40]

This passage, then, is significant both because it acknowledges that there are problems beyond need and delight—Aristotle had said that no one becomes a tyrant just to keep warm—and because it recognizes the ease with which philosophers can overthrow the civil order. The remedy is philosophy itself. In short, right thought is a cause of civil peace because it prevents the would-be philosophers from turning on the civil order as they seek to resolve metaphysical questions. Metaphysicians who turn on the civil order are the most dangerous of our kind. The question is, nevertheless: how sufficient is philosophy for this purpose? To what does it apply?

Again referring to Phaleas in Aristotle, Aquinas took up the question of what causes us not to do evil besides a sufficiency of possessions, moderation, and coercion. "Even if someone arranges for moderate possessions among all the citizens," he wrote, "still this is not enough for the good life of all the citizens. More important is the regulation of internal desires of the soul, namely that it does not desire things so that external goods be desired immoderately. But that the desires of men be regulated, this does not happen except that man be sufficiently instructed by the laws, which Phaleas does not do. He

---

40. *Ibid.*, II, 8, p. 87.

deals insufficiently with those things that belong to the citizens. . . . And it is necessary to say what in particular this discipline is by which all citizens are informed."[41] The significance of this passage ought not to be overlooked. It lays the whole groundwork for Aquinas's treatise on law, particularly the relation of human and divine positive law, of revelation, to the capacity to touch internal acts from which external deeds flow.[42]

Aristotle held that but a few philosophers might be so instructed as to observe the meaning of law to achieve the right choices by themselves. Aquinas, however, was concerned with both the polity and the highest end of each human individual, the philosopher and everyone else. He left open a place for an "instruction," addressed indeed to intelligence, an instruction that was not merely political even though, indirectly, it would touch the essential good by which each person could act exteriorly. Aquinas's position, however, left the coercion of the human law intact when necessary without denying that there were motives that transcend the letter of the law to reach the particular case and the good it was to achieve.

FRIENDSHIP AND POLITICAL PHILOSOPHY

Many of these points, it seems, can be brought out more clearly and deepened if we examine Aquinas's commentary on Aristotle's discussion of friendship in Books VIII and IX of *The Ethics*. No doubt the most beautiful passages in all of Aristotelian literature are those found in his discussion of friendship. Indeed, it is often remarked that Aristotle devoted more time and space to friendship than he did to justice, presumably the political virtue. In fact, friendship for Aristotle seems more important to the polity than even justice, however much both are needed. This itself is the philosophic foundation for the theme of "superabundance," which frequently appears in Aquinas's commentaries, to account for what really cannot be wholly accounted for by human intelligence. This theme reflected Aquinas's fundamental the-

41. *Ibid.*, II, 8, p. 86.
42. Thomas Aquinas, *Summa theologiae*, I–II, 91, 4.

sis that the world is made in "mercy" rather than in "justice," which is to say that no wholly deterministic cause can be assigned that anything exists at all. At this essential point Christian and neo-Platonic systems of thought differed most radically (see Chapter 3).

The relevant passage in the *Summa theologiae* is worth citing in this context:

> The work of divine justice always presupposes the work of mercy and is founded thereon. Creatures have no rights except because of something pre-existing or pre-considered in them. And since we cannot go back and back, we must come to something founded on the sole generosity of the divine will, which is the ultimate end. The possession of hands is owing to human nature because of the rational soul; the possession of a rational soul is demanded if we are to be men, but why should we have a human nature except because of divine generosity?
>
> And so mercy is the root in each and every divine work, and its virtue persists in everything and grows out of that, and even more vehemently flourishes there. The first cause enters into effects more strongly than do secondary causes. Even with regard to things which are a creature's due, God more abundantly dispenses them than the proportion of the claim demands. The order of justice would be served by much less than in fact is granted by divine generosity, which far exceeds what is owing.[43]

This passage would argue that the most difficult aspects of human life, indeed of reality itself, are those that seem to reveal something more, something more generous and unexpected than what we would anticipate by a strict analysis of equality and justice. The natural evidence of this "superabundance" in the practical sciences that deal with man as man lies in the nature of equity and friendship in particular, in which something quite beyond justice needs to be accounted for if we are to have a complete treatment of what it is to be human.

"Equity is the last thing in justice, but the first in friendship," Aquinas noted.[44] And this "equity" is the virtue that corrects law and jus-

---

43. Thomas Aquinas, *Summa theologiae*, I, 21, 4, I, N. 332.
44. Thomas Aquinas, *In decem libros ethicorum ad Nicomachum expositio*, N. 1632.

tice because of their incapacity to treat adequately the variety of singular circumstances in which actual life takes place.⁴⁵ "The infinity of singulars cannot be comprehended by human reason," Aquinas noted in the *Summa theologiae*.⁴⁶ "The reason why what is legally just needs direction is this," Aquinas likewise remarked in his commentary, "that every law is given universally. For, since particulars are infinite, they cannot be comprehended by a human intellect. In order that the law may deal with all particulars, the law, thus, must be universally posited."⁴⁷ This awareness of the variety of singular instances, in which human actions occur, requires the virtue of *"epichaia,* equity," which recognizes the necessity of taking this infinite variety into consideration when dealing with the reality of singular events and actions.

In this context, however, there is a connection between this aspect of Aquinas's understanding of the limits of justice because of singular acts with their circumstances and the need for a discussion of friendship which, at its highest, deals with singulars or particulars which lie beyond justice, even though it includes the universal or contemplative truths. And this higher reach of friendship, which both Aristotle and Aquinas are at pains to elaborate, reveals most strikingly the limits of politics and the direction which metaphysical reflection takes as a result of that which is exchanged between friends. Again, in Aquinas's commentaries on Aristotle, certain key passages indicate how friendship itself likewise poses questions to politics and to philosophy which seem impossible to solve by rational means, even though they legitimately arise from experience and reflection on it.⁴⁸ The issue of despair at finding any adequate solution is posed at this point, or at least the suspicion that man is poorly made, so that he exists in ultimate contradiction.

The condition of having no proper philosophic solutions naturally

---

45. *Ibid.*, N. 1078–90.
46. Thomas Aquinas, *Summa theologiae*, II–II, 47, 3, ad 2, I, N. 969.
47. Thomas Aquinas, *In decem libros ethicorum ad Nicomachum expositio*, N. 1083.
48. See James V. Schall, "The Totality of Society: From Justice to Friendship," *Thomist*, XX (January, 1957), 1–26.

gives rise to utopian or Gnostic answers which, however elaborate, somehow abstract from the particular individuals in whom and for whom the questions arose as a reality in the first place. Just as in the questions dealing with the origin and destiny of the human individual, (*i.e.*, Socrates, Plato, or Mary), so also friendship questions deal with particular human beings, not abstractions or universal propositions. "An individual who is governed for the sake of the species," Aquinas wrote, "is not governed because of any inherent worth. But human persons come under divine providence in their own right. For the activities of rational creatures alone are divinely directed for the sake of the individual as well as of the species."[49]

The theoretic grounding of the inherent worth of each individual of the human species, Socrates, Plato, or Mary, is perhaps the most urgent task of political philosophy. The reabsorption of the individual into the species has been one of the main characteristics of much modern political philosophy and practice, often in the name of community or social goals. In this context, then, the emphasis on the particular nature and abidingness of friends serves to prevent the activity of the mind or the speculations of thought from substituting for the being of the particular persons who actually think and live. This latter is and must remain the ground for what human beings know to be their own good and happiness as communicated by themselves to their friends and, in turn, received back from their friends.

In this sense, the reality of friendship prevents abstractions from ruling the real life of human beings. It is the ground of Aquinas's identifying charity and friendship.[50] In this context, then, one of the most perplexing passages in all of philosophy is Aristotle's observation that we cannot have more than a few real friends in our lives and that the highest forms of friendship are not political. Civil friendships, like the practical virtues that ground them—what is called, as we have seen, "the proper human good"—do lead to speculative truth. Aristotle did not think, however, that things were necessarily bad be-

---

49. Thomas Aquinas, *Summa contra Gentiles*, III, 113, I, N. 1109.
50. Thomas Aquinas, *Summa theologiae*, I–II, 65, 5; 66, 6, ad 2; I–II, 23, 1; 24, 2.

cause they were useful or delightful in themselves. Quite the contrary, this most sane of all men recognized the value of use and delight, but he simply did not consider them to be the highest things open to man. Friendship at the highest level exists in "superabundance" and freedom, in an exchange of the highest things—which are not simply useful or delightful as such.

As we saw earlier, Aquinas, following Aristotle, held that the perfection of knowledge was in the knower. The soul was "potentially" all things so that the good of the world could in fact exist in one knowing being. This led some philosophers to hold that the final end of man would be in knowing with its perfections. Aquinas warned that this was a possibly dangerous position if it placed the final end of man exclusively in man's knowing powers and their activities and not in God, who is the end and cause of knowing in the ultimate sense.[51] The significance of this position in political philosophy is to be marked, since it gives the outline of the direction modern theory will take toward the elevation of the abstract species "man" as the goal of political man in his actions. In contrast, Aquinas recognized the extension of human knowledge to all being in principle but did not leave aside the question of friendship for the individual and the limitations of the cosmos itself and knowledge of it, even if politics were to be the highest science by a denial of the speculative order.

In Aristotle, an account of friendship was needed to complete the discussion both of justice and of metaphysics. At the end of Book VI of *The Ethics,* Aristotle remarked that the practical sciences, which correspond to human actions as human, our proper life (1139b17–19), are not supreme over philosophic wisdom, which contemplates the things that cannot be otherwise. Aquinas will not disagree with Aristotle that our highest good does consist in our intellectual vision of the First Being, which is thought thinking itself.[52] Moreover, the highest good is not wanted for someone else but for the individual human being himself. This is the import of the remark that, when we

---

51. Thomas Aquinas, II *De veritate,* 2, I, N. 1117.
52. Thomas Aquinas, *Summa contra Gentiles,* III, 37, IV, 11. See also Thomas Aquinas, *In Metaphysicam Aristotelis, Commentaria* (Turin, 1935), N. 2519–2663.

wish good to our friends, we do not wish them to cease being the particular humans they are, even though we acknowledge that there is a higher form of life than the human.

Aquinas's remarks are clear here. "There is some doubt whether friends desire for their own friends the highest good," he wrote, "such that they be gods or kings or especially virtuous. And it does not seem that they do, since in that case, they would not remain friends, and they would lose the highest good, that is, their friends. . . . Thus, a friend wishes good to a friend so that in the process, he remains what he is. For a friend wishes the highest good to a friend as to an existing human being, not to someone about to be transformed into a god."[53] This is yet philosophy, but the question is posed properly, namely, is our seeking the highest good a threat to a singular good each person is? And this question takes on particular urgency, since what friends exchange, the basis of their highest friendship, is the knowledge and truth of *what is,* the knowledge of God and all the cosmos which is available to each individual through his intellect, to Socrates, Plato, or Mary.

Friendship, moreover, is not something that everyone can have with everyone else at its highest levels. Indeed, it can be had only with another human being or at the most, with a very few, in one lifetime.[54] Friends do not wish to cease to be what they are—that is, human beings—nor do they wish to cease this friendship because of death or even to have the lives of those before or after their time closed to them, especially about the highest things. Each one nevertheless wants to reach the highest good himself and knows that a friend is another being, like himself, not the highest good. In this context, it is proper to talk, as Aristotle and Aquinas do, of both the happiness available in this life and that which transcends it as pertaining to the same individual, who is born and lives in the polity and likewise seeks transcendent truth, which he wishes to exchange with a friend.[55]

Furthermore, no one wishes to be perfectly happy at the risk of be-

---

53. Thomas Aquinas, *In decem libros ethicorum ad Nicomachum expositio,* N. 1636–37.
54. *Ibid.,* N. 1609, N. 1921.
55. *Ibid.,* N. 1912.

coming someone else. And yet, we cannot seem to be friends with God. "Everyone wishes to be himself in so far as he has kept that which he himself is. But that which keeps him in his very being is God." Aquinas was careful to stress the force of these arguments as they stood in ethical and political experience. He noted, furthermore, that no one would want the whole world without friends. "Concerning all those things which are necessary to human life, the most necessary is friendship, such that no one would agree to live on the condition that he could have all other good things, but not friends."[56] This is the highest expression of the principle that man is a social animal by nature at the human level, even with regard to the highest things.

And if this is indeed the highest of the realities that exist at the human level, is there not something wrong when it appears that the First Mover does not have friendship?[57] Aquinas did interpret Aristotle as suggesting some kind of friendship with God: "Children have friendship with their parents, as to some sort of super-excellent good insofar as the parents are the cause of being, nutrition, and discipline in the children, and such also is the friendship of men to God."[58] These seemingly insolvable issues arising out of the very nature of friendship—its desire for permanence, its desire to reach the highest good, its concern for *what is* "in itself"—are not changed in the final solutions that Aquinas suggested from revelation, the two central ideas that God, thought thinking on itself, is Trinity, a society of persons in one nature, and that the Incarnation took place, so that the friendship of man with God is first one not of man becoming God but of God first becoming man.

In the *Summa contra Gentiles,* moreover, Aquinas put the question in this manner: "Since friendship consists in a certain equality (VIII *Ethics,* v, 5; 1157b), those things which are very unequal, do not seem to be able to be joined in friendship. To this end, then, that a more familiar friendship exist between God and man, it was expedient for man that God became man, since also man is naturally a friend

56. *Ibid.,* N. 1807.
57. *Ibid.,* N. 1600.
58. *Ibid.,* N. 1715, N. 1752. See also N. 1807.

to man (*ibid.*, i, 3; 1155a)."[59] Again, this revelational solution will not therefore be true in philosophy, but it will be noncontradictory, that is to say, it does not violate the evidence as argued in *The Ethics* and *The Politics* on the basis of reason.

On the other hand, the rejection of this solution, even from philosophy, will set particularly political thought off in the only direction in which it can go, the denial of individual destiny and ultimately uniqueness, so that the highest being reappears as the highest thing of the practical intellect, the polity. This historical alternative in political philosophy—that is, the record of the alternative solutions—supports the validity of the positions in political philosophy as argued by Aquinas on the basis of Aristotle. What needs to be followed, then, is the intellectual statement of the alternative to this classic position of Aquinas as it has worked itself out in modern political theory. It will subsequently be possible to repropose the foundations of political philosophy on the basis of both the historical record and the intellectual comprehension of what it means to locate properly the City of God in political discourse. This approach is ultimately the defense of moderation in political philosophy, a moderation that in fact has been philosophically more completely achieved through the challenge of revelation to the city.

59. Thomas Aquinas, *Summa contra Gentiles*, IV, 54, p. 513.

5

THE HUMANIZATION AND "HISTORICIZATION" OF THE PRACTICAL ORDER

Since Machiavelli and Hobbes, political philosophy has gradually gained in importance among the intellectual disciplines. The reason is not always appreciated, for its gains were not accidental. As long as Aristotle and the Judaeo-Christian tradition dominated the thought of the West, the place of politics was limited. Theoretical energies were devoted to theology, metaphysics, cosmology, psychology, and ethics before they were expended on politics. Politics, although esteemed, itself depended on speculative knowledge or rectitude for the definition of its own goals. Politics did not construct man but accepted him from nature as something already formed. Politics strove to make man good, not to make man as such, or at least it tried to prevent the worst, which it could at least understand.

Machiavelli, following perhaps a lead from Marsilius of Padua, was the first to remove politics from this hierarchical order of Western tradition. Politics, he believed, had its own goals and methods completely independent of speculative guidance. Descartes, on the other hand, perhaps the first figure of modern philosophy, had little formal political thought himself. Nevertheless, he stands at the source of modern political thought because of his position with regard to the speculative order as imitable by the human intellect. In a sense, Descartes went beyond Machiavelli. For with Descartes, not only could man use politics as an art, as Machiavelli already held, but he could approach the whole speculative order as something to be made by man.[1]

Yet this ideal of Descartes was not to last either. A new spirit came

---

1. See Ernst Cassirer, *The Philosophy of the Englightenment*, trans. Fritz C. Koelin and James P. Pettegrove (Boston, 1951), 51. See also James V. Schall, "Cartesianism and Political Theory," *Review of Politics*, XXIV (April, 1962), 260–82.

into modern science and philosophy with Newton and the scientific movement. This transformed the clear and deductive ideal of Descartes into an analytic historical method which sought to formulate its principles at the end of empiric investigation rather than a priori at its inception. "For Descartes the certainty and stability of all knowledge," Ernst Cassirer wrote, "was founded in its first principles, while everything factual as such remained uncertain and problematical. We cannot trust the appearances of things to the senses, for sense perception always involves the possibility of sense deception. . . . The certainty of facts is subordinated to that of principles and dependent on the latter. The new physical theory of knowledge, which owes its existence to Newton and Locke, reverses, however, this relationship. The principle is derivative; the fact as such is original."[2] Mind as such is no longer the source of the construction of the world, or at least, not apparently so.

To trace the exact nature of the development of philosophy from the Middle Ages to the eighteenth century would perhaps be to extend this discussion too far beyond its limits. Descartes, Hobbes, Spinoza, Locke, and Leibniz in particular deserve extended attention. Especially through Hobbes, political thought avowedly placed all societal reality, state and church, under the control of the Leviathan. If this effort be seen in the general scientific spirit of the times, it is again an effort to reduce the manifold complex of politics to a predictable and orderable unity based on certain and basic scientific precepts. The mechanical interpretation of reality, which is associated with one side of Descartes's thinking and which is also evident in Hobbes, was not, however, destined to last. Newer historical and biological interpretations of reality were to replace the strong mechanical influence of early science on philosophy.

To understand the dynamism of thought behind modern political philosophy, it is well to realize that to it fell much of the type of thought traditionally associated with doctrines of human perfection,

2. *Ibid.*, 54–55.

salvation, original sin, knowledge, and nature.³ This is another aspect of the relation of immortality and political philosophy. When man no longer believed in life after death in any sense, he did not evidently give up the ideals and attitudes which that idea had inspired. He did not fully "lower his sights," as Machiavelli had thought. Rather, man experienced a shift in the ideas associated with immortality into operative ideals to be attained vicariously in this life and located in the ongoing collectivity. The minute this shift had occurred, these ideas necessarily became political ideals. The theory of progress, original contract, the invisible hand, the state of nature, and the general will—the classless society even—were ideas that arose during the Enlightenment, though the thought of the late medieval period often paved the way for them. And essentially they are secularized theological dogmas which originally revolved around man's life after death.

The idea of progress is perhaps the most obvious example of this whole trend, with its relation to salvation history. Crane Brinton noted the meaning of this movement: "In the widest terms, the change in the attitude of Western men toward the universe and everything in it was the change from the Christian supernatural heaven after death to the rationalist natural heaven on this earth, now—or at least very shortly."⁴ The whole corpus of ideas that Christianity attributed to the supernatural order—perfectibility, happiness, and personal salvation—now became relocated and reshaped into ideas that served the dynamics of the political order.

Condorcet first noted that progress was based on "the principle that the general laws, known or unknown, which regulate the phenomena of the universe are regular and constant."⁵ Into this belief in a progress based on regular laws came a new notion, that of history, to form a foundation for prediction of the direction of man's advancement.

---

3. See J. B. Bury, *The Idea of Progress* (New York, 1955); Carl Becker, *The Heavenly City of the Eighteenth-Century Philosophers* (New Haven, 1931); Robert Nisbet, *History of the Idea of Progress* (New York, 1980).

4. Crane Brinton, *The Shaping of the Modern Mind* (New York, 1959), 118.

5. Marquis de Condorcet, *Equisse d'un tableau historique des progrès de l'esprit humain*, in *The Making of the Modern French Mind*, ed. Hans Kohn (New York, 1955), 93.

Ortega y Gasset remarked how this new idea of progress differed from rationalism and the Cartesian spirit: "The idea of progress is perhaps the first great vision of human life as historicity, as process, as constitutive change. It is the dawn of the 'historical sense'."[6] The City of God no longer seemed to be out of man's immediate reach. With "progress" man could eventually in this life obtain it or at least something that was said to look like it.

The manner in which history, or better, "historicism," became an intrinsic part of political theory can be seen in Montesquieu. Montesquieu strove to apply the newer scientific methods to politics. This effort entailed an exhaustive investigation of facts in order to find the generalized laws guiding their spirit. Franz Neumann indicated how Montesquieu regarded history. "Each society has, according to him, a specific structure and follows its own inner logic," Newmann wrote. "The inner logic can be grasped only through the medium of facts. A type of society (a republic, a monarchy, or a despotism) is thus not an addition or an aggregate of facts, but the expression of a structure. These ideal types are not arrived at by induction, that is, by the collection of data and the elimination of irrelevant ones, but by reading into the historical facts a meaning that illuminates them and reveals their structural principles."[7] Montesquieu's essential insight, then, was his belief that actual historical facts, sociological conditions, climate, and geographical conditions were the loci in which the law or system of society was working itself out. In this sense, Meinecke rightly called Montesquieu one of the founders of historicism.[8]

Montesquieu believed that he gained insight into reality: "I have not drawn my principles from my prejudices, but from the nature of

---

6. José Ortega y Gasset, "The Past and Future of Western Thought," *Modern Age*, II (September, 1958), 253. See also F. C. Green, *Rousseau and the Idea of Progress* (Oxford, 1950), 1–20.

7. Franz Neumann, "Editor's Introduction," in Baron de Montesquieu, *The Spirit of the Laws*, trans. Thomas Nugent, ed. Franz Neumann (New York, 1949), xxxv.

8. Leo Strauss specifically argued that Montesquieu was closer to the classics than Aquinas, that is, that Aquinas "restricted the latitude of the statesmen because of his revelational teaching" (*Natural Right and History* [Chicago, 1953], 164). However, Strauss also noted that Montesquieu prevented Rousseau from completely cutting himself off from man (*ibid.*, 277).

things."⁹ Montesquieu held that "laws . . . are the necessary relations arising from the nature of things."¹⁰ He observed that originally men were in a state of war and gained strength only when they entered society. Law became a means to restore liberty and security. "Law in general is human reason, inasmuch as it governs all the inhabitants of the earth: the political and civil laws of each nation ought to be only the particular cases in which human reason is applied."¹¹ The particular arrangement is the "spirit of the law." Montesquieu, then, enabled the detailed historical and geographical knowledge to be elevated into a general theory. Careful attention to the facts and their ordering into an intelligible whole enabled him to reunite facts with reason rather than to deduce facts from the clear and distinct notions of reason. It is noteworthy, however, that this "reading into the data" by the mind does not depend on some "intelligence," direct or substitute, already in nature indicating *what is*.

Rousseau differed from Montesquieu in that Rousseau combined history and scientific investigation with the questions of evil and General Will. In this sense, Rousseau was an echo of Plato and a forerunner of Kant and Hegel. Where Montesquieu incorporated history into the process of political science, Rousseau would attempt to give a direction to the historical process itself through the reconstitution of community in opposition to the individualism of the earlier modern thinkers. The older teleological or Aristotelian notions placed God or the First Mover at the head of the totality of human drives. But with the secularization of the drives that had formerly led to God, and then only perfectly after the end of this life, something was needed to replace the function of God, as it were, in the process. Rousseau turned to this kind of a problem.

The *Discours de l'inégalité parmi les hommes* begins: "The most useful and least advanced of all human knowledge appears to me to be that of

---

9. Baron de Montesquieu, "Montesquieu's Preface," *The Spirit of the Laws*, lxvii.
10. Montesquieu, *The Spirit of the Laws*, Bk. I, Chap. 1, p. 1.
11. *Ibid.*, Bk. 1, Chap. 3, p. 6.

man."¹² It is necessary to know what man is to know the sources of inequality. There are two types of inequality, that which comes from nature and that which comes from society. Rousseau, in terms much like those of Montesquieu, held "that inequality being almost nil in the state of nature draws its force and increase from the development of our faculties and from the progress of the human spirit and finally becomes stable and legitimate by the establishment of property and law."¹³ The problem, therefore, that arose is how this development of society which makes men unequal can be regularized to keep the advantages of development and also to restore equality. Rousseau gave the clue to this resolution in his discussion of natural law. "That it be a law it is necessary that the will of him whom it obliges can submit itself to it with knowledge, but it is also necessary in order that it be natural that it speak immediately by the voice of nature."¹⁴ The problem, then, is to show how this law can be freely chosen.

Ulrich Allers traced the line of this development in Rousseau's Second Discourse. Man in nature is good but is not yet rational or moral. The development of man's wants brings with it pleasure which incites the passions. From this development reason is incited to increase pleasure. Reason enables men to solve common problems. "Reflection begins its activity, and men know themselves and others as human beings."¹⁵ Men come to recognize their common humanity. This sets up a norm which each sees he must recognize. Morality for Rousseau meant freedom under law. But such freedom would be impossible unless the man who is free gave himself the law under which he is obliged. The law to which man submits cannot simply be nature's interests, which are merely natural. It must be universal. What is this universal good? It is the "concept of humanity" derived from man's recognition of other people and the need to respect them.

---

12. Jean-Jacques Rousseau, *De L'Inegalité parmi les hommes* (Geneva, 1946), 21. My translation.
13. *Ibid.*, 106.
14. *Ibid.*, 25.
15. Ulrich S. Allers, "Rousseau's Second Discourse," *Review of Politics*, XX (January, 1958), 102.

Here the *Social Contract* became important. The Second Discourse explained how the state is the natural development of institutionalized inequality. The social contract is designed to replace this natural inequality. "Instead of destroying the natural equality of mankind, the fundamental compact substitutes, on the contrary, a moral and legal equality for that physical inequality which nature placed among men, and, let men be ever so unequal in strength or in genius, they are all equalized by convention and legal right."[16] Rousseau's *Social Contract* was intended to be a scientific tract.[17] It endeavored to apply the historical-scientific analysis to man in order to arrive at his very definition. The social contract attempted to combine freedom with obedience. It did so, not unmindful of Hobbes, by "the total alienation of each associate, and all his rights, to the whole community. . . . each person gives himself to all, and so not to any one individual." Each individual is an "indivisible part of the whole." There exists now a moral, free body which "from this art receives its unity, its common self, its life, and its will."[18] Rousseau identified the individual with the General Will not for all purposes but only for the common ones.

The effect of this contract was to make man man. He now possessed moral liberty for the first time.

> Although he is deprived in this new state of many advantages which he enjoyed from nature, he gains in return others so great, his faculties so unfold themselves by being exercised, his ideas are so extended, his sentiments so exalted, and his whole mind so enlarged and refined, that if, by abusing his new condition, he did not sometimes degrade it even below that from which he emerged, he ought to bless continually the happy moment that snatched him forever from it, and transformed him from a circumscribed and stupid animal *to an intelligent being and a man.*
>
> In order to draw a balance between the advantages and disadvantages attending his new situation, let us state them in such a manner

---

16. Jean-Jacques Rousseau, *The Social Contract,* ed. Charles Frankel (New York, 1955), Bk. I, Chap. 9, p. 22.
17. Cassirer, *The Philosophy of the Englightenment,* 270–71.
18. Rousseau, *The Social Contract,* Bk. I, Chap. 6, pp. 15–16.

that they may be easily compared. Man loses by the social contract his *natural* liberty, and an unlimited right to all which tempts him, and which he can obtain; in return he acquires *civil* liberty, and proprietorship of all he possesses.[19]

To this extent, alienation of nature is overcome. Montesquieu's laws are transformed into human laws. The experience of liberty is added to security through law. Everyone now has the experience of participating in all public acts. The state is indeed the product of man. "Those who dare to undertake the institution of a people must feel themselves capable, as it were, of changing human nature, of transforming each individual, who by himself is a perfect and solitary whole, into a part of a much larger whole, from which he in some measure receives his being and his life; of altering the constitution of man for the purpose of strengthening it; of substituting a moral and partial existence instead of the physical and independent existence which we have all received from nature."[20] The significance of Rousseau's thought here must be seen in the light of his discussion of civil religion.

In the pagan states, Rousseau maintained, religion was part of the state. To convert was to conquer. But with Christianity's doctrine of another life, men were ill at ease in the state. For this inability to give full attention to the state, the pagans persecuted the Christians. But when Christianity gained the power itself, it divided every state within itself. Hobbes was the only philosopher to see that what was needed to save the state was the submission of the church to the state. But Hobbes failed to see that "the interests of the priesthood would always triumph over the state."[21] (Marsilius of Padua had argued that this same priesthood was the new cause of revolution of which Aristotle could not have been aware.)

---

19. *Ibid.*, Bk. I, Chap. 8, p. 19.
20. *Ibid.*, Bk. II, Chap. 7, p. 36. See also Bk. I, Chaps. 4–6, pp. 34–36, Bk. III, Chap. 9, pp. 79–80.
21. *Ibid.*, Bk. IX, Chap. 8, p. 118.

Rousseau divided religion into two parts.

> The religion of man, and the religion of the citizens. The former, without temples, altars, or rites, and confined entirely to the purely internal cult of the supreme God and the eternal duties of morality, is the pure and simple religion of the Gospel, the true theism, and what he justly called the 'natural divine law'. The other, set down only for one country, gives it its gods, and its own tutelary patrons; it has its dogmas, its rites, and its external cult prescribed by the law; but if you pass the boundaries where this religion prevails, its followers consider every human being as a stranger, an infidel, a barbarian; they will allow the rights or the duties of man only to those who live in the circle of their own altars.

The doctrine of the General Will demanded that "whatever breaks social unity is worthless; all institutions which set man in contradiction with himself are worthless." On this basis, Rousseau entirely rejected the tradition of the two powers. Religion could have no place in the formal social life of man unless it was under the control of the General Will. In this, Rousseau transferred Hobbes's Leviathan into the General Will. Indeed, Rousseau specifically said "that a society of true Christians *would not be a society of men.*" Why not? "Christianity is a religion entirely spiritual and occupied only with the things of heaven; the country of the Christians is not of this world."[22]

But it is important to recognize that religion—at least the Christian religion—is completely removed from this life. Men are what the state forms. For this reason, Christians are not men, since they are not formed by the state. Rousseau left out of the state many aspects of life, however.[23] "The right which the social compact gives the sovereign over the subjects extends no further than the public good. No sovereign can therefore have a right to control the opinions of the subjects any further than as these opinions may affect the community."[24] For

---

22. *Ibid.*, 121. Italics added.
23. This no doubt reflects the tradition of Marsilius of Padua. See Strauss, "Marsilius of Padua," 251–60.
24. Rousseau, *The Social Contract,* Bk. IV, Chap. 8, p. 123.

this reservation Marx will hold that Rousseau still left part of man alienated from himself and subjected to outside authorities. The General Will itself was only abstract if it did not include all that is possible to the species, man. Rousseau's discussion on civil religion left man, the composite of body and soul, split within himself. Internally, man was wholly free, but externally he must be part of the General Will, which was man's true self and liberation. Religion in the Christian sense was for Rousseau like Luther's religion: it was cut off from all externals.[25] The contemplative order could no longer exercise any influence on the practical. Indeed, the practical now exercised the function previously thought to be the property of the contemplative order.

Charles N. R. McCoy indicated the overall significance of this whole trend in Rousseau. Rousseau to be understood must be seen from the viewpoint of the Greeks on the one end and Marx on the other.[26] Kant said that Rousseau attributed the ethical sense to the man of nature, not to the man of civilization. In the eighteenth century, reason meant something like energy, an elemental force in nature, not so much a set of principles. "The autonomy of the intellect corresponds to the pure autonomy of nature. In one and the same intellectual process of emancipation, the philosophy of the Enlightenment attempts to show the self-sufficiency of both nature and intellect." The two sources need no transcendent power to unify them. Nature is not created; the "divine process pervades nature itself. The dualism between creator and creature is abolished." Nature now became "an original formative principle which moves from within."[27] As a result, Rousseau could, in his *Origin of Inequality,* hold that the traditional divorce of man from nature enabled civilized man to construct philosophy, theology, and other disciplines apart from the real

---

25. See James V. Schall, "Luther and Political Philosophy," *Faith and Reason,* VIII (Summer, 1982), 7–31.

26. Charles N. R. McCoy, "The Meaning of Jean-Jacques Rousseau and the Structure of Political Theory," in *Proceedings of the American Catholic Philosophical Association* (Washington, D.C., 1956), 51.

27. Cassirer, *The Philosophy of the Enlightenment,* 45, 40–41.

world of nature. "The distinctions constituted by birth, wealth, position, and education destroyed man's 'essentiality' because they made some men dependent on others, thus severing the individual from his original generic capacities by making his life have his reason outside itself."[28] The modern project of utopian equality, on its intellectual and scientific side, will consist in a systematic attack on these distinctions which are based on the uniquenesses of differing persons.

Kant was shaken by Rousseau's belief that intellectual progress would not improve men. Kant thought Rousseau's belief that no one should rule over another was the political expression of a deeper liberation, that is, a liberation of the theoretic intellect so that it could exist independently of nature and produce pure ethics as independent of nature. Marx thought Rousseau did not see this deeper level. The state substituted for the ruling classes. Man would then have a double life, one in the state and one in society. The political was thus opposed to the human in Marx. The area of civil society was still individualistic. Man's real being was thus in the state alienated from the individual. This was an advance, Marx thought, but it left real being as an abstract General Will.[29]

For Greek thought, the autonomy of nature did not correspond simply to the autonomy of intellect. Aristotle said in the *Physics* that nature acts for an end, but its principle is not intrinsic to itself (198b1–10; 199a4–33). It needs the First Mover. Nature is a substitute intelligence, not an original one. It does not vary artifacts.

> It is because nature is a substitute intelligence that it operates "always or for the most part in the same way," not varying its artifacts. . . . And this would not be the case if it operated by intelligence and art. Thus, the uniformity of nature as well as its chance deviations are equally signs of its having no intellectual principle for itself. But architects do not all build the same kind of house; for being capable of judging about the form of artifacts, the architect can vary them. Thus

---

28. McCoy, "The Meaning of Jean-Jacques Rousseau and the Structure of Political Theory," 54.
29. *Ibid.*, 54–56.

it is evident that it is not in the line of the "pure autonomy" of nature that art proceeds; the "autonomy of intellect" does not simply correspond to the "pure autonomy of nature."[30]

In political philosophy, then, should this approach be followed, man would move toward perfection by moving toward the position of a self-creator, if he becomes himself nature's substitute intelligence. Nature, in acting always or for the most part in the same way, does not, in its own teleology as being purely autonomous, intend any particular individual. "It intends individuals only so far as the species cannot be man without them."[31] When nature and reason are identified, the species must be intended and not the individual. The individuals are absorbed into nature, whose reality is not rooted in this or that individual. The remote intellectual apparatus for grounding reality in something other than the concrete, given being, then, is already on the horizon here.

On the political level, this grounding happens when ruler and ruled are absorbed into the General Will. We have in mind this absorption when we speak of nature as being perfected by reason. Marx held that Rousseau's theoretical mind was still outside the individual. The conflict of individual and species must be grounded in the real. Real life for Marx was identified with the autonomy of nature, which implied the negation and overcoming of the General Will and the state, which were both separate from the individual as such. Marx will hold that any element in the species that comes from the theoretic order—religion, philosophy, or science—is a source of alienation and must be overcome.[32] Nothing can remain that is not formed by man. What is formed by nature as substitute intelligence—which includes man's proper ends for Aristotle—is regarded as an alienation which must be overcome if man is to have full autonomy presupposed only to himself.

Rousseau's insight here was to make nature not a substitute intelli-

30. *Ibid.*, 57.
31. *Ibid.*
32. *Ibid.*, 57–60. See James V. Schall, "Atheism and Politics," in *Christianity and Politics* (Boston, 1981), 94–117.

gence formed by what it was that made nature what it was, but something simply to be formed. No distinction in the moral or physical world could stand. "This appears to be the intelligible root of Rousseau's thought: the conception of man not as specifically rational animal, but as 'specifically infinitely malleable'."[33] The world is now a thing ready to be "made" by man. Rousseau had eliminated the Aristotelian notion that the ends of man were given, to be compared to mathematical axioms, which cannot be changed by man, though they can and ought to be discovered by him as given to his intelligence. Man's nature, for Rousseau, was now free. It did not depend on God or First Mover to make man individually. Nature intended the species—not Socrates, Plato, or Mary, but man. The intelligence that now guided man was independent of an external power and depended, as a result, on whoever controlled the formation of man in society. And this cannot be, as Rousseau specifically said, the Christian God.

The trends in philosophy during the Reformation and the Enlightenment had thus introduced a further development beyond the position of Descartes. There had been a definite secularization of Christian drives. This secularization had its meaning in the attempt to apply the doctrines associated with immortality to this life. However, when one attempted to create a "substitute immortality," as it were, it was necessary also to replace in some sense the intellectual answers provided by the Christian faith or by Aristotle to questions found posed to reason. That is, a new definition of nature, man, and society was needed to replace the older concepts.

Montesquieu and Rousseau provided at least a partial solution to the problem. With Aristotle, the ends of man's nature were fixed by the First Mover. With a philosophy incited by revelation, the concrete and ultimate goal of this nature, existing only in each concrete human being, was finally found to lie outside this life, although man as such had legitimate goals in this life. Each person was a single continuum, not two persons, one for this life and one for some other life. When

33. McCoy, "The Meaning of Jean-Jacques Rousseau and the Structure of Political Theory," 61.

these ideas lost their dominance, a substitute was needed to define both the sources of the peculiar nature of man and the ultimate direction toward which it tended. These goals were found in history and man himself. History, the long record of man on earth, could apparently give itself a concrete description of the kind of a thing man was. In conformity with the scientific spirit, there was a need for a detailed examination of the facts from which it could be learned what man was.

Rousseau, however, saw that the record of man's progress could also lead to a retrogression. Man seemed to have been freer in the beginning than at the end. As a result, there was a need for an ideal or goal in terms of which man could, by his own intelligence, define and measure progress or regress. Rousseau thought he had found this definition in the General Will, which could accept all that history had produced but which at the same time would enable man to avoid the slavery of what he did not cause. This accomplishment was possible if each man willingly yielded his freedom to a higher freedom which in turn would be a law he himself made. Rousseau then provided the outlines of a goal, humanity itself, which could presumably replace the inroads of the First Mover or God on human nature. Man in independence of these religious or philosophical alienations could form the truly human city. The solution of Rousseau, however, while it seemed to provide a concrete goal which accepted the processes of history, still lacked a true unity and dynamism which would hold all elements together. The story of how this unity and dynamism were achieved leads immediately to Kant and Hegel.

6

THE INTELLECTUALIZATION OF POLITICAL REALITY

KANT

According to Christian theology, man's highest end, that which answers to questions of what he is ultimately "for," can be attained only after his own death, after the conclusion of his own single, personal life. This end consisted essentially in each human being's own individual vision of God, the Alpha and Omega of *all that is,* and secondarily in the knowledge and love of all else that God has created.[1] To one holding such a position and the intellectual grounds about why it is noncontradictory, politics cannot be that discipline which guides man to his ultimate end as its proper and distinctive task.

Politics does, however, deal with a necessary, elevated good, an end, the proper life of man in the polity, the life of man insofar as he is mortal, insofar as he is a being capable of making choices in a context of other beings like himself, choices with real consequences. Moreover, as Aristotle, Albert, and Aquinas held, politics deals with the proper good of man in the sense that it is the highest natural good of a being composed of body and spirit insofar as he is so composed, a being for whom it is "normal" to die in three score years and ten. Insofar as man is destined for something higher and beyond this life, he was considered by the philosophers at least to be composed not of body and soul, but only of soul.[2]

In intellectual history, Christian revelation alone, with its doctrine of eventual bodily resurrection, carried with it the notion of personal immortality after death of the precise being of Socrates, Plato, or Mary. As a direct consequence of this idea, politics could be consid-

---

1. See Thomas Aquinas, *Summa theologiae,* I–II, 3–8.
2. *Ibid.,* I–II, 4.

ered the proper avenue or mode not of man's eternal life but only of his life on earth. Politics was thus limited to this life, to the erection of a suitable home for men who are destined to die but a home properly the product of their own activities. Yet this restriction implied a continuity of ultimate being which made actions even in the polity of ultimate importance, since they revealed, by their choices, how the particular persons stood to the world given to them. Likewise, the unity of being, of the good, meant that particular good actions, even in the polity, contributed to its good.

The hope of resurrection, however, could and sometimes did lessen man's efforts to improve the earthly city on the grounds that life would soon end anyhow for its members. But such an attitude, while legitimate to the extent that it stressed the obvious fact of man's mortality, falsified the connection between this life and the next in this understanding. The attempt to restate the proper relationship, so that the values of both kinds of life, relative to a single being, could be preserved in their proper perspectives, was the burden and importance of medieval Christian political philosophy. Albert and Aquinas held that, while it is true that politics properly belonged only to this life, still it is the natural and proper task of man. Politics was the architectonic science and was not intended to substitute itself for all other tasks. The neglect of the political task on earth would also mean the failure to achieve a happy immortal life, since grace built on nature, and to neglect nature was to reject grace. All being had a unity and consistency that elevated what it distinguished so that a contribution to a higher order was implicit in any properly functioning being.

Consequently, the shape of the human city and the efforts to enable it to withstand time were, in this view, proper tasks for men who were ultimately destined each for a personal immortality beyond the grave. The mark of a particularly "Christian" politics—and in this it is like Aristotelian theory, in contradistinction to much of post-Aristotelian and modern theory—lies in the fact that it sought to provide for man's life both in this "passing" world, that is, as the "mortal," and in the next by accepting the only conditions which in fact made the achievements of these respective ends possible, ends which were thus not conceived to be related to each other as contradictories.

Politics, in this view, was the limited, oftentimes slow, effort of men on this earth to define and institutionalize in a working manner the actual human condition, the time of their "mortality." Neither virtue nor vice were to be factually excluded from the abiding reality of a polity. Though this life had already begun in the life of each "political animal," immortality was the life after death, in which all man's highest desires were to be achieved. In this same position, however, man could also finally reject *all that is* except the permanence of the self. The two sorts of life, political and contemplative, would destroy each other if the dynamism proper to one were applied to the other.

Modern political theory has not for the most part accepted this classical Christian solution to perennial problems that in fact always arise in political living and philosophy. This point must be understood if we are to reach any complete understanding of the meaning of the alternatives to it which also occur precisely as "political theories," the more radical Gnostic ideologies. Modern political philosophy really broke with the Christian and Aristotelian tradition at the point where it ceased to look upon nature and man as the "products," as it were, of a "Maker" outside nature and outside man himself. The steps in the long process were many. The previous chapters have traced the central trends in this evolution.

In essence, however, the main endeavor, it seems, was to see "nature" and its operations as formative through the mind of man, a reversal of the classical notion that truth was first a conformity of the human mind with a reality it did not itself make. Nature came to be regarded not as something made or given but as something being made and being made intelligible by man's own scientific and rational intellect. Man himself was regarded as a malleable form which was undetermined in itself and thus originally formless. Man's destiny, his Promethean destiny indeed, was to give himself shape and purpose through his own mastery of nature, society, history, and finally himself, even his very corpus. Once man was no longer regarded as something whose ends were fixed by the Maker of nature, he became free, as it were, to form his own world and purpose independently of any "limits" given in his own existence.

Any claim, therefore, that man's proper end was not defined by man himself was regarded as an alienation which must be "overcome" if man were to prove himself radically "free." But man did in fact possess a desire to know and experience all things. This was a commonplace in the classical theory of knowledge, which held that the object of the intellect was simply *that which is*. To overcome any obligatory response to *what is* became the prevailing constant underlying all the various forms which men have employed to give content to this desire themselves to form all reality by their own power. Once the Aristotelian and Christian answers to the problem of a natural and supernatural end beyond this life ceased to be comprehensible realities, the peculiar dynamism attached to man's desire for contemplation became transformed into categories of this life and consequently into this life's highest natural task as acknowledged by classical political philosophy itself, the task of politics.

The secularization of metaphysics and correlative theological notions gave modern politics the idea of progress, the General Will, the classless society, the idea that evil is caused by societal institutions, that life is man's highest good, that the ongoing species is the highest being, that physical death is the greatest evil. Machiavelli and Descartes left man the idea that the theoretic order could pass under his mastery. Once theoretic order became "practical," in the classical sense of that word, that is, subject to man's artistic powers, it needed to be given depth and content—it needed to be, if I may use somewhat awkward but descriptive terms, "historicized" and "humanized." The humanization of the practical order meant that man's task was to create conditions, goals, and techniques which would leave him in possession of all that he was and wanted to be, presupposed to nothing but himself. He would only respond to questions and answers he himself formulated and controlled. He would accept nothing he did not legislate for himself, including even man's own past. He would admit no experience to be valid for one man and not for another. Collectivities, in one form or another, replaced the ontological reality of the individual as the center of ultimate meaning. Rule would only mean rule over his own life, presupposed to nothing but what man gave to himself.

The reduction of reality to history, "historicization," furthermore, would come to mean that man must overcome everything in his past record that could alienate him from himself, that was not put properly under his own control. The implication was first that man must eliminate the idea of a "Creator" outside time who defined man's ends and being for him as his own highest good. Second, any alien, heteronomous or paternal rule of one man over another, however rational in classical and Christian theory, must be removed as incompatible with man's full freedom.[3] And finally, what history shows men able to enjoy and experience must be open to everyone, so that all distinctions based on a diversity of will or talent are invalid and dangerous. History consequently became the record, even the "metaphysics," of the only being, that is, of man's own being but his own being presumed to no personal immortality. This is the key. Political philosophy, at its ultimate level, is about the ways in which these ideas work themselves out when the religious and philosophical alternatives are by choice closed as a matter of legitimate consideration.

However, the task was not yet completed when the theoretic order was made practical and the practical was in turn historicized and humanized.[4] When personal immortality beyond this life was denied to each man, particularly in the Christian understanding of it as addressed to questions in classical political philosophy, it meant that a substitute "immortality" must be elaborated which would somehow fit into the confines of life on earth. Intellectually, it was no easy effort to make this adjustment. Nevertheless, the attempt to explain how all nature and history could fall under man's primacy and causality was

---

3. See E. B. F. Midgley, "Authority, Alienation, and Revolt," *Aberdeen University Review*, XLVI (Autumn, 1976), 372–83.
4. For this reason Strauss and Voegelin were right to see in historicism an attack on man himself. See Strauss, *Natural Right and History;* Eric Voegelin, *The New Science of Politics* (Chicago, 1952).

the distinctive note of modern intellectual history. What was needed above all was some unity or unifying matrix which could combine historicized and humanized reality into one overarching view.

In the Judaeo-Christian and Aristotelian systems, God and the First Mover supplied the matrix. But with this alternative gone, the only substitute to Divine Reason was, in the end, human reason, but a human reason having implicitly rejected the alternatives opened to reason by revelation. Modern political philosophy has wrestled in effect with the question of what it means for human reason to operate "as if" there were no God, a position which originated in Grotius's analysis of the natural law. Also, as Leo Strauss noted in Machiavelli, it has retained the elevated ends inspired by revelation while denying the methods of revelation to understand and achieve them.[5]

To save reality from blind purposelessness it was necessary, then, to substitute human reason for the divine intellect as the cause of all reality—physical, social, and even spiritual. The next step in this process was the work of Kant and Hegel. Essentially it consisted in identifying all the scientific and historical work of man with the species "man" while assuming, at the same time, that the total dynamic content of the species as it existed in time was to be identified with the Absolute, with *what is*. In Kant, each individual became capable of intellectual and moral acts that were exactly like, if not actually identified with those of every other man. Hegel took this process a step further by making all individuals moments in the Absolute Whole, so that in a sense everything became the One and the One a "part" or aspect of everything else.[6] Both in Kant and Hegel, the unifying principle which gave coherence and unity was always the human knowing process.

In 1783, Kant wrote his *Prolegomena to Every Future Metaphysics That May Be Presented as a Science*. Here he asked his readers to "suspend their work, look upon all that has gone before as non-existent and above all, first ask the question: 'Whether such a thing as meta-

---

5. Leo Strauss, "Niccolo Machiavelli," *Studies in Platonic Political Philosophy*, 213.
6. Georg Wilhelm Friedrich Hegel, *The Philosophy of History*, trans. J. Sibree (New York, 1956), 37.

physics is even possible at all.'" The cause of this question, Kant confessed, was "the attack made upon it [metaphysics] by David Hume." Hume's famous attack was of enormous importance because, in effect, he was said to have undermined the very basis of traditional metaphysics, "that of the connection of cause and effect." For Kant, Hume showed that the connection of cause and effect could not be a product of experience. Kant expanded this question to include all the concepts of metaphysics. But Kant did not believe that these ideas of causality, form, and time were entirely independent of reality. They were found to originate not in experience but "in the pure intellect." Kant's whole effort was to find a way to protect God, immortality, and freedom from the implications of Hume's criticism.[7]

The function of the *Critique of Pure Reason* was to safeguard knowledge from Hume's criticism that knowledge arises from "a repeated association of that which happens with that which precedes, and from a custom of connecting images, a custom originating in this repeated association, and constituting therefore a merely subjective necessity." Kant admitted with Hume and Aristotle that "all our knowledge begins with experience," but he denied that all knowledge "arises out of experience."[8] He sought to recognize the spiritual stability of knowledge.

A priori knowledge is "absolutely independent of all experience." Whatever does not derive from experience is a priori knowledge, the criterion of which is "necessity and strict universality." Kant wanted to show, therefore, that a priori principles were "indispensable for the possibility of experience." These principles, moreover, made it possible to extend "the scope of our judgment beyond all limits of experience, and this by means of concepts to which no corresponding object

---

7. Immanuel Kant, *Prolegomena to Every Future Metaphysics That May Be Presented as a Science*, Introduction, in *The Philosophy of Kant*, ed. Carl J. Friedrich (New York, 1949), 41–42, 46. (Hereafter this work will be cited as Kant, *Prolegomena Metaphysics*, in Friedrich, 41.) "God, freedom, and the immortality of the soul are the problems to whose solution, as their ultimate and unique goal, the laborious preparations of metaphysics are directed" (Kant, *Critique of Judgment*, Appendix: *Theory of the Method of Applying the Teleological Judgment*, N. 91, in Friederich, 362).
8. Kant, *Critique of Pure Reason*, Int. Chap. 2 and I, in Friedrich, 27, 24.

can ever be given in experience." Thus reason operating beyond sense confronted the basic problems of God, freedom, and immortality, which existed in an area "where experience can yield neither guidance nor correction."[9]

Metaphysics is directed to establishing these a priori principles. And as Kant had set up the problem, Hume's objections could not apply to God, freedom, or immortality, since these objections of Hume could refer only to experience.[10] In order to prove this thesis, Kant formulated his famous doctrine of analytic and synthetic judgments, a priori and a posteriori knowledge. Kant wanted to show that metaphysics could have a priori, synthetic knowledge, which did not depend on experience but which contained something new. Analytic, a priori judgments added "nothing through the predicate to the concept of the subject," while synthetic judgments "add to the concept of the subject a predicate which has not been in any wise thought in it, and which no analysis could possibly extract from it."[11] An a priori judgment did not derive from experience; an a posteriori judgment did. What, then, was the business of metaphysics? "[It] is not merely to analyze concepts which we make for ourselves *a priori* of things, and thereby clarify them analytically, but to extend our *a priori* knowledge. And for this purpose we must employ principles which add to the given concept something that was not contained in it, and through *a priori*, synthetic judgments venture so far that experience is quite unable to follow us."[12] In this way, Kant hoped to obviate the Humian notion that the denial of causality in nature meant the denial of God, immortality, and freedom.

Aristotelian metaphysics concerned itself rather with beings as they were given in experience or at least whose knowledge required experience. Aquinas in turn spelled out the meaning of this trait for the individual and the way in which what was revealed related to it. For

---

9. *Ibid.*, Int. Chap. 1, 2, 3, in Friedrich, 24, 25, 26, 27, 28.
10. Kant, *Prolegomena Metaphysics*, Chap. 27, in Friedrich, 82–83.
11. Kant, *Critique of Pure Reason*, Intro. 5, Chap. 4, in Friedrich, p. 30–31. See also Kant, *Prolegomena Metaphysics*, Chap. 2, in Friedrich, p. 51–58.
12. Kant, *Critique of Pure Reason*, Intro., Chap. 5, in Friedrich, p. 35–36. See also Kant, *Prolegomena Metaphysics*, Chap. 2, in Friedrich, 57.

Kant, however, the knowledge of God or soul as such was not the proper subject of metaphysics. Kant's significance lay in his radical separation of something very fundamental in classical metaphysics, namely, the existing thing which is known, from the mode of knowing that is based on it. And in making the distinction, he elevated the way of knowing to a prime place and removed the thing-in-itself from experience. What is common is no longer things—rocks, men, trees, Socrates, Plato, and Mary—but a priori concepts and judgments which impose forms on reality. All men have the same a priori concepts, whereas it was not certain that they all know the same things. Reason was the faculty "which supplies the principles of *a priori* knowledge" independent of experience. Kant was therefore concerned with transcendental knowledge, that is, with "all knowledge which is occupied not so much with objects as with the mode of our knowledge of objects in so far as this mode of knowledge is to be possible *a priori.*"[13] The thing-in-itself was, with the possible exception of the self as such, utterly unknown.[14] Phenomena appear, not things.

Kant's application of this system to nature enabled him to define nature as "the existence of things in so far as their existence is determined by universal laws." When this nature is known, it is the result of the application of laws which are a priori. Nature considered materially is "the sum total of all the objects of experience." The formal order in nature is caused by the laws "which regulate all the objects of experience, and, insofar as they are known *a priori,* these laws constitute the necessary regularity of nature." Considered in themselves, however, the things of nature cannot be known. Therefore, what is important are things "as the objects of a possible experience. The sum total of these is what we properly call nature." He added, "But we must distinguish the empirical laws of nature, which always presuppose particular perceptions, from the pure or universal laws of nature, which, without being based upon any particular perceptions, merely contain the conditions of the necessary association of such perceptions

---

13. Kant, *Critique of Pure Reason,* Intro., Chap. 7, in Friedrich, 36.
14. See Allers, "Rousseau's Second Discourse," 67.

in experience; in respect of the last, nature and possible experience are the same thing. . . . The intellect does not derive its laws *(a priori)* from nature but prescribes them to nature."[15] The categories of reason are forever the same. They organize whatever is given to them according to their own formal modality.

The real object, therefore, can never be known. What is known is what is imposed on nature. "The object in itself always remains unknown." Kant could now answer Hume because intellectual concepts as such did not refer to *noumena*. These intellectual concepts, however, were the cause of experience; "experience is derived from them," and thus Hume's problem is avoided. "The synthetic *a priori* principles can never refer to anything more than mere phenomena and can only represent that which makes experience in general possible, or which, inasmuch as experience is derived from these principles, must always be capable of being presented in some possible experience."[16] There is, then, a constant use of intellect in the very formation of reality.

Kant admitted the temptation to believe in *noumena* that are pure spiritual beings. Nor did he think that his system made them impossible. What was impossible was that these beings be known by speculative knowledge. "Our pure intellectual concepts, no less than our pure images, refer to nothing but objects of a possible experience, to mere beings of sense."[17] Intellectual concepts, moreover, refer only to the field of experience because they "merely prescribe the logical form of judgment in respect to images or things-looked-at." As a result, Kant believed these *noumena* are "notions of a task whose object is conceivable in itself but whose execution is utterly impossible because of the nature of our intellect. Our intellect is a faculty not for looking at things but merely for joining given images into experiences."[18] At every point, Kant reversed the common way of viewing reality. Man causes his experience; experience does not cause him to know.

15. Kant, *Prolegomena Metaphysics*, Chaps. 14, 16, 17, 36, in Friedrich, 67, 68, 69, 91.
16. *Ibid.*, Chaps. 19, 30, in Friedrich, 72, 85. See also Chap. 28, in Friedrich, 83.
17. *Ibid.*, Chap. 22, in Friedrich, 87. Recall again the questions in Thomas Aquinas, *Summa theologiae*, I–II, 3–8.
18. Kant, *Prolegomena Metaphysics*, Chap. 34, in Friedrich, 88.

One of Kant's original intentions was to save God, freedom, and immortality from skepticism. In order for him to accomplish this task, he had to establish a universal good which did not depend upon theology or metaphysics. "What?" he wrote in an early work, echoing the questions asked by the young men in the beginning of Book II of Plato's *Republic,* "Is it good to be virtuous only because there is another world; or will not actions be rewarded rather because they were good and virtuous in themselves?" But such a good for Kant would have to be the product of both freedom and universality; otherwise it could not be applied to all. Practical reason differed from theoretical reason because the will, "a faculty for determining its own causality," made its own objects and therefore the objects always correspond to the concepts.[19]

But the will needed a guide which could not come from experience, since "all moral concepts have their seat and origin completely *a priori* in the reason, and have it in the commonest reason just as truly as in what is speculative in the highest degree. Moral concepts cannot be obtained by abstraction from any experience and hence merely contingent knowledge." Moral laws hold for all rational beings and are therefore derived "from the general concept of a rational being." Morality is just as independent as metaphysics. Kant, however, excluded teleology from morals; "The moral worth of an action does not consist in the effect expected from it." Whence, then, is the moral worth? From the idea of law as such as it determines the will. "The will is a faculty for choosing only that which reason, independently of inclination, recognizes as practically necessary, that is, as good."[20]

Consequently, in order to avoid teleological morality, Kant introduced a morality which derived its criterion from its own universality. "Duty is the necessity of an action, resulting from respect for the law." Kant looked not to the particular act and circumstances as they reveal a unique situation but to the situation as it represents a universal form

---

19. Kant, *Critique of Practical Reason,* Intro., in Friedrich, 209. See also Kant, *Prolegomena Metaphysics,* Chap. 56, in Friedrich, 98.
20. Kant, *Metaphysical Foundations of Morals,* 2nd Sect. in Friedrich, 159, 160; 1st Sect., 148; 2nd Sect., 161.

capable of being applied to all humanity. Such was its very form. Thus every moral act was an act for the whole human race. "The will of every rational being is a will giving general laws." And the will which gives these principles is one's own will. "By virtue of this principle all maxims are rejected which cannot co-exist with the will as the general legislator," Kant wrote. "Thus the will is not being subjected simply to law, but is so subjected that it must be regarded *as giving itself the law,* and for this very reason is subject to the law of which it may consider itself the author. . . . Thus, the principle that every human will *gives general laws through all its maxims* if otherwise correct, could very well be *suited as* to the categorical imperative because it is *not grounded in any interest* but rather in the idea of universal lawgiving. Therefore, it alone among all possible imperatives can be unconditional."[21] The will which has no interest determining it is autonomous.

"Of what sort would a will be which could be determined not by any material condition but by the pure form of law?" Germain Grisez asked. "Such a will would be wholly independent of the natural law of appearances, the physical law of nature. For the determining ground of any actualization in nature must be found in sensible appearance. Independence of this natural law is freedom. Therefore, such a will would be free. Again of what sort would a law be which could serve as the determining ground of a free will? It clearly must be a law which determines by its mere form, for if it were by any reference to the object which it has that it is determined, there would be causality exercised by the empirical conditions and such causality is always necessary."[22] Freedom and law can now coexist, and nature's necessity is likewise retained.

The principle of the autonomous will, moreover, applies equally to all human beings. Consequently a universal law can be formed on this basis "that each must treat himself and all other such beings, never

---

21. *Ibid.,* 1st Sect., 148; 2nd Sect., 180.
22. Germain G. Grisez, "Kant and Aquinas: Ethical Theory," *Thomist,* XXI (January, 1958), 57.

merely as means, but also always as ends in themselves." Here the idea of teleology, which Kant had excluded from nature, can enter into morals. "A rational being belongs as a member to the realm of ends to the extent to which he is himself subject to these general laws, although giving them to himself." The historical destiny of man can now reenter as an end and definite purpose to be achieved by men. "Rational nature is distinguished from the rest of nature by setting itself an end. This end would be the content of every good will." An independent morality now existed which was "the relation of actions to the autonomy of the will." Mankind's dignity "consists just in this capacity of making general laws, always provided that it is itself subject to these laws." Kant clearly separated morality from any purpose that came from outside man himself. "Autonomy of the will is that property by which will is a law unto itself, independent of any property of objects of volition . . . the principle of autonomy is the sole principle of morals."[23]

In Kant, then, there is, both in metaphysics and in morals, a philosophy that identifies individual human experience with the race or species as such.[24] The maxims of duty and universality of moral actions make all men the same in their activity. The progress of history has for its purpose the development of the species as such. Indeed, the species seems to have a priori principles and universal maxims, since one individual cannot be distinguished from another in the source and knowledge of these universal notions. Even though each man is to be treated as an end in himself, he still appears as man in indistinction, not as the unique individual, Socrates, Plato, or Mary. We see a definite similarity between Kant and Plato here. The logical notion of common man seems to be more real than living particular individuals. Indeed, logically, the individuals do not differ at all if man is understood to be the logical notion or universal, not the distinct,

23. Kant, *Metaphysical Foundations of Morals*, 2nd Sect., in Friedrich, 182, 185, 187. See also Grisez, "Kant and Aquinas: Ethical Theory," 73.
24. See Kant, *Idea for a Universal History with Cosmopolitan Intent*, in Friedrich, 116–31.

unique individual whose own knowledge derives from his own individual experience and intellectual capacities in contact with *what is*.[25]

Kant's metaphysics posited a faculty in each human mind that produced an objective phenomenon just like that produced in every other man. This similarity came not from the thing-in-itself, which was unknown, but from the structure of the mind. Consequently the direction of Kant's thought turned to a path which subsumed practical or better existing objects into the mind itself. This subsuming gave them unity; just as in the moral and historical realms, it was not a relation to objects beyond man in which some order already existed that defined man's good but the conformity of man to his own universal laws. Thus in Kant, reality was gradually becoming absorbed into the intellect of man, which served as a matrix for *all that is*.

Charles Sentroul noted the significance of this position in Kant. "Descartes has said: 'I think, therefore I am'; Kant would have been able to say: 'I think, therefore that thing is'; and Aristotle: 'I think that which is.'"[26] This apt analogy clearly suggests the ultimate significance of Kant when he is compared to Aristotle and the Stoics. Kant finally established the primacy of the practical reason as will. The Stoics had stressed the primacy of the practical but from the side of intelligence, not will. Sentroul wrote:

> That (originality) of Kant holds especially to the doctrine of the *primacy of the practical reason*. Toward that doctrine converge all the secondary theses. . . . It constitutes a response which for many thinkers is definitive regarding the eternal questions of the good and the true. . . . Now, the good or the true, which is the primordial notion? From the intelligence or the will, which is the preponderant faculty? Kant has reedited the answers of the ancient Stoics and has supported with subtle reasons the simple—very human, in any case—phrase of Pascal: "the heart has some reasons which the reason does not understand." For in contrast to Pascal and the others after him who have said

---

25. "Perfectum judicium intellectus in nobis non potest haberi, nisi per resolutionem ad sensibilia quae sunt prima principia nostrae cognitionis" (Thomas Aquinas, *Summa theologiae*, II–II, 173, 2; see I, 76, 2; 79, 3).

26. Charles Sentroul, *Kant et Aristote* (Paris, 1913), 328 (my translation).

that phrase with their heart, Kant has said it with his reason! In order to prove it, he has refashioned one more time the examination of theoretic knowledge; and that examination he has pushed, we freely believe, as far and as profoundly as perhaps any other person.[27]

Kant regarded everything as a knowing maker who unified all reality in the order of knowledge because he imposed his own order on reality.

HEGEL

The connection between Kant and Hegel is, of course, quite close, one of the most fertile cross-influences in the history of thought. But Hegel felt that Kant's dualism of noumenon and phenomenon needed to be broken. If noumenon and phenomenon were merged, then man would have a direct insight into reason itself. God, freedom, and morality could no longer lie outside or beyond phenomenon but must be within reason.[28] The effect of this union was quite vast. For now, not only God, freedom, and immortality could be incorporated into reason but likewise history, which Kant, Montesquieu, and other thinkers had already attempted to incorporate into reason. With the placement of history at the center of intellectual discussion, the political life, which formed history from generation to generation, assumed new importance in Hegel.

Hegel, then, saw and accepted what had been implicit in political philosophy since Machiavelli and Descartes, namely, the full identification of what ought to be with what was in fact made in society by man. "The insight, that to which . . . philosophy is to lead us," Hegel wrote, "is, that the real world is as it ought to be—that the truly good—the universal divine reason—is not a mere abstraction, but a vital principle capable of realizing itself. This *Good*, this *Reason*, in its most concrete form, is God. God governs the world; the actual working of his government—the carrying out of his plan—is the History of the World. This plan philosophy strives to comprehend; for only that which has been developed as the result of it, possesses *bona fide*

---

27. *Ibid.*, 330–331.
28. See James Collins, *A History of Modern European Philosophy* (Milwaukee, 1954), 604.

reality."[29] What Hegel needed, consequently, was a model on which he could unify all of this historical reality with the movement in the Absolute.

This model he found in thought structure itself. Hegel's *Logic* penetrated into the nature of abstract intellectual relationships occasioned by the realization that an order of reason somehow lay behind external things. But Hegel did not stop here. If behind things stood reason, behind reason taken as human thought, there must lie a thinking something to which those abstract concepts which men experience were properly real. What did Hegel do with these data? Quite clearly, he insisted that men were part of an a priori thought process in some manner. But he maintained, in addition, that reality is this process of the Absolute Spirit. Consequently, the way this Spirit came to know itself, through a process of self-externalization and reembodiment of itself into itself, was actually what the world was in its being. Everything thus became a phase or moment in this process, which brought to consciousness some phase implicit in the initial reason.

Actually, for Hegel, politics came before history. That is, the record of what the Absolute Spirit did must follow its own activity, which, strictly speaking, was not really capable of being otherwise than it was. In this, Hegel reflected something of the position of Plotinus. Politics recorded the objective spirit as it developed content, which in turn could be reassimilated into the Absolute Spirit. The first thing to remember, however, when treating Hegel's politics was that it was not a "practical science," in Aristotle's sense, by which things were changed or ordered. Rather, as Hegel himself wrote, "This book, *The Philosophy of Right,* then, containing as it does the science of the state, is to be nothing other than the endeavor to apprehend and portray the state as something inherently rational. As a work of philosophy, it must be poles apart from the attempt to construct a state as it ought to be. The instruction which it may contain cannot consist in teaching the state what it ought to be; it can only

---

29. Hegel, *The Philosophy of History,* 36.

show how the state, the ethical universe, is to be understood. . . . To comprehend what is, that is the task of philosophy, because what is, is reason."[30]

Hegel's "reason" came into the world, then, as an active, dynamic spirit. "But by 'reason' we must no longer understand the 'practical reason' of Kant. It is not a mere abstract and formal principle, a moral demand like the Kantian categorical imperative. It is reason that lives in the historical world and organizes it."[31] When reason actually entered into politics as such, therefore, everything that happened, good and evil, was equally a part of reason. "To recognize reason as the rose in the cross of the present and thereby to enjoy the present," was how Hegel put it.[32]

The dynamism of politics took place apart from man's making. Yet man's actions were the moments of the Spirit. Hegel, quite in opposition to Kant, insisted on man's interested intrusion into reality. "If men are to act, they must not only intend the Good, but must have decided for themselves whether this or that particular thing is a good."[33] The full involvement of all reality in the Absolute is the eternal present complete with the content history has given to it. The Ideal appears only when history has ripened it.

The proper context of the state, then, is history. But history itself was actually the ultimate process of the consciousness of the Absolute Spirit. The mind externalized to itself in history returned to full self-consciousness. Consequently, for Hegel, what is is right; what does take place must take place. Everything was part of order and spirit and act. Nothing is wrong, only opposed in such a manner that it can bring out a truth which can be subsumed into the full Spirit. Everything is rational, therefore real. "The only Thought which Philosophy brings with it to the contemplation of History is the simple concep-

---

30. Georg Wilhelm Friedrich Hegel, *The Philosophy of Right*, trans. T. M. Knox (Oxford, 1942), 11.
31. Ernst Cassirer, *The Myth of the State* (New Haven, 1946), 323–24.
32. Hegel, *The Philosophy of Right*, 9.
33. Hegel, *The Philosophy of History*, 128.

tion of Reason: that reason is the sovereign of the World: that the History of the World, therefore, presents us with a rational process."[34]

Kant had stressed the primacy of practical reason. Hegel differed from Kant by his union of the noumenon and phenomenon into a single notion of Reason. Everything must be combined in the same system. Time and eternity were no longer opposed. "In history the two factors of 'time' and 'eternity' are not separated from one another; they interpenetrate each other. Eternity does not transcend time: it is, on the contrary, to be found in time itself."[35] The identification of the speculative order with the practical order in a formal unity elevated political life to the highest form of the Divine on earth. And as such, it needed no longer to conform to the ends higher than itself; "there is no longer any moral obligation for the state."[36] Here Hegel's treatment of war and the hero acquires its revolutionary meaning. Without speculative rectitude in the classical or Christian sense, the state was free to make its own ends; indeed, it must make its own ends. And the very pursuit of these ends was the judgment of the world. "The History of the World is not the theatre of happiness."[37] It is the realm of action and making.

But Hegel, like Rousseau and Kant, used the 'species', man, as the proper context or reality which survives individual mortality. Hegel too believed that man was free by society, not by nature. "The state of Nature is, therefore, predominantly that of injustice and violence, of untamed natural impulses, of inhuman deeds and feelings." But this state refers to "mere brute emotions and rude instincts." In another sense—that in which Hegel joined Rousseau and Kant—man is free by nature. "That man is free by Nature is quite correct in one sense; viz., that he is so according to the *Idea of Humanity;* but we imply thereby that he is such only in virtue of his destiny—that he has an

---

34. *Ibid.*, 9.
35. Cassirer, *The Myth of the State*, 327.
36. Hegel, *The Philosophy of History*, 26. For discussions of Hegel's political thought, see Christopher Dawson, "The Politics of Hegel," *Dublin Review*, CCXII (October, 1943), 97–107; George H. Sabine, "Hegel's Political Philosophy," *Philosophical Review*, XLI (May, 1932), 261–82.
37. Hegel, *The Philosophy of History*, 26.

undeveloped power to become such."[38] In other words, humanity is something to be fulfilled by the history of man; it needs to be given shape and content by history.

The state, then, has its "generic" existence in its citizens, and this generic existence must be embodied in each citizen. "The State is an *abstraction* having even its generic existence in its citizens; but it is an actuality, and its simple generic existence must embody itself in individual will and activity."[39] Hegel, however, recognized the problem of morality. Like Kant, he was forced to apply the full realization of humanity to the species, not the individual, even though he insisted that this content of man really existed in individuals at each phase of history.

Indeed, Hegel held that the influence of Protestant Christianity in particular was the main realization of this trend.

> But first we must observe how the life which proceeds from death is itself, on the other hand, only individual life; so that, regarding the species as such as the real and substantial in this vicissitude, the perishing of the individual is a regress of the species into individuality. The perpetuation of the race is, therefore, nothing other than the monotonous repetition of the same kind of existence. Further, we must remark how perception—the comprehension of being by thought—is the source and birthplace of a new, and in fact higher form, in a principle which while it preserves, dignifies its material. For Thought is that Universal—that Species which is immortal, which preserves identity with itself.[40]

The full realization of this potential of the species belonged to the whole species. All of this content was finally unified and realized in a rational context modeled after the knowing process as it is applied to history. Consequently, for Hegel, political reality was intellectualized; it was given the absolute freedom to define its own goals. And the goal it strove to achieve was that which gave intellectual support to

38. *Ibid.*, 41, 41, 40.
39. *Ibid.*, 43.
40. *Ibid.*, 77–78.

the freedom of nature. It was, in other words, the full development and consciousness of the idea of humanity as such in a mystic vision of unity that included all of the classical providential order of secondary causes but without a relation to the First Cause of Being, since this was now replaced by the species mind in history.

The systems of Kant and Hegel thus provided a means to unify historical, political, and economic, as well as intellectual and mental concepts, into a unified system which sought to satisfy man's ultimate drives for unity and intelligibility. Yet both of these systems always appeared abstract and unreal to the average person. They seemed to miss the vitality of the daily life of human beings. This aspect left open the thread of thought which Feuerbach and Marx were to take up, which would attempt to concretize and materialize these visions into something that seemed, at least, to be more compatible with the experience of real people.

The legacy of Kant and Hegel was, then, of profound meaning and importance. It represented a real and concerted effort to account for all of man's basic drives, intellectual, supernatural, and political, in one complete system. The peculiar relation of the First Mover to the world, of Yahweh to creation, and of the Christian God to the redeemed tended to have lost its clarity and sharp differentiation. There was now a hope that all reality was somehow open to and under the control of the mind of man and that alone, but this mind no longer presupposed to a contemplative order, to a personal transcendence, or even to a separate individual existence. Indeed, it seemed to portend some superbeing into which each person would be absorbed as a mere "part."

7

THE PRACTICAL ORDER MATERIALIZED

Aristotelian and Judaeo-Christian philosophy had held that God was a real, infinite, eternal Being, who was the proper and ultimate origin and end of each man and of all men. Man was not the highest being in the universe. Political life, the proper life of mortal man, which distinguished him from all other creatures in the universe, both gods and beasts, differed consequently from the speculative life, because political life as such was limited to this life. Speculative life, however, was "above man" and higher than the practical life, without denying either the reality or vitality of the practical life. The theoretical order was something that man did not make himself, though he was open to it also by his given nature. Man's nature and ultimate ends were thought to belong to the speculative order, to the order that man found but did not make. But Christian theology, in particular, did envision a union of the theoretical and human life in its doctrine of real personal immortality. The same man who was political was immortal, was to be resurrected.

The doctrine of immortality in its Christian formulation affirmed that the individual, living, particular man would personally reach the highest Being in the universe. However, he would reach this only after death, his own and all others, and then not by his own efforts or plans but only on condition of his own free response to the goodness of reality in which the distinction of good and evil was within the structure of being and was known by man as such.[1] Since such an end consisting in the personal vision of God was considered beyond the natural powers of man, a separate means and institution were formed to

---

1. See Thomas Aquinas, *Summa theologiae*, I–II, 3, 8.

direct and guide man to this "supernatural" end, grace and the Church. But this supernatural end, since it was to be attained only after death, did not supplant or undermine the natural order of this life but rather subsumed and enhanced it. The natural order of this life was considered to be worthy of human effort and achievement. The Christian dogma of immortality, however—resurrection, with its philosophical import toward properly human and political questions—did imply that the characteristics of the unlimited, immortal, complete life after death could not be duplicated by politics, economics, psychology, or the culture of this earthly life. These were two essentially different types of life, so that to confuse the two or to conceive that one had the typical characteristics of the other was to disrupt both orders, which dealt, nevertheless, with the same human beings.

Much modern philosophy, however, could not accept this view. The classical and Judaeo-Christian view held that man's ends and nature should be outside man's power to make himself. The nature and end of man were considered the proper object of man's own activity but something to be discovered as already formed and not by man. To say that a supernatural Being "created" man and established his ends would, in much modern political philosophy, be to "alienate" man from himself—in other words, to make him inhuman. The evolution of modern thought has revealed a concentrated, indeed often profound, effort to attribute to man the powers and dynamism formerly attributed to the theoretical and supernatural orders. In this effort, many classical and Christian ideas, such as creation, individual immortality, and evil, have been secularized and transformed into the confines of this life or at least into the life of the human species as a whole over time.

In this process, the doctrine of immortality was of particular importance. The significance of the doctrine itself, even for those who did not accept it, lay in its claim to be dealing with real, individual, polis-*living* men who were personally to attain resurrection and beatitude. Christian immortality was to enable man to embrace all being and God, in an eternal, personal manner, personal to man himself in his individuality. But if this drive to participate in all reality were confined to this life, it would seem to follow that politics, the highest good of this life, would actually have to become a kind of metaphysics or theology. A "new politics," then, which sought to do this could somehow embrace *all that is,* so that man could feel that he actually experienced in this life all the reality there was. The marvellous structure of the Hegelian system seemed to be inadequate at just this point, because it left man in an abstract and partial participation in the Absolute Spirit. The world was a rational whole, but no true man could feel that such rationality was "real" to him. His autonomy was still incomplete.

FEUERBACH

An attempt to confront such a situation was made by Ludwig Feuerbach. Feuerbach transformed Christian and Hegelian notions into the real, tangible world, "I attach myself, in direct opposition to Hegelian philosophy, only to realism."[2] This realism, he thought, would enable him to make ideas and beliefs that were only abstract into concrete realities for men. With this point in mind, he held that Christianity was really an abstract analysis of man. "Man is the God of Christianity, anthropology the mystery of Christian theology."[3]

Feuerbach's method was to transform every dogmatic and moral idea of Christianity—salvation, Trinity, Providence, celibacy, Mariology, faith, prayer, charity, sin, miracle, immortality, even heaven—into abstractions of real human desires and experiences. He thus believed that Kant's "God, immortality, freedom, in the supernaturalistic sense, exist only in the heart. The heart is itself the existence of God, the existence of immortality."[4] The Christian God, then, should be seen as the abstract species of humanity. Religion is the devotion to this abstraction. "But religion is man's consciousness of himself in his concrete or living totality," Feuerbach wrote, "in which the identity of self-consciousness exists only as the pregnant, complete point of *I* and *thou.* Religion, at least the Christian, is abstraction from the world; it

---

2. Ludwig Feuerbach, *The Essence of Christianity,* trans. George Eliot (New York, 1957), Preface to the 2nd ed., xxxiv.
3. *Ibid.,* App. N. 22, 336.
4. *Ibid.,* App. N. 4, 285.

is essentially inward. . . . God, as an extramundane being, is however nothing else than the nature of man withdrawn from the world and concentrated in itself."[5]

Feuerbach therefore claimed that Christianity denied the significance of human multiplicity as such because it identified the species, man, with Christ. "The most unequivocal expression, the characteristic symbol of this immediate identity of the species and individuality in Christianity is Christ, the real God of the Christians."[6] But if the full perfection of humanity is concentrated in Christ, men must, in Feuerbach's analysis, love Christ, not one another. On this basis, the Christian does not have to worry about the world or about real people, only about Christ. Culture and politics could be ignored, since they were not essential. Thus God was interpreted between man and man, and man was not loved for his own sake.[7]

Feuerbach held, consequently, that man was his own object. "Consciousness in the strictest sense is present only in a being to whom his species, his essential nature, is an object of thought." For Aristotle and Thomas Aquinas, the species as such could not have been an "object" of thought; individual men or beings were objects of thought. By transforming the object of thought into its logical expression or abstraction, Feuerbach hoped to enable every man to participate in the real species. "Man is himself at once I and thou; he can put himself in the place of another, for this reason, that to him his species, his essential nature, and not merely his individuality, is an object of thought." Nevertheless, the nature of man was always concrete for Feuerbach. The real task was "to know man's own concrete nature."[8]

Christianity understood this point, apparently, but made it abstract rather than concrete. "Religion, at least the Christian, is the relation of man to himself, or more correctly to his own nature (i.e., his subjective nature); but a relation to it viewed as a nature apart

---

5. *Ibid.*, 66. For a further analysis of the importance of these ideas of Feuerbach, see Martin Buber, *Between Man and Man*, trans. Ronald Gregor Smith (Boston, 1955), 145–48.
6. Feuerbach, *The Essence of Christianity*, 154.
7. *Ibid.*, 154; see 160, 213–15, 267, 268–72.
8. *Ibid.*, 1, 5; see 2–3.

from his own. The divine being is nothing else than the human being. . . . All the attributes of the divine nature are, therefore, attributes of human nature." Feuerbach, then, posited that the multiplicity of men in the species man was the real God. "Man has his highest being, his God, in himself; not in himself as an individual, but in his essential nature, his species. No individual is an adequate representation of his species, but only the human individual is conscious of the distinction between the species and the individual; in the sense of this distinction lies the root of religion. The yearning to be free from himself, i.e., from the limits and defects of his individuality. . . . Man feels nothing toward God which he does not also feel towards man. *Homo homini deus est.*"[9] This multiplicity makes politics and culture necessary; it makes men work for and love each other because they see the true value of others, an idea that is itself quasi-religious, as Feuerbach seems to have held.

The Christians, on the other hand, in Feuerbach's view, did not need this world to achieve this perfection. They could ignore this participation in the concrete species or multiplicity of men.[10] "Nature, the world, has no value, no interest for Christians. The Christian thinks only of himself and the salvation of his soul." Any effort of the Christian to participate in human culture or love simply violated the Christian longing for Christ, the absolute ideal of the human species. "True, religious Christianity has within it no principle of scientific and material culture, no motive to it. The practical end and object of Christians is solely heaven, i.e., the realized salvation of the soul."[11]

Christian ideas of celibacy and immortality were related to the notion that each individual attained a personal immortality without others. "The unwedded and ascetic life is the direct way to the heavenly, immortal life, for heaven is nothing else than life liberated from

---

9. *Ibid.*, 5; N. 1, 281.
10. Arendt, *The Human Condition*, 21, 35.
11. Feuerbach, *The Essence of Christianity*, App. N, 5, 287, 288. "The individual attains his end by himself alone; he attains it in God. . . . God only is the want of the Christian; others, the human race, the world, are not necessary to him; he is not the inward need of others" (*ibid.*, 160).

the conditions of the species, supernatural, sexless, absolutely subjective life." Immortality was the idealization of the celibate life which *ipso facto* removed real love and participation of man from the species. And "the doctrine of immortality is the final doctrine of religion."[12]

The belief in immortality was, then, an attempt to idealize real human perfection, according to Feuerbach. "The future life is the feeling, the conception of freedom from those limits which here circumscribe the feeling of self, the existence of the individual." But faith in immortality was the "faith of man in himself. . . . The Divine Being is the subjective human being in his absolute freedom and unlimitedness." Feuerbach's thesis was now complete. "Our most essential task is now fulfilled," he wrote. "We have reduced the supramundane, supernatural, and superhuman nature of God to the elements of human nature as its fundamental elements. Our process of analysis has brought us again to the position with which we set out. The beginning, middle and end of religion is MAN."[13] Feuerbach held reality to be man as a real, living, communicating species of individual men and women. He had, in a manner, transposed the abstractness connected with the Kantian and Hegelian systems into the real, sensuous world.

Feuerbach was consequently of great importance in this discussion of immortality and political philosophy because he insisted that immortality destroyed any real participation in the politics and culture of this life. As a result, immortality was dangerous to this life because it withdrew men from communication with others in the species. Feuerbach, furthermore, attempted to face the obvious objection to his position, which was that man does in fact have a real desire for personal immortality. He tried to show how all desires connected with immortality arose from human relationships and from the desire to idealize them. In this sense, he was directly concerned with the classical discussions of friendship. Assuming that this was all that the supernatural reality was, he believed that man could forget such ultimate desires and could concentrate on the human tasks at hand, those primarily rooted in human love.

12. *Ibid.*, 170, 174.
13. *Ibid.*, 181, 184.

MARX

Feuerbach had a particular importance beyond the value of his own system in itself because of his influence on Marx. Though he was not as influential as Hegel, Feuerbach did nevertheless contribute much to Marx's thinking. Engels noted the effect on him of *The Essence of Christianity*. "Then came Feuerbach's *Essence of Christianity*," he wrote. "With one blow it pulverized the contradiction, in that without circumlocutions, it placed materialism on the throne again. Nature exists independently of all philosophy. It is the foundation upon which we human beings, ourselves products of nature, have grown up. Nothing exists outside nature and man, and the higher beings our religious fantasies have created are only the fantastic reflection of our own essence. The spell was broken, the 'system' was exploded. . . . One must himself have experienced the liberating effect of this book to get an idea of it. Enthusasm was general; we all became at once Feuerbachians."[14] But Engels could not fully accept Feuerbach. He felt that Feuerbach had elevated sex love to the highest religion. In this, Hegel still seemed superior to Feuerbach.[15]

Hegel's ethical and political doctrines dealt with real content, though their form was ideal. Feuerbach, on the other hand, "in form . . . is realistic, since he takes his start from man; but there is absolutely no mention of the world in which man lives; hence his man remains always the same abstract man who occupies the field in the philosophy of religion."[16]

Engels saw that Feuerbach's theory did not really involve historical man. For Engels, Feuerbach's message was simply "love one another—fall into each other's arms regardless of distinctions of sex or estate—a universal orgy of reconciliation." Engels's contempt here was obvious. The root problem, Engels felt, was that Feuerbach's ideal did not take into account history. "It is designed to suit all periods, all peoples and

---

14. Friedrich Engels, "Ludwig Feuerbach and the End of Classical German Philosophy," Chap. 1, in Karl Marx and Friedrich Engels, *Basic Writings on Politics and Philosophy*, ed. Lewis S. Feuer (Garden City, N.Y., 1959), 205.
15. *Ibid.*, 216–17.
16. *Ibid.*, 219.

all conditions, and precisely for that reason it is never and nowhere applicable. . . . He is incapable of telling us anything definitive either about real nature or real men. But from the abstract man of Feuerbach one arrives at real men only when one considers them as participants in history."[17]

The lesson of Hegel, then, was not lost. Marx too felt that Feuerbach did not escape abstractions. Marx's very first *Thesis on Feuerbach* stated that Feuerbach still only contemplated sensuous reality. Feuerbach regarded man's proper attitude as theoretical, an attitude which inhibited him from seeing the meaning of revolutionary activity.

> The chief defect of all hitherto existing materialism—that of Feuerbach included—is that the thing, reality, sensuousness, is conceived only in the form of the object of contemplation, but not as human sensuous activity, practice, not subjectivity. Hence it happened that the active side, in contradistinction to materialism, was developed by idealism—but only abstractly since, of course, idealism does not know real, sensuous activity as such. Feuerbach wanted sensuous objects really differentiated from the thought objects, but he does not conceive human activity itself as objective activity. Hence, in the *Essence of Christianity,* he regards the theoretical attitude as the only genuinely human attitude, while practice is conceived and fixed only in its duty-juridical form of appearance. Hence, he does not grasp the significance of 'revolutionary', of 'practical-critical', activity.[18]

Marx held that Feuerbach's belief in materialism was valid but that Feuerbach failed to consider the further implications of materialism, namely, that the historical progress of mankind revealed development. Feuerbach's man did not seem to show the effect of history, which revealed that men at the beginning were not as free and as human as they would come to be. Here we may usefully contrast Marx with Aristotle, whom Marx himself called, significantly, "the greatest thinker of antiquity."[19] Aristotle considered the theoretical order to be higher

---

17. *Ibid.,* 223.
18. Karl Marx, *Theses on Feuerbach,* N. 1, *Basic Writings on Politics and Philosophy,* 243.
19. Karl Marx, *Capital,* trans. Samuel Moore and Edward Avelling (New York, 1936), Bk. I, Pt. 4, p. 446.

than the practical order. Man was a species whose ends were defined by the First Mover. Man and his ends belonged to the class of things that could not be otherwise, even according to man's proper mode of action, which was in freedom.

The development of modern philosophy had made a radical change in the Aristotelian system, of course, for it could no longer consider the theoretic order to be something stable and given. Following a line of development that led from Machiavelli, Descartes, Hobbes, and the origins of the scientific movement to Kant and Hegel, the hypothetical necessity which Aristotle placed in nature, which Aquinas called a "substitute intelligence," an intelligence placed in things, was gradually replaced by autonomous nature and finally by the human knowing process as the principle of organization, so to speak, which unified and distinguished nature and history.

Feuerbach's significance, as Marx rightly saw, was his insight that the unity of men and nature must be sensuous and real, that is, "material," not intellectual alone. This point gave Marx an initial and most important clue. Feuerbach was right but he was too contemplative; he did not see that man must exercise his practical activity—that activity which Aristotle saw to be peculiarly human—against all alienation of and from himself, whether the alienation was religious, social, economic, or political. Marx felt that man could show his independence only by destroying every historical institution or being that the older philosophies and religions had claimed to be "natural" or superior to man. Man could thus, in the very act of the destruction of given natural institutions and norms, demonstrate to himself his complete autonomy and independence. Marx wanted to make the Hegelian dialectic sensuous and real. He gave it a real historical task.

The endeavor which Marx set for himself was to translate Feuerbach's contemplative attitude of human society into a real, practical dynamism which was simultaneously metaphysical and practical. "Feuerbach's whole deduction with regard to the relation of men to one another goes only so far as to prove that men need and always have needed each other. He wants to establish consciousness of this fact, that is to say, like other theorists, merely to produce a correct consciousness about an existing fact; whereas for the real communist it is a question of overthrowing the existing state of things."[20] Feuerbach thought that the world is a "given" reality, something from all eternity, whereas in fact the sensuous world is "the product of industry and of the state of society; and indeed in this sense that it is an historical product, the result of the activity of a whole succession of generations, each standing on the shoulders of the preceding."[21] For this reason Marx would insist on the application of Hegelian method to historical reality.

The connection between the generations is a dialectical one of necessary historical progress, with real enemies and real tasks to perform. Marx strove to evade pure thought as an explanation of reality. The economic theories of Marx would transform the ideas of human alienation into economic conditions and structures. In this context he could rightly claim that alienation could be overcome only by abandoning Feuerbach's contemplative attitude. "It is a question of revolutionizing the existing world, of practically attacking and changing existing things."[22]

Marx could not accept the idealistic abstractions of his time. He particularly disliked the belief that society was some kind of being separate from the individuals who composed it.[23] "Society, the 'totality of existence', is conceived by our author [Bruno Bauer] not as the interaction of the constituent individual existences, but as a separate existence which undergoes another and separate interaction with these individual existences."[24] On this basis, Marx insisted that society cannot be an abstraction from the lives of real men in history. "The abstraction, the category taken as such, as apart from men and their ma-

20. Karl Marx and Friedrich Engels, *The German Ideology*, trans. R. Pascal (New York, 1939), 33.
21. *Ibid.*, 35.
22. *Ibid.*, 34. "The philosophers have only interpreted the world, in various ways; the point, however, is to change it" (Marx, *Theses on Feuerbach*, N. 11, *Basic Writings on Politics and Philosophy*, 245).
23. See Karl Marx, *Die Heilige Familie*, in Karl Marx, *Die Frühschriften*, ed. Siegfried Landshut (Stuttgart, 1953), 234, 317–38.
24. Marx and Engles, *The German Ideology*, *Basic Writings on Politics and Philosophy*, 107.

terial categories, is of course immortal, unmoved, unchangeable; it is only one form of the being of pure reason."[25]

Marx, consequently, saw society in terms of the relation of real, sensuous, that is, tangible men. "What is society, whatever its form may be? The product of men's reciprocal activity."[26] But the aim or direction of society was to develop the individual. "Man is in the most literal sense of the word a *zoon politikon*, not only a social animal, but an animal which can develop into an individual only in society."[27]

Real society for Marx must consider man in historical context, reflective of the modes of production, if it is to be understood. But production was social; it represented the interchanges of men.[28] Consequently, the way for men actually to participate in the wealth of the species was via the labor process.

> The social relations are intimately attached to the productive forces. In acquiring new productive forces men change their mode of production, and in changing their mode of production, their manner of gaining a living; they change all their social relations. . . .
>
> The same men who establish social relations conformable with their material productivity, produce also the principles, the ideas, the categories, conformable with their social relations.
>
> Thus, these ideas, these categories, are not more eternal than the ideas they express. They are historical and transitory products.
>
> There is a continual movement of growth in the productive forces, of destruction in the social relations, of formation in ideas; there is nothing immutable but the abstraction of movements—*mors immortalis*.[29]

Marx thus transferred the intellectual order into historical reflections of the productive process.

Consequently, insofar as each man did not participate in the prod-

---

25. Karl Marx, "Letter to P. V. Annenkov, December 28, 1846," in Marx and Engels, *Correspondence, 1846–95*, trans. Dona Torr (London, 1934), 14.

26. *Ibid.*, 7.

27. Karl Marx, *A Contribution to the Critique of Political Economy*, trans. N. I. Stone (Chicago, 1904), App. I, 268.

28. "The total product of our community is a social product" (Marx, *Capital*, Bk. I, Pt. 1, p. 90; see p. 83).

29. Karl Marx, *The Poverty of Philosophy*, trans. H. Quelch (Chicago, 1920), 119.

ucts of his own labor, products which embodied the reality of the time in which he lived, he was alienated from himself and from other men. Marx's violent hatred of capitalism really reflected his belief that, since a man's personal labor was objectified in produced goods, he who controlled the goods controlled the man. His metaphysics allowed nothing of wonder or superfluity or superabundance. The worker was exploited by the power of the owner. Thus, Marx believed, men were prevented from enjoying the fruits of their own labor. And likewise, in being kept from the fruits of their own efforts, they were also kept from the fruits of the combined social labor of all men by the classes that controlled the ownership of the means of production. The only effective way to restore to man his real being, that is, the reality produced by his labor, however, was to abolish all classes as such by socializing property, a theme suggestive of passages in *The Republic* of Plato. The property classes always controlled the goods of mankind for themselves and not for all men.

"The essential condition of the emancipation of the working class is the abolition of all classes," Marx wrote. "The working class will substitute, in the course of its development, for the old order of civil society an association which will exclude classes and their power, properly speaking, since political power is simply the official form of the antagonism in civil society."[30] Clearly, then, even the state represents the alienation of man from himself, though Marx was quite willing to admit that the state could and must help restore man to himself through its own ultimate destruction. In this sense, Marx did not hold the natural necessity of the state but, like early Christian writers, attributed it to some sort of fall or deviation.

The classless society in the eyes of Marx played a very special role. "But man is no abstract being, squatting outside the world. Man is the world of man, the state, society."[31] Social production led to the production of the proletariat, which was deprived of all human riches, completely alienated from this world. But the alienated men of the

---

30. *Ibid.*, 190.
31. Karl Marx, *Toward the Critique of Hegel's Philosophy of Right*, in *Basic Writings on Politics and Philosophy*, 232.

proletariat are one, united in their indistinction. Indeed, such an idea was not at all unlike the Platonic Man or separated Form, which conceived man's essential nature as something common, something left over after the individuating circumstances had been subtracted. As these proletarian men were indistinguishable, they had no determination from outside, neither from God nor from society.

Thus, Marx reasoned, if proletarian man gained the whole world, he gained it for himself. He owed his success to no one else. The proletarian classes consequently affirmed their unity and power through a Hegelian dialectical feat by which the proletariat took back what rightfully belonged to it, the products of its labor which had been taken by the capitalist classes. In this light Marx's defiant prayer made sense: "I am nothing, but I must be everything."[32] The proletarian was nothing; he must become everything. This seemed, furthermore, to be a metaphysical need, as it were, the ultimate secularization of man's desire for ultimate happiness and participation in all being.

Social production, the cooperation of men in labor, produced the world of values. In *Das Kapital,* Marx explained how the dynamism of the economy in capitalism universalized human labor, the source of the production of the human world. Consequently, through money, which was the abstract embodiment of all values, every value could be exchanged for every other value. As a result, all values became equalized and interchangeable.[33] But the total product of men's labor represented the union of men with one another in making the real world of society—and hence also of ideas, values, and culture, which are the superstructures of the mode of production. Therefore, the whole species, man, produced the human world. And since labor was equalized in exchange where all men needed each other's contribution, it became possible for all men to participate in the classless, perfect society.

Communism represented for Marx the destruction of all alienation which could keep something man produced for himself. "It is therefore the return of man himself as a social, that is, really human,

---

32. *Ibid.,* 264.
33. Marx, *Capital,* Bk. I, Pt. 1, p. 76, 110, 123.

being, a complete and conscious return which assimilates all the wealth of previous development. Communism as a complete naturalism is humanism, and as a complete humanism is naturalism. It is the definitive resolution of the antagonism between man and Nature, and between man and man. It is the true solution of the conflict between existence and essence, between objectification and self-affirmation, between freedom and necessity, between individual and species. It is the solution of the riddle of history and knows itself to be this solution." Marx transformed the Hegelian and Feuerbachian concepts of religion, state, and family as alienations into basically economic alienations. "Religious alienation only occurs in the sphere of consciousness, in the inner life of man, but economic alienation is that of real life, and its abolition therefore affects both aspects."[34] All abstract alienations in Marx ultimately depended on economic life, which Marx held to be the real life, since it took place in the sensuous world, not in the mind.

In analyzing human progress, Marx held that all human progress was social, so that man *as man* was produced by man in society. Nature too, insofar as it existed independently of man, must be humanized, but humanization could be accomplished only by man in society. In the common appropriation of nature by men, they could experience their bond with other men through their work on nature. "It is only there that the natural existence becomes for him his human existence and nature becomes for him man." And as a result, nature rose out of itself to form the "naturalism of man and the realized humanism of nature."[35] On this basis Marx held that man's "own existence was a social activity." Scientific work itself was a social and human act, not an isolated individual one. Consequently the scientist produced for society, not for himself. Knowledge was merely the abstract form of what really existed. If the social activity of all men was what formed

---

34. Marx, *Nationalökonomie und Philosophie, Frühschriften*, 236. Translations of this work, unless otherwise indicated, are from Karl Marx, *Selected Writings in Sociology and Social Science*, ed. T. B. Bottomore and Maximilian Rubel (London, 1956), 243–44. Hereafter translations from this work will be cited as *BR*; N. 5, 236, *BR*, 244.
35. *Ibid.*, N. 5, 237 (my translation); N. 5, *BR*, 246; N. 6, 238, *BR*, 77.

the world, then, the theoretic form of this social activity was man's "own theoretic existence as a social being," since his own being is made by society.

Marx did not fail to note the significance of death, which he admitted seemed to contradict the unity of this participation of man in production. His answer was consistent with his system. Yet the answer also seemed to reveal the system's limits, for "the determinate individual was only a determinate generic being, and as such is mortal." Marx could thus offer only the type of participation in being which his system itself envisioned, the being produced by the species in its labor. When Marx faced the problem of the theoretic versus the practical attitude to life, he insisted that man's real life was practical—the work of this life—because theory as such could not aid man in his essential task. "The resolution of theoretical contradictions is possible only through practical means, only through the practical energy of man."[36]

These contradictions were solved in life, not in philosophy or theory. Now, since what has been produced has been socially produced, one must look to the "history of industry" for a concrete knowledge of the development of man. Natural science was ineffective as long as it failed to consider human work. Philosophy too remained aloof. But actually the natural sciences had penetrated into human life through industry. "They have prepared the emancipation of humanity." Through industry mankind has transformed nature. Therefore, industry defined the relation of nature to man. By this means, the natural sciences became human sciences, for they served industry in transforming the earth into man's image. And this was a social, historical development. "Nature, as it develops in human history, in the genesis of human society, is the real nature of man; thus nature, as it develops through industry, though in an alienated form, is truly anthropological nature."[37] Here, as not in Feuerbach, nature was real, standing within history.

36. *Ibid.*, N. 6, 239 (my translation); N. 8, 243, *BR*, 72.
37. *Ibid.*, N. 9, 244, *BR*, 73.

Science must consequently be based on sense experience because this kept it in the real world. From this foundation Marx concluded that the "whole of history is a preparation for 'man' to become an object of sense perception. . . . History itself is a real part of natural history, of the development of nature into man." Nature became an object of sense perception when everything that was formerly disorganized and scattered in the universe had been transformed by man for his own purposes. This mutual interconnection of man and nature will, in the end, leave only one science, the science of man. "Natural science will one day incorporate the science of man, just as the science of man will incorporate natural science; there will be a single science."[38] Science became a tool with which to remake the earth through industry into human objects. Nature became human when the earth was reorganized to suit man's own ends.

"Man is the direct object of the natural sciences." This is the result of the transformation of industry. Since man's own consciousness of himself first arose through the objects of his senses, and man was the object of science, it followed, it seems, that man's relation to other men was primarily through humanized nature, the product of the labors of men. Speech itself was sensible. Nature thus met man always through the mediation of sensibility. "The social science of man and the human natural science or natural science of man are identical expressions." If man lived by means of another, he was dependent. He would thus have the sources of his own existence outside himself. Socialism held that the labor of a man was the source of all value. Thus the history of the world was the actual creation of man by human labor. "Once the essence of man and of nature, man as a natural being and nature as a human reality, has become evident in practical life, in sense experience, the search for an alien being, or being outside man and nature (a search which is an avowal of the unreality of man and nature) becomes impossible in practice."[39] Here Marx seemed to have

---

38. *Ibid.*, N. 9, 245, *BR*, 70.
39. *Ibid.*, N. 10, 245, 246 (my translations); N. 11, 248, *BR*, 246.

brought the world of man fully under the control of man. The final vestiges of a God or First Mover were eliminated.

In his analysis of Hegel's *Phenomenology,* Marx drew the conclusion for his system that God did not exist and that the object of nature was man. Hegel, Marx saw, viewed man's self-production as a historical process. Hegel also recognized that human work actually changed and organized nature so that, by work on nature, man produced his own human world. But this production was possible only if man activated all of his "generic powers."[40] Man had his own vital forces. Through the work of man, everything became transformed into the human system by the labor of men.

Marx had consequently incorporated Feuerbach's concern for real men and real multiplicity into his own system under the influence of the Hegelian dialectical method. Marx excluded everything which did not immediately fit the sensuous criterion. Man was a "human natural being, that is, a being existing for himself, therefore, a generic being; as such he must affirm himself both in his being and in his own knowledge." Human beings did not present themselves immediately in the objective order. Objective and subjective orders needed to be made explicit—needed, in other words, to be defined as human. The Marxian labor theory of value in economics was an endeavor to define the way in which this humanization took place. Marx constantly tried to make the objects of the eyes and ears, in short of all the senses, into human objects through the transformation of the world by social labor. Wherever man looked, he should, in Marx's view, see man. Thus all knowledge drawn from the sensuous world would be human knowledge. And since the material world was to be organized by the history of social man, man communicated with man through sensation because the objects of sensation were products of man himself.[41]

Marx was very conscious of human fraternity and communication.

---

40. *Ibid.*, N. 22, 269; "Gattungswesen," N. 34, 289.
41. *Ibid.*, N. 26. 275 (my translation); see 285–303, N. 7, 240–241. See also Sidney Hook, *Marx and the Marxists: Ambiguous Legacy* (New York, 1955), 22–23.

In this sense, he was related to Aristotle and Aquinas's notion of friendship and the sensory basis of knowledge. Marx did not abandon Feuerbach's vision, but he transformed it into the real sensuous and historical world. Through man's participation in the object of nature, he became all men in a way, since all men mutually made the world through their social labor. All men were, in this sense, one being. Marx was quite violent in his castigations against capitalism because he thought it prevented men from sharing in their mutual production and communication. The products were created for man, not just the ruling class.[42] Marx held that the objects seen by man should be human objects produced by all men for all men, not for some men. In this way he hoped to enable all men to participate in the human world.

Marx, then, constructed a quasi-immortality in this life. That is, he attempted to define the economic task of man in such wise that it would account for all significant reality. The task of man in society was to reconquer all that man had produced for himself. Anything such as religion, philosophy, or art which tended to attribute reality to the theoretic world must be radically eliminated because it was only a chain to bind man, not something to free him. Marx added the element of violence and aggression to Hegel's dialectical process because he felt it necessary to overcome these alienations in a positive manner. Each element of religion in particular had to be consciously eliminated. Everything had to be rejected by a conscious choice.

Like Hegel, Marx believed that the process would eventually overturn the alienations. But like Feuerbach, he felt that the process had to have something more tangible and real. For this reason he always insisted on materialism to stress and prove his theory. But in the end Marx's thesis retained much of its theoretical foundation in the sense that its validity still rested on an identification of the theoretical and practical orders in an effort to provide man with a world that belonged exclusively to man. He simply defined man as what he could himself

42. Marx, *Nationalökonomie, Frühschriften,* N. 52–54, 298–300.

overcome. Somehow the main notion of the older concepts of immortality and resurrection, the value and permanence of the person, was lost. Only the *Gattungswesen,* the generic being, was immortal. The human person disappeared into the species. This seemed, in the end, the final result and cost of attempting to think in opposition to classical and revelational ideas as they concerned political philosophy.

8

JERUSALEM, ATHENS, ROME

POLITICAL PHILOSOPHY AND THE MODERN "GNOSTIC" PROJECT

With the young Marx, political philosophy reached both an intrinsic conclusion and an impasse that could result only in sending its "ideas" into the world for enfleshment, for testing by experience to see how and whether ideas and being conformed. The "conclusion" this development represented was the logical extreme to which the denial of classical and revelational theory could reach by a thinking and acting out of the alternatives that necessarily followed when central doctrines and classical reason were denied step by step through intellectual and practical history. The "generic being," that is, the individual who is species, in which no possibility of differences or openness to anything but self-made man is allowed, is, indeed, an "intelligible" conception. But it forms an utterly antihuman sort of "humanness." Yet to do it justice, it is, granted its premises, a thoroughly consistent position in seeking to reach what seem to be the highest goals, themselves reformulations in terms of what thought must think, thinking of itself by itself.

These results are, as they turn out, however, mere parodies of what is found in classical reason and revelation. In this intellectual conclusion, the individual does seem at least to participate in "all being," and all being is "his." There is, by hypothesis, *nothing* else. All that is present historically, metaphysically, or theologically is actively, positively rejected. What has any higher claim from nature, history, culture, philosophy, or God is "overcome," overthrown by a positive, voluntary, collective act of defiance, which directly claims in its very positing the falsity of what men have held about the highest things in reason and revelation. Man, as "restored" to himself, must, then, confront nothing but what he has made, including himself, in which "generic being" is equally one and indistinct in every being. This is the "all" that is.

On this basis, therefore, it is no wonder that Nietzsche, taking stock of this impasse, had to propose something beyond atheist, collective man, something which, in a sense, must reject as such the whole human enterprise as a dead end and a mistake from the beginning. The distance between the "generic man" of Marx and the "superman" of Nietzsche is not, in this sense, so difficult to traverse. Eric Voegelin, at the end of *From the Enlightenment to Revolution,* stated the situation exactly:

> The interrelation of science and power and the consequent cancerous growth of the utilitarian segment of existence have injected a strong element of magic culture into modern civilization. The tendency to narrow the field of human experience to the area of reason, science, and pragmatic action, the tendency to overvalue this area in relation to the *bios theoretikos* and the life of the spirit, the tendency to make it the exclusive preoccupation of man, the tendency to make it socially preponderant through economic pressure in the so-called free societies and through violence in totalitarian states—all these tendencies are part of a cultural process that is dominated by the idea of operating on the substance of man through the instrumentality of pragmatically planning will. The climax of this is the magic dream of creating the Superman, the man-made-Being that will succeed the sorry creature of God's making. This is the great dream that first appeared imaginatively in the works of Condorcet, Comte, Marx and Nietzsche and later pragmatically in the Communist and National Socialist Movements.[1]

Nietzsche, in a sense, reversed the step taken from Hobbes's Leviathan to Rousseau's General Will, only this time, with Nietzsche, the direction was toward a Leviathan that rejected any pretense of the philosophic or revelational human. The "spirit" is no longer one that cares for ordinary individuals, as kings or paupers or citizens, of the earthly

---

1. Eric Voegelin, *From the Enlightenment to Revolution,* ed. John Hallowell (Durham, N.C., 1975), 301–302.

or the heavenly city. The distinction of the twentieth century is that it has watched such controversies about *what man is* work themselves out no longer in mere thought but in political reality. Here political philosophies try to translate the "being" of thought into sensuous reality as a rejection of what is not itself self-thought.

How is it possible to interpret this experience of political philosophy to locate its meaning more exactly and restore some sense of classical and revelational wisdom? The first step, which has been followed thus far, is the necessary one of intelligence. What has happened? But as Aristotle insisted, man is a whole, so that thought alone, particularly in politics, is not sufficient to describe the alternatives to revolutionary and radical humanism, which would deliberately deny the proper being of man on the grounds that there is no "nature" in man as such. Unavoidably the implication is that political philosophy must reopen the whole range of thought, including that which is called revelation, which is addressed to the particular questions posed in political experience and pondered by the philosophers.

Eric Voegelin, in his letter to Albert Schutz, again put the point well: "The traditional treatments of the history of philosophy and particularly of political ideas recognize antiquity and modernity, while the 1500 years of Christian thought and Christian politics are treated as a kind of hole in the evolution of mankind. . . . A general history of ideas must be capable of treating the phenomenon of Christianity with no less theoretical care than that devoted to Plato or Hegel."[2] The peculiar shape of modern political philosophy is constituted also by this failure to attend properly to the unique response given by revelation, both Jewish and Christian, to questions arising in political experience, wherever such experience occurs.

However valuable this added revelational reflection might be, the

---

2. Eric Voegelin, *The Philosophy of Order: Essays on History, Consciousness, and Politics,* ed. P. J. Opitz and Gregor Sebba (Stuttgart, 1981), 449–50. See also John Hallowell, "Obstacles to the Recovery of a Christian Perspective on Human Nature," *Modern Age,* XXVII (Winter, 1983), 2–14; Dante Germino, "Voegelin, Christianity, and Political Philosophy" (paper presented at the annual meeting of the American Political Science Association, Chicago, 1983); George Carey and James V. Schall (eds.), *Essays in Christianity and Political Philosophy* (Lanham, Md., 1984).

question occurs, nevertheless, as to whether it is anything more than a sort of abstract intelligence which leaves no particular hope of concrete results before the success of the modern ideologies. At times, Voegelin himself seemed to doubt its efficacy. He was skeptical of neo-Thomists and felt that St. Paul's analysis of the law was not reduplicated in modern times. Voegelin insisted that Christianity ought to provide meaning to the movements of history and civilization, but modern men do not find the Church providing this meaning in an era that differs so much from that of the classics. "In the face of this abandonment of the magisterium," Voegelin wrote, "it is futile when Christian thinkers accuse the *superbia* of modern man who will not submit to the authority of the Church. There is always enough *superbia* in man to bolster the accusation plausibly, but the complaint dodges the real issue: that man in search of authority cannot find it in the Church, through no fault of his own. From the dissatisfaction of being engaged in a civilizational process without meaning, there are engendered attempts, beginning with Voltaire, at a reconstruction of meaning through the evocation of a new 'sacred history'. And with Voltaire begins also an image of man in the cosmos under the guidance of intraworldly reason."[3]

And in his beautiful and penetrating memorial to Leo Strauss, Harry Jaffa wrote:

> Strauss did not believe that the principles of reason and revelation could ever be reduced, one to the other. Nor did he believe in the possibility of a synthesis, since any synthesis would require a higher principle than either. Catholic Christianity, which found its highest expression in Thomas Aquinas, attempted such a synthesis. Strauss admired the magnificence of Thomas' efforts, and he saw in them a great humanizing and moderating of Catholic theology. Perhaps the greatest gain from the Thomistic synthesis was that Aristotle, after being a forbidden author, eventually became a recommended one. But only in traditional Judaism did the idea of revelation, and of a tradi-

---

3. Voegelin, *From the Enlightenment to Revolution*, 22–23. See also Eric Voegelin, *Science, Politics, and Gnosticism* (Chicago, 1968); Henri de Lubac, *Nature and Grace*.

tion undivided and uncompromised by syncretism, find its full expression. And Western civilization at its highest expressed the tension between Greek rationalism and Jewish revelation.[4]

In both of these open and observant writers, the specifically Thomist position of the relation of reason and revelation, or at least, the adequacy and uniqueness of this response, is rejected, though not without a careful hearing. Christianity, it is held, is valuable for preserving Aristotle or for showing an original synthesis of Pagan, Jewish, and its own unique elements. But its capacity for confronting modernity is doubted. Western civilization is unique because of Greek and Jewish sources, or when the basic Christian elements are recognized, as with Voegelin, they are not fully adequate for the problem at hand.

There are writers, such as E. B. F. Midgley in Scotland, who hold rather that the Thomist position is the proper response to the problems and issues resulting from the dangerous directions and conclusions of specifically modern political philosophy and practice flowing from it. What seems to be needed is not merely a revival of the classics and the Bible, however necessary that both be reconsidered, but also the interpenetration of these two sources in a full Christian philosophy, one that can account also for the actual facts of the modern experience. This is to be seen, of course, in the unsettling context of a contemporary Christianity which has itself, at least in several fundamental areas, often rejected this enterprise in favor of an attempt to "Christianize" the very modern Gnostic project itself. In this sense, both the Voegelinian and the Straussian views have a most valid point to make.

Midgley, however, wrote:

> The Thomists remain to remind their contemporaries that whatever evils there may be in modern, as in earlier, political life, there is no necessity to ignore the truth about the ends of political life or to despair of it or to revolt against it. So long as it is feasible, the good man in politics will continue to do what can be done in furtherance of the

---

4. Harry Jaffa, "Leo Strauss, 1899–1973," in *The Conditions of Freedom: Essays in Political Philosophy* (Baltimore, 1975), 6.

common good. Sometimes he may have to resign; sometimes he may have to suffer persecution and even, in the extreme case, martyrdom, but whatever the outcome, the truth remains. Accordingly, the Thomists will not seek to 'go beyond' an erroneous nihilism, nor will they shrink back, in pusillanimous fashion, into pre-modern contradictions. Whatever intellectual acrobatics may be performed by those who actively participate in the modernist subversion (or those who, ensnared by traditionalism, are unable to defeat the modernist subversion), the immutable truth about the fundamental nature of political life (and about the fundamental nature of the contemplative life) does not change. . . .[5]

The case for a renewed statement of the classical position of Thomas Aquinas seems clear. What is needed is this alternative statement itself. The position required has not itself been well understood within modern political philosophy as such nor by the efforts to judge it within the terms of the classics.

Yet we can wonder whether the endeavor to explain the modern world to itself in some terms other than the Judaeo-Christian responses to the questions of political philosophy, a process we have sought to describe, is not itself an illusion. If we assume, for the sake of argument, that we do not know what the world would be like, whether the revelational response has validity, and that the truth of political philosophy as operative within actual systems has only been approximated, then the endeavor of Aquinas to think in the light of classical questions of political thought again makes sense. Many, under the name of 'political theology' or 'civil religion,' have sought to baptize the fundamental outlooks of the socialist or liberal, or even absolutist, state, of the products of the modern project. They valiantly strive to rewrite religion as if support of this modern system ought to be its essential tool or goal. Radical versions of religion itself are capable of turning against what Aquinas argued, so that both polity and *ecclesia* become objects of transformed political ideology.

5. E. B. F. Midgley, "Concerning the Modernist Subversion of Political Philosophy," *New Scholasticism*, LIII (Spring, 1979), 190. See also Frederick D. Wilhelmsen, *Christianity and Political Philosophy* (Athens, Ga., 1978); Josef Pieper, *The Silence of St. Thomas* (Chicago, 1957).

Many acute endeavors to evaluate the essential nature of modern political philosophy, as Ernest Fortin has written, "are all the more striking as the New Testament has practically nothing to say about these things. For better or worse, it is notoriously indifferent to questions of political organization, societal arrangements, public reform, and most of what goes now under the ambiguous name of 'social justice'. It does not favor, let alone prescribe, any particular regime and leaves it up to us to devise whatever system of government may be best suited to our needs and circumstances.... What we really need is a recovery of both philosophy and theology."[6] The implication is that attending to what the New Testament itself considered to be mankind's most essential task, man's personal destiny and his relation to God, would allow politics to do what politics is about and not open itself as an arena for the playing out of Gnostic and modernist projects.

These latter positions, however, are to be constructed according to another definition of what man is, because they do not and cannot answer the ultimate questions that appear in terms other than those of human self-creation, questions posed properly by reason to revelation. The need for a recovery of both philosophy and theology in this context can be seen best perhaps in what Leo Strauss called "the modern project" and how it related to what he called Jerusalem and Athens. The relative silence about "Rome" is, in its own way, the clue to that core of ideas and practices that would prevent the Gnostic modern project from coming about, while not, at the same time, denying the possibility that truth would be found both in reason and revelation, a truth that is more than merely a conformity of the mind to itself.[7]

In his famous essay, "Jerusalem and Athens," on the nature of the whole scope of political philosophy, Leo Strauss argued that Western civilization was composed of two essential elements.[8] These two elements he called Jerusalem (the Bible) and Athens (Greek philosophy).

---

6. Ernest Fortin, "Comment," *This World,* II (Spring–Summer, 1984), 102–103.

7. See Ernest Fortin, "Rational Theologians and Irrational Philosophers: A Straussian Perspective," *Interpretation,* XII (August–September, 1984), 349–56.

8. Leo Strauss, "Jerusalem and Athens," 147–73. See the review of *Studies in Platonic Political Philosophy,* in James V. Schall, "Classical Politics," *Reflections* (Summer, 1984), 12. See also

The civilization composed of both was unique because its component parts were each devoted to the truth as such, as universal to all, not merely to those "truths" separately formulated by this or that nation, religion, or ethnic grouping. These two traditions were both facts, both inseparable culturally, both responsible for the vitality and energy manifest in Western civilization. Their combination, their abiding contrasts, their meaning, it seems, turned out to serve as direct challenges to every other civilization, since every realm of man was confronted with its truth, itself initially by the meeting of revelation with philosophy.

Strauss held, further, that "the modern project"—what Eric Voegelin called "Gnosticism," to suggest its perennial nature—beginning with Machiavelli, Descartes, and Hobbes, consisted in an attempt to reject the core of the classical and biblical traditions, while it sought to achieve their universal goals, still elevated by revelation, through the instrumentality of modern science, including social science.[9] In its turn, modern science was itself a reduction of knowledge to what could be learned by certain methods and processes of analysis. This "science," which sought to include classical political science, insisted upon using science not as Aristotle had held, as a term that varied according to the object of investigation, but according to the experimental procedures of the natural sciences as they developed through modern theories, without Aristotle's caution regarding the nature of the experimental sciences.

The "new science" was held to prescind from the recognition of any higher order either in nature or in man. Both man and nature were held to be "true" only by following these newer verifiable scientific "norms," themselves, however constantly variable, presupposed to no permanent nature of abiding divine will. Whatever "higher" goals there might be, as described in classical philosophy or religion, these

---

M. F. Burnyeat, "Sphinx Without a Secret," *New York Review of Books,* May 30, 1985, 30–36; Harry Jaffa, "The Legacy of Leo Strauss," *Claremont Review of Books,* III (Fall, 1984), 14–21.

9. Leo Strauss, *City and Man* (Chicago, 1964), Intro. Eric Voegelin, *The New Science of Politics,* Chap. 5.

were deprived of any "scientific" standing. They became instead mere "opinions" or "values" but not "scientific" or "true."

As a result, the highest questions of *what is,* of why man is man, of what is his personal end and happiness, these were "privatized" and finally "humanized," so that they became identified with what could be put into the world by man himself. In its most extreme form, "humanization" itself came to mean the active removal by politics of what was not derived from an exclusively human source. The description of what was being "formed" in the modern project could be aptly called "Gnostic" because it implied a conception of man presupposed to nothing normative except man himself. Simultaneously, this approach rejected any mind or content discovered about man from classical philosophy or revelation.

What became increasingly evident in the twentieth century, however, was not merely that such "alternative" descriptions of man could be "thought," as with the ancient Gnostics or even classical philosophers, but that they could be, in some sense—such was the reality of modern power—put into physical and political existence as a living statement of what man is in his individual and corporate existence. This evidence of lived Gnostic politics, economy, or even religion, in turn, itself posed a question to the classical and revelational tradition about its own structure and validity. The sort of "freedom" envisioned in the modern project was a freedom which presupposed no ends in man or "substitute intelligence" in nature, which persuaded the human intellect by its discovered truth. It turned out, in practice, to be an effort to remove any "limits" or "moderation" associated with the classical endeavor to keep politics as politics or the Judaeo-Christian effort not to locate the Kingdom of God in this world.

Strauss held that the initial step in saving mankind from the disastrous political consequences of the modern project, now put into existence for all to see by the ideological results of modern political philosophy, was to return to classical political philosophy. There the proper relation of science, man, and the contemplative order might be rediscovered and restored. Strauss seemed less aware that the biological consequences of this same modern project might also follow an attempt to establish literally the norms of Plato's eugenic state as a fact. This seems to be one of the central points at which Strauss's remarks on Aquinas seem less persuasive, since the attack on man's very corpus and the kind of being following from it is itself a part of the modern project.[10]

But this is indeed a critical point, as Strauss understood, about the relation of particularly Christian revelation to his analysis of the direction of modern political thought and its relation to the classics and revelation. Once this renewed attention to classical political philosophy had become a reality, however, it might again be possible, Strauss thought, to call attention slowly to the existence and importance of revelation, though neither the reason nor revelation could be resolved into each other or could effectively deny the validity of the other.[11] Science could never eliminate the possibility of revelation, since science could never itself manage a full description of *what is*. And without reason, revelation could not ever be recognized as a result of a properly human act. This awareness of the limits of science was itself sufficient to undermine the essential features of the modern project, the Gnostic view that man's ends and meaning, the distinction of good and evil, virtue and vice, were solely under man's own artistic faculties, even in politics.

Without this moderation, consequently, no metaphysical or revelational input could limit what could be "imagined" or finally put into experimental reality as possible and as theoretically good. The truth of politics was, consequently, to be like truth in art, something whose validity depended solely on the polity's conformity with what the maker of the political order—one, few, or many—wanted to be. Political existence came to refer only to the truth of the mind presupposed to no being but still creative of the civil order by its own calculations.

10. Strauss, *Natural Right and History*, 164. See James V. Schall, *Human Dignity and Human Numbers* (Staten Island, N.Y., 1971); *Christianity and Life* (San Francisco, 1981); Julian Simon, *The Ultimate Resource* (Princeton, 1980).
11. See Leo Strauss, "The Mutual Influence of Philosophy and Theology," *Independent Journal of Philosophy*, III (1979), 111–18.

Strauss, however, had very little to say about the third element generally thought to compose the unique dynamic of Western civilization, namely, Christianity itself. Strauss, of course, was famous for being silent about what he wanted to be silent about. However, his generally sympathetic references to Aquinas (rarely to Augustine) suggested the nature of this reticence. Strauss appreciated Aquinas as a commentator on Aristotle. In that sense, Aquinas did in his age what Strauss hoped to do in his own age, namely, restore a consideration of reason by its own powers to the center of intellectual life. If Strauss finally seemed more attentive to Plato than to Aristotle, this silence, especially about Augustine, becomes more important. Aquinas had argued that the questions posed to reason by revelation were best formulated by Aristotle because of Aristotle's attentiveness to matter and to reason existing in each particular individual. Aquinas was constantly aware from the demands of revelation of the need for a true philosophy that could allow for revelation's possibility.

Augustine, on the other hand, as we saw (Chapter 3), was not critical of Plato because he formulated incorrectly the question of the best polity. Rather, Augustine's main contribution was to free politics itself from ever being the location of this "polity" or republic. Augustine argued that revelation, Old and New Testament, alone allowed politics to be free of the claim to offer man a kingdom posed in his own terms. The Gnostic project, in this sense, was a claim to do precisely this, to formulate entirely a man-made kingdom. What Aquinas did in his commentaries on Aristotle was not himself to embrace the extreme reaches of the Platonic project become Gnostic but to reestablish the limits of politics as a legitimate human enterprise, an expression of proper human being, but not one in which man's attainment of the highest things was to take place as such. This position would have the effect of legitimizing politics and its limits. It would thereby remove from politics the hope that it might be remade into an instrument for transcendent goals.

In this analysis of the foundations of political philosophy, then, it remains to repose the Jerusalem and Athens thesis over against the Gnostic modern project to include Christianity. As it developed, this position was much less concerned to hold that the dichotomy Jerusalem-Athens, valid in its own way, was quite so stark as Strauss, with much erudition and insight, apparently made it seem. Likewise, on the very basis of a return to the classics, keeping in mind Aristotle's notion that particular experience does open one to the intelligence of being, does all modern science, economics, and politics need to be seen solely in terms of opposition to the classics? How did the Aristotelian-Thomistic insight into the nature of the practical sciences continue, sometimes in spite of the aberrations of the theoretic order?

The practice of modern politics and economics, quite often, was more a completion and carrying out of the ideas of the classical and Christian authors when they considered politics and economics as being limited to the *temporal* order. This is the import of the controversy about the relation of the American and French revolutions, of the nature of Burke's own political thought, and even of that of a modern Thomist such as Jacques Maritain. This is likewise the question of how to analyze and confront the reality of the nations that appeared in the world after World Wars I and II, with their performance and their problems, of the universal good as existing in a variety of polities which can be classified according to the structure of the classical nomenclature of regimes. The notion of planetary organization under the aegis of the nation-state, in which everyone achieves freedom and abundance, with the requisite knowledge of how to do so, has been in one sense the location of the struggle between the advocates of the modern project, with their socialist-utopian experiences that seldom work and the more practically oriented, enterprising systems which have grown from experience, craft, and personal freedom to establish the physical conditions which Aristotle himself had argued were needed for a liberal life in the world of the polity inhabited by mortal men. Strauss seemed to have held that the modern project, as a theoretical endeavor, corrupted this more practical possibility.

Strauss seemed perfectly correct to have underscored the particular dangers of the modern project when it has rejected both its philosophical and revelational norms. These rejections seem to be the real causes for the failure of the modern state and the theory on which it was based. The intelligibility of ideas and their direction is not necessarily coterminous with a particular modern state's actual performance. The remains of traditional belief (Jerusalem and Rome) and classical philosophy contained, until recently at least, enough solidity of practice and hold on the people to keep alive for the majority the classical sense of virtue, of what man is and his limited political destiny. What is perhaps unique in the decades after Strauss himself is not that he failed to consider adequately Jerusalem, Athens, *and* Christian Rome but that this latter often seems itself to have embraced the very elements of the modern project which Strauss most abhorred. As an unbeliever in Christianity, of course, Strauss would not have been totally surprised by a "Marxist Christianity" or a "revolutionary Christianity" or versions of the natural law that were indistinguishable from modern natural right, which so essentially changed the meaning of man from a received being (even of revelation) to a self-maker (even of revelation).

What needs to be argued, then, is that the central Augustinian-Thomistic tradition within Christianity, whatever its practical status for Christians, themselves often influenced by the modern project, was the proper direction in which to develop, if politics as politics were to be preserved. At the same time, this would allow philosophy to consider, without lapsing into some Gnostic solution, those higher questions posed to it by the very experience of being and thinking. This latter would substitute an actual man-made political order for the highest things. But the final answers were intimated by revelation to a properly reasoning human being. They were not to be located in any existing or conceivably existing polity.

"Political ideas will vary," Thomas Aquinas remarked in his commentary on Aristotle's *Politics*, "according to man's views on human destiny."[12] The human intelligence, actually abiding in each particular individual over time, though not independently of him, can understand, classify, and judge that complexus of human actions and communications established by law and custom which we call the civil

---

12. Thomas Aquinas, Commentary, *Politics*, II, 1, I, N. 1079.

polity. Likewise, what politics is can be misunderstood or deliberately distorted. The human mind and will are evidently free to follow argument, having previously excluded this or that relevant fact or principle from consideration. The enterprise of political philosophy over time, as we have followed its terms and directions, is to grasp its own limits by understanding what the polity is.

Understanding will necessarily suggest, however, that philosophy is, in some basic sense, broader than political philosophy. *What is* and what is political are not identical questions. The former is broader than the latter. "What is political?" however, makes "what is?" possible to ask in any state that does not claim for itself the complete definition of reality and its content. Even the existence of personal intelligence in each human being will tend to undermine any absolute state however tyrannical, though political philosophy has not and ought not to underestimate the power of modern totalitarian states in this regard, something already intimated in Aristotle's discussion of tyranny (1312a1–14a29).

The classical writers, furthermore, thought that the question "what is politics?" would include a consideration of the consequences which theoretically and practically follow from rejecting or wrongly locating the limits of politics, which are themselves rooted in *what man is* as a distinct being within the cosmos. Political philosophy included a description of the worst regime and all deviations from the good regime that were less than the worst. Political philosophy, likewise, seeks to clarify why politics is open to the overturning of its own limits. The reason is that man is individually more than a political animal, something he understands first by being a political animal. The issues, rooted in real experience, which tempt political philosophy to become a "radical humanism" or Gnosticism, closed to anything but human input, are addressed initially within political philosophy itself. The foundations of political philosophy are to be found, then, in the questions addressed to human intelligence by the experience of public life.

These questions, moreover, seek resolution in politics itself, or in metaphysics, including skepticism, or in revelation. The most fundamental of these issues, arising in part from the failure to achieve full rewards of good actions or full punishment for evil ones in the polity, are those of personal immortality, friendship, and the location of happiness with due regard to the sort of limited happiness available proportionately in existing polities. A return to the classics, to the manner in which such questions were posed in Greek philosophy or Hebrew revelation, is not an irrational or dated way to examine why modern political philosophy has produced errant political systems intelligible primarily as brilliant intellectual alternatives to the impasses found in classical philosophy or Hebrew revelation. These alternatives, however intelligible, in this sense cannot escape their own limits and meaning. Likewise, they cannot obviate the availability also of a series of Christian intellectual answers, which lie at the actual core of Western civilization and which also affirm the truth of both the classical and Hebrew traditions, though not their completeness for the questions as posed.

In his short, curious treatise "On Prophesying by Dreams," Aristotle wrote, "It is absurd to combine the idea that the sender of such dreams should be God with the fact that those to whom he sends them are not the best, but commonplace persons."[13] In his famous argument about why revelation might in fact be "necessary," that is, reasonable to believe, Aquinas held that particularly commonplace persons, not merely the saints or the philosophers, required guidance which would enable them to achieve the highest things for themselves (I–II, 91, 4). Life is too short, too busy with other things, too confused by difficult and subtle arguments, for most people to be expected to reach the correct understanding of the highest things. The point of revelation in this sense was to assure the possibility that everyone, philosopher and common man, could arrive at the highest good as such, as a personal possession, as it were. In this sense, revelation was eminently democratic.

This position thus expected the philosopher and the common folk

---

13. Aristotle, "On Prophesying by Dreams," *The Basic Works of Aristotle*, 3, 462b20–23, p. 626.

to achieve a common end, one in a sense beyond the natural expectations of either but one for which ultimately each existed. There were not two ends, one open to the philosopher and a lesser good, open to common folks or citizens of whatever regime. The two truths of Averroes, the idea that reason and revelation can contradict each other, are rejected consistently, as is the notion that certain men (philosophers) have a higher end than ordinary people. But this orthodox position did not deny that, in revelation, degrees of holiness or nearness to God are not necessarily related to intelligence as such. Nevertheless, the knowing of the highest things was also properly of man's highest faculties—intellect and will.

Aquinas, in other words, contrary to Machiavelli's famous dictum, did not "lower the sights" to include in a common political project everyone who was indifferent to contemplative rectitude. But he raised the possibilities for everyone, not directly through politics, though not denying its own limited validity, by connecting each individual in his inner and outer life to the highest things. The classical distinction between the philosopher and the nonphilosopher regarding the contemplative devotion to the highest things, though not simply eliminated, is replaced by a will and a truth which can reject, even in the philosopher, the highest destiny offered to each person or can accept it. The City of God, in this sense, became itself a risk.

The intellectual desire, so well elaborated by Eric Voegelin, that all men be open to the transcendent, must parallel at least the possibility of its rejection by even the most intelligent, by the philosopher whose life of leisure arises within the city, however much his life also transcends it. The hoped-for common destiny of each human therefore cannot exclude the possibility that a City of Man deliberately rejects the invitation to the highest things as they are revealed in nature and grace. The realization of this position is, no doubt, the highest meaning of Augustine in political philosophy. Revelation, then, was not a sort of "myth" to assuage the masses incapable of a contemplative or philosophic life, as it sometimes seemed to be in the classics, but rather the answer to the perplexities that arose especially for the philosophers in the most poignant sense as representative of each man at his best, in the best regime, but one confronted by every man in some basic fashion.

The denial of the possibility of the highest thing both to the philosopher and to the citizen is the beginning of "modern political philosophy." The theoretical extreme or end of this modern political philosophy is reached by the humanization of all reality according to norms formulated against the classic content of both reason and revelation. This was the ultimate significance of Marx's "generic being," which was by itself a brilliant insight into the direction and meaning of modern political philosophy cut off from the classical and revelational roots.

Strauss, however, in his essay on "The Three Waves of Modernity," added that Marx had not yet penetrated to ultimate humanistic radicalism because he felt that the generic man, who has concentrated all being *that is* in himself, so that nothing lies between man and man, was yet a product of historic determinism. The more radical insight was that of Nietzsche, who understood that man must freely will this rejection of nature and divinity. "The transvaluation of all values which Nietzsche tries to achieve," Strauss observed, "is ultimately justified by the fact that its root is the highest will to power—a higher will to power than the one which gave rise to all earlier values. . . . Nietzsche does not, like Hegel, claim that the final insight succeeds the actualization of the final ideal but rather that the final insight opens the way for the actualization of the final ideal. In this respect, Nietzsche's view resembles Marx's. But there is this fundamental difference between Nietzsche and Marx: for Marx the coming of the classless society is necessary, whereas for Nietzsche, the coming of the Over-man depends on man's free choice."[14] This emphasis of Nietzsche seems especially right if we argue that the modern project itself is not a full and necessary conclusion from intelligible premises but rather a chosen alternative which follows from rejecting the structure of classical and revelational thought.

14. Leo Strauss, "The Three Waves of Modernity," *Political Philosophy: Six Essays by Leo Strauss,* ed. Hilail Gildin (Indianapolis, 1975), 96–97.

"The true masters of history," the British historian Christopher Dawson wrote, "are not to be found in the surface events among the successful politicians or successful revolutionaries: these are the servants of events. Their masters are the spiritual men whom the world knows not, the unregarded agents of the creative actions of the spirit."[15] Is this doctrine, which places the true meaning in spiritual forces, as Hannah Arendt suspected, also "antipolitical"?[16] Is the immortality of the individual, who is the frailest of beings by classical standards, the enemy of politics itself, since the polity was rather the locus of immortality, of abidingness in the classics, not the individual? Does immortality dethrone the very core of politics by locating the motive forces of man in a reality other than a civil society? Socrates held that he must remain a private citizen to be safe philosophizing, but even Socrates was not safe. And do we not expect the saints and the philosophers, often unknown and common men by public criteria, to live in this world of politicians and revolutionaries precisely to change it?

The exaltation of the private and the ordinary in contemporary historiography, however, has often been philosophically directed against any notion of the exceptional or the extraordinarily good in which human actions are seen as specifically good and noble because they accept a standard made not by but for man.[17] The denigration of the excellent and the good is often part of the very modern project itself and its denial of any individual nobility or good in the name of common man, or "generic man." Such denigration requires us, as Machiavelli understood, to exalt whatever men do as good, whatever they do presupposed to no moderation not imposed by themselves.

The Prince, the Leviathan, the General Will, the Generic Man, and the Superman in this sense are the same. The excellent and the good are thus seen as hostile to the ordinary, whereas in the classics, the

---

15. Christopher Dawson, *The Dynamics of World History*, ed. John J. Mulloy (Lasalle, Ill., 1978), 364.
16. Arendt, *The Human Condition*, 73–78.
17. Gertrude Himmelfarb, "Denigrating the Rule of Reason," *Harper's*, CCLXVIII (April, 1984), 84–90.

excellent and the good were seen as that which gave meaning and dignity to what was only potentially present in the ordinary but to which the ordinary desired also to tend. Everyone had a desire for happiness as such. The revelational tradition, which also addressed the ordinary to call it to the highest things, even in its ordinariness, did not, like Machiavelli, directly approve what men did do. But it instructed them—as Aristotle maintained that law should—in what they ought to do (the Commandments), even about the things they could know themselves as well as the opening of a destiny beyond the polity. Revelation was designed not to deny the existence of the deviations described in the classics, let alone exalt them, but to define them accurately as deviations corruptive of the human good as that is related to the good as such. The "shalt nots" of the Commandments were principles of intelligence about *what man is,* not despairing counsels about what he could also be expected to do, even the worst.

Too, revelation, while agreeing with and exalting human excellence in a way that seemed even more demanding than Aristotle's philosopher, was still capable with St. Paul of calling the wisdom of the Greeks "foolish" because it failed to understand how the very questions about the highest things received their adequate answers in a revelation directed also to philosophy. The philosophers, having rejected voluntarily the instruction of reason, were held by Paul to lapse precisely into "myths" (I Corinthians 1:20–25; Colossians 2:8–9; I Timothy 4:1–8; II Timothy 3:1–9). The "myths" in modern political philosophy, insofar as they are themselves Gnostic reconstructions of a form of order imposed on reality by man, are, in their intelligibility, related to Paul's uneasiness with the philosophers, who did not open themselves initially, even before a question of revelation, to being as such. In the New Testament, Greek philosophy was expected to understand from its own sources at least when something was directed to its own questions. Reason and revelation, in this sense, are not two parallel origins of truth, but part of a consistent, noncontradictory whole in which their interrelationship is based on the nature and origin of the whole, man and universe.

REASON AND REVELATION IN POLITICAL PHILOSOPHY

The argument of these considerations regarding political philosophy, and of its understanding of itself, then, has been that the intelligibility of what has occurred in specifically political philosophy from Plato and Aristotle, through Cicero, Augustine, and Aquinas, into modern political philosophy, to the young Marx, Nietzsche, and beyond, has been that the classical and revelational limits of politics were replaced by an anthropological substitute metaphysics. This political metaphysics, the possibility of which was implied in the very structure of Greek philosophy and Judaeo-Christian revelation, is not completely arbitrary. It corresponds in a clear-cut but curious fashion to questions that everywhere and legitimately arise from the political experience described most accurately in the Greek classics, particularly Thucydides, Plato, and Aristotle. Perhaps unique to this argument is the inclusion of the revelational tradition as a necessary element in comprehending both the nature of this result and why it happened.

What is new, however, is the suspicion, not totally anticipated either by Strauss or Voegelin, that revelation itself needs genuine political philosophy if it is to remain revelation and not merely to become itself, as Voegelin put it, an "imminentization of the eschaton," merely another contender for the modern project, another ideology. What needs to be added is that the "higher sights," which Machiavelli attributed to revelation, were less "lowered" by the modern project than retained without the spiritual means to achieve them. For this reason modern political philosophy will propose a total solution to man's problems by political means, will attempt a Kingdom of God on Earth, however designated.

Two questions persistently arise. (1) What is the origin and destiny of each particular human individual (microcosmos, person) conceived and born into this world and into a polity (the question of immortality)? (2) What are the consequences of the interrelated activities of these individuals with each other and, individually, with the First Being, especially as formulated in Books VIII and IX of *The Ethics* of

Aristotle (the question of friendship)? Such questions are by no means neutral or unrelated. According to the way they are differently answered, because of the legitimate perplexity they pose in their very existence, different political systems will be founded. We must add, however, that, in the modern era, it is not merely a question of one of the differing forms of regime described in various ways from the classical authors even up to the writers of the American *Federalist Papers*. As contrasted with classical and revelational reflections on politics, which distinguished between action and contemplation, between the City of God and the City of Man, the modern project is not essentially a "limited" political theory but implies a complete metaphysics, which purports to describe *what is* apart from what was found in either the classical authors or revelation.

In the history of Western culture, furthermore, the philosophical answers to such legitimate questions, rising naturally in political experience and found discussed in political books, were not the only ones that the citizens knew about. In this sense, and this is what has been argued here, the revelational answers do not "bind" the philosopher, however much they might incite him to be more of a philosopher, because something more than human reason fell in his ken, so that he had to reflect on its meaning and possibility. The common folks could know more about political truth in relation to the highest things from revelation than the philosopher in this sense. The philosopher still had to ponder the philosophical truths which the revelational statements and acts implied. Revelational tradition, however, had no difficulty in accepting the elevated place of one who was both a philosopher and a saint or even a politician who was a saint.

On the other hand, the revelational "answers" meant nothing in a philosophic sense unless the questions to which answers were directed were themselves properly discovered and reflected upon *as* philosophy. This is the significance of that perplexing and profound passage in Strauss's *City and Man,* on the modern political philosophers, which began: "It is not sufficient for everyone to obey and to listen to the Divine Message of the City of Righteousness, the Faithful City. In order to propagate that message among the heathen, nay, in order to understand it clearly and as fully as is humanly possible, one must also consider to what extent man could discover the outlines of that City if left to himself, to the proper exercise of his own powers. But in our age, it is much less urgent to show that political philosophy is the indispensable handmaiden of theology than to show that political philosophy is the rightful queen of the social sciences, the sciences of man and of human affairs."[18]

It seems necessary to add to these lines, some quarter of a century after they were written, however, that, although this very Gnostic modern project has often closed off recollection of what this "Divine Message of the City of Righteousness" might be among the political philosophers, still a revival of a specifically Christian political philosophy might make it possible again to consider the outlines of the city left to ourselves. In this sense, Machiavelli and Augustine would be most helpful, whereas a Christianized ideology of the modern project would be fatal. Thus this reconsideration of political philosophy must not proceed as if revelation or its possibility did not exist, a revelation as itself also directed to human intelligence in its speculative and practical dimensions. These outlines appear again in those questions of friendship, immortality, virtue, and the experience of living in actual cities, such as Athens, Jerusalem, and Rome, which in fact killed both Socrates and Christ, both Cicero and Paul.

The Gnostic modern project which leads to the "generic man," inclusive of all men, which must deliberately destroy and replace notions of natural, divine, and historical norms in order to allow man to be only himself, consequently, suddenly becomes free to form a city which *must* be built upon the denial of the classical distinctions of good and evil, of the revelational location of the ultimate City of God. Etienne Gilson wrote in 1941, characterizing what happens when a successful Gnostic rational modernity has replaced revelation and philosophy:

> Mankind is doomed to live more and more under the spell of a new scientific, social and political mythology, unless we resolutely exorcise

18. Strauss, *City and Man*, 1.

these befuddled notions whose influence on modern life is becoming appalling. Millions of men are starving and bleeding to death because two or three of these pseudo-scientific of pseudo-social deified abstractions are now at war. For when the gods fight among themselves, men have to die. . . . The trouble with so many of our contemporaries is not that they are agnostics, but rather that they are misguided theologians. Real agnostics are exceedingly rare, and they harm nobody but themselves. . . . Much more common, unfortunately, are those pseudo-agnostics who, because they combine scientific knowledge and social generosity with a complete lack of philosophical culture, substitute dangerous mythologies for the natural theology which they do not even understand.[19]

This description of the Gnostic modern project corresponds at almost every point with that projected by Voegelin and Strauss—the combination of science and social enthusiasm with a lack of any corresponding connection with the classics. The result is dangerous mythologies projected actually into the world. "[Many] have celebrated the 'return of the sacred'; a 'powerful counterattack by religion' in a 'syncretistic context'," Henri de Lubac has commented. "With no regard for genuine Christianity, today every species of the 'sacred', or even every tawdry imitation thereof, every religion, every spirituality, every culture is being exalted, amid total confusion and with no effort at discrimination. Here and there clerics, who despite their name had been asleep in profoundest ignorance, are dazzled by the discovery of the vast universe; they are quite prepared to admire everything about it without understanding it and have no critical resources (or what they believe to be such) except against the faith which nourished them. They have become blind to the unique contribution of Judaeo-Christian revelation, as well as to the lights, overpowering or discreet, shed by holiness."[20]

How, then, in this context is it possible to formulate for contemporary political philosophy at least a statement of the potentiality for

19. Gilson, *God and Philosophy*, 136–37. See Ronald Knox, *Enthusiasm* (New York, 1950).
20. Henri de Lubac, *Nature and Grace*, 98–99.

reconciling reason and revelation, without fusing one with the other or, like an Averroes, holding some modernized version of the "two truth" theory, which would allow faith and reason to be contradictory? Moreover, how is it possible to suggest further that a revival of the classic positions, while necessary, is by itself incomplete without including Rome in the complexity of answers addressed to the authentic questions of the political philosophers? This notion seems, in addition, to be the other side of the function of political philosophy itself, namely, to serve as a grounding for revelation itself, to prevent it from embracing a new sort of ideological fundamentalism, which would seek to make the newness of revelation and its responses conform to the man-made ideologies which have arisen historically within political philosophy to replace revelation, if not also reason.

The New Testament dictum of rendering to Caesar and to God implied not merely that revelation was not designed to replace or destroy the things of Caesar but that the knowledge of what is politics will be a constitutive part of fully understanding what is revelation, a knowledge (politics) found only vaguely or indirectly in the sources of revelation. Revelation, in this sense, presupposes political philosophy and is incomplete without it. Revelation at its highest human intelligibility requires the "queen of the social sciences" to be just that but no more than that.

Strauss had argued, as we noted earlier, that political philosophy was less necessary as the "indispensable handmaid of theology" for his era. But the subsequent degree to which politics became ideologized after his time would seem rather to suggest that unless revelation addressed political philosophy in its own terms, and authentic to itself, what would follow is not a moderate political philosophy as such. Rather, a political philosophy transformed into a radical metaphysics would appear which would seek to rival revelation itself as an explanation of the highest things. The obvious danger, which seems to have in fact occurred to some degree, is that politics and certain interpretations of revelation combined to form a Gnostic project proposing perfect peace and order in this world as a result of this interpenetration of theology and politics.[21] In this sense, the forces of atheism and religion have never before been so interallied as a political force.[22]

The classical political philosophers and revelation had understood the need to identify and limit the sphere of the polity and of religion on the basis of what they were. If neither revelation nor political philosophy recognized its respective nature and limits, the result would necessarily be a sort of Gnosticism. This would be a man-made salvation, inimical both to a livable city for mortals who will die and for the unique individuals within the city ultimately destined for immortality and resurrection but not as a direct product of any sort of political or ideological action.

Here, then, it is important not only to affirm the validity of Strauss's central thesis about a return to classical political philosophy but also to indicate at least a way in which the Jerusalem-Athens dichotomy might be reassessed in terms of a greater harmony, for which something Strauss himself in fact did most of the work. At stake is the possibility of a civil society in which freedom and virtue are located in the heart and actions of individual human beings. This endeavor involves a description of the higher things (philosophy) that is not exhausted by an attempt to answer all man's effective questions about his meaning as a political being by some soon-to-be-established political order in which they receive pseudo-answers much lower in dignity and philosophical acumen than those posed in revelation or in the constant search for truth symbolized by a philosopher, a Socrates.

In his essay "Progress or Return? The Twentieth Century Crisis," Strauss listed again the three characteristics of modern thought against which he wrote. The first characteristic was that it was anthropocentric rather than theocentric or cosmocentric. (The alternative, "Christocentric," does not appear in Strauss, though it does in Voegelin and of course in Aquinas and Augustine.) By this statement Strauss understood, following theses of Hobbes and Kant, that "all truths or all meanings, all order, all beauty, originate in the thinking

21. *Ibid.*, 100–105.
22. See James V. Schall, *Liberation Theology* (San Francisco, 1982).

subject, in human thought, in the mind."[23] The mind did not "discover" these as given in reality but literally "created" them by its own power.

Second, the notion of "human rights" replaced the idea of primary human duties or natural law, whereas these "modern" human rights were in turn based on passion, not reason. Freedom replaced virtue. "The good life does not consist, as it did according to the earlier notion, in compliance with a pattern antedating the human will, but consists primarily in originating the pattern itself. The good life does not consist of both a 'what' and a 'how', but only of a 'how'. To state it somewhat differently . . . , man has no nature to speak of. He makes himself what he is; man's very humanity is acquired."[24] And third, man's freedom is limited only by his own earlier use of his freedom, not "by his nature or by the whole order of nature or creation." This "historicization" of reality is itself visible in man's technical accomplishments, which were, in the modern project, designed to serve man's estate in charity but by prescinding from any necessity of individual virtue or recognition of given ends which man did not himself make.

If, to recover a sense of virtue and personal, distinct dignity, however, we are to turn away from such concepts of the modern project to the origins of Western culture from which they arose as problematic answers, it becomes evident that we must encounter both the Bible and Greek philosophy. Yet however many their similarities, these two, Athens and Jerusalem, in Strauss's initial formulation and analysis were incompatible with each other. Nonetheless, one did not force the apodictic rejection of the other. Strauss specifically, it seems, rejected what in retrospect must be considered classic Thomism, that is, "the whole history of the West presents itself at first glance as the attempt to harmonize or synthesize the Bible and Greek philosophy."[25] But this "attempted harmonization" was never achieved, because what the Bible presents as necessary, namely, "obedient love," is opposed to the

23. Strauss, "Progress or Return? The Contemporary Crisis," 31.
24. Ibid., 32.
25. Ibid., 33.

Greek idea of a life devoted to "autonomous understanding." The one can use the other in a sense, but finally the two are irreconcilable.

This statement would seem, at first sight, to end the matter, but Strauss went on to acknowledge that the Bible and Greek philosophy had many things in common, such as the indentification of virtue with the second section of the Decalogue. "Those theologians who identified the Second Table of the Decalogue, as the Christians call it, with the natural law of Greek philosophy, were well-advised."[26] Both traditions refused to worship any human being and regarded justice as the highest virtue (the Old Testament, Plato), understanding it as "obedience to the law." Both end with a promise of prosperity for the just. Again with no reference to Christianity, Strauss noted the parallel of the famous passage in Book II of *The Republic,* about the fate of the just man in any city—that he would be reviled, scourged, and crucified—with Isaiah's description of the Man of Sorrows, a parallel that deserves much reflection and one common in Christian sources.[27]

In discussing the difference between these traditions, Strauss observed that the Greek philosopher was to have a noble pride with adequate economic underpinnings and civil honors but a pride that was no more than an honest reflection of the reality of the virtuous man as he in fact was.[28] The Bible praised the poor and opposed the haughty, so that fear of the Lord was a virtue in the Old Testament. Strauss found the Jews community oriented, whereas the philosopher was lonely. Complete morality was not defined in the same way for both traditions, though both praised morality. Strauss detected a certain lack of depth in the philosopher because the philosopher did not see how the object of contemplation, God, was concerned with the individual man. "The force of the moral demand is weakened in Greek philosophy because in Greek philosophy this demand is not backed up by divine promises."[29]

---

26. *Ibid.,* 34.
27. *Ibid.,* 35.
28. Recall from Chapter 2 the discussion of pride, Stoicism, and Christianity, particularly the analysis of Cassirer.
29. Strauss, "Progress or Return? The Contemporary Crisis," 38.

Behind this analysis, then, Strauss discovered the question of the relation of the doctrine of creation to that of the eternity of the world in Greek philosophy. The Bible in its doctrine of creation from nothing thus had a notion of divine omnipotence, which Strauss held to be contrary to Greek philosophy, something that Aquinas, seeking to explain the same problem, did not see in such absolute terms (I, 46, 1 and 2). The concept of essence or nature, in Strauss's view, did not exist in the Bible, whereas it was fundamental to Greek thought. "In Greek thought we find in one form or another an impersonal necessity higher than any personal being," Strauss noted, "whereas in the Bible the first cause is, as people say now, a person. This is connected with the fact that the concern of God with man is absolutely, if we may say so, essential to the biblical God; whereas that concern is, to put it very mildly, a problem for every Greek philosopher."[30] The Christian doctrine of the triune God in three persons, who are not therefore merely 'lonely', even apart from creation questions, makes Strauss's point, if anything, even more strongly. The relation between revelation and political philosophy is, no doubt, at its deepest when the question is the nature of the inner life of God, one nature and three persons.

Strauss remarked that the notion of divine law was common to both Greek and biblical thinking. He used this concept to suggest how it was possible to relate the notion of philosophy to that of the biblical God. The law of God was from an omnipotent source. God's essence was not knowable, yet he was trustworthy. Yahweh kept his promises. As a result divine law was understood to be something to be obeyed, something originating in a source beyond the human intellect. It was not understood except as an expression of a covenant which was God's will. Still, it could be understood by man at least with respect to what it wanted or commanded. In this context, Strauss remarked that even Aristotle understood the notion that "maybe it is bad to devote oneself to the philosophical rebellion against God."[31] This passage of Aris-

---

30. *Ibid.*, 39. See in this context "The Trinity: God Is Not Alone," in Schall, *Redeeming the Time*, Chap. 3.
31. Strauss, "Progress or Return? The Contemporary Crisis," 41.

totle, as I noted in Chapter 1, was found in the *Metaphysics* wherein Aristotle suggested that man's nature seems somehow in bondage (982b29).

But Strauss's final resolution of the relation of knowledge and God was very close to that of Paul and Aquinas—so close, indeed, that one can perhaps wonder why he did not specifically note the resemblance.

> Fundamentally, the institution of human kingship (I *Samuel*) is bad—it is a kind of rebellion against God, as is the polis and the arts and knowledge. But then it becomes possible by divine dispensation that these things, which originate in human rebellion, become dedicated to the service of God, and thus become holy. And I think that this is the biblical solution to the problem of human knowledge: human knowledge if it is dedicated to the service of God, and only then, can be good, and perhaps, in that sense, it is even necessary. But without that dedication, it is a rebellion. Man was given understanding in order to understand God's commands. He could not be freely obedient if he did not have understanding. But at the same time, this very fact allows man to emancipate the understanding from the service, from the subservient function for which it was meant, and this emancipation is the origin of philosophy or science from the biblical point of view. And so the antagonism between them.[32]

Strauss concluded that these two separate positions, Greek philosophy and the Bible, must remain in tension, that they are the source of life for Western culture, a position with which Christopher Dawson, in his own way, agreed.[33] "No one can be both a philosopher and a theologian," Strauss noted, "or, for that matter, some possibility which transcends the conflict between philosophy and theology, or pretends to be a synthesis of both."[34]

These conclusions of Strauss may seem strange, since at every point they embrace, incipiently at least, precisely Aquinas's position about

---

32. *Ibid.*, 42.
33. Christopher Dawson, *Religion and the Rise of Western Culture* (New York, 1950).
34. Strauss, "Progress or Return? The Contemporary Crisis," 41–42. See Strauss, "The Mutual Influence of Philosophy and Theology," 111–18. See also Maurice Auerbach, "The Philosophical Politics of Leo Strauss," *Teaching Political Science*, XII (Winter, 1984–85), 52–60.

the proper relation of reason and revelation. They also embrace the way in which Aquinas's own philosophy is related to Aristotle as well as to the discussions of philosophy in Paul of Tarsus. Aquinas would have said that human knowledge and nature as such were good but that in its present fallen condition, which did not completely "corrupt" nature, they tended to perform as Strauss (or Augustine, for that matter) described them, following the Book of Samuel. To hold that the biblical God created man in his image to communicate knowledge to him implies, as Aquinas saw in Aristotle, that although the human intellect remains finite, it demands a certain kind of unique power capable of properly knowing what is communicated both in nature and in revelation. Greek nature need not, as such, be so opposed to the Bible if nature is itself understood as needing explanation.

The whole point of the discussion of "substitute intelligence" in nature, or nature itself, from Aristotle's *Physics,* Book II, and Aquinas's commentary on it, was, as we saw (Chapter 1), to show that the ends in man and nature were in fact dependent on the First Mover, or God. Thus stability of essences did not necessarily imply creation or existence from eternity, as Aristotle and the Greeks held in lieu of a better explanation. The logic of Strauss's own argument does not, it seems, require the radical separation of reason and revelation that Strauss himself insisted upon, although at the same time the attention to the fundamental difference between finite and infinite intelligence, which is implicit in Strauss, seems quite valid in this context.[35]

What is perhaps even more striking in the light of Strauss's remarkable discussion, however, is Josef Pieper's analysis indicating how we are to understand the notion of personal immortality, which follows from the condition that there is a creature capable of understanding and following God's commands. Strauss, using much the same evidence and argumentation as Pieper, concluded that philosophy and theology must remain incapable of resolution. Pieper, on the other hand, wrote: "We have now at last touched, and perhaps somewhat

---

35. See James V. Schall, "Reason, Revelation, and Politics: Catholic Reflections on Strauss," *Gregorianum,* LXII, Nos. 2 and 3 (1981), 349–65, 467–97.

overstepped, the boundary which is set for the philosophical inquirer. Really to reach this boundary—therein lies, I think, the true meaning and distinctive opportunity of philosophy. The great philosophers have always seen in philosophy a challenge to penetrate beyond philosophizing. If this challenge presents itself to us more sharply than usual in the present case, this only indicates once more that death is a philosophical subject in a special sense."[36] The "penetration beyond philosophy" and the dogmatic insistence that philosophy and theology cannot be "reconciled" can in a way mean the same thing, particularly in the case of immortality for the soul, if the limits of philosophy still leave us with legitimate questions unanswered. Moreover, it is to be recalled that this very question of immortality arose in Greek philosophy in the political context of the death of Socrates, or more broadly in the context of the inability of the polity to reward all good and punish all evil. (See Book X of *The Republic*.)

This issue of immortality, however arose also from a self-reflective philosophical analysis of what it is we know and the status of this truth that we do know. Strauss and Pieper did not disagree in the understanding of creation nor even in the idea that nature must itself be made what it is by a command which had to be rooted in the divine intelligence to be what it was. Josef Pieper, in a carefully reasoned argument, held that the Englightenment view of immortality, which downplayed the body and the significance of death and erroneously identified its view with Plato's, tended to identify man fully with the soul but in a way that distorted what Plato himself came to hold on the subject. In the *Phaedo* (107C, 113E) and the *Phaedrus* (246C), Plato recognized, in some sense at least, that the wholeness of man was necessarily inclusive of the body and the soul.

This question of immortality, likewise, is a question of the soul's indestructibility. In revelation, the notion of an immortal or inde-

---

36. Pieper, *Death and Immortality*, 129–30. See also Mieczław A. Krąpiec, *I-Man: An Outline of Philosophical Anthropology*, trans. Francis Lescoe, Andrew Woznicki, *et al.* (New Britain, Conn., 1983), 335–62.

structible soul cannot mean the existence of something which, by its own power, exists as it is and continues to do so, such that death is no significant event to the being which undergoes it. The Old Testament doctrine of creation meant that the soul also came from nothing, so that its indestructibility was not of itself.[37] It is thus a form of rationalism or idealism, not strict Platonism or revelation, to conceive the soul as an externally existing form with no other cause for its being what it is and its abidingness but itself.[38]

The revelational idea of personal immortality (and eventual resurrection), then, did not argue that the essence or nature of a soul (only existing actually in each living individual human being) gives itself its imperishability. Strauss was thus quite correct to deny a Greek idea of nature in the Bible, when that idea was taken to mean a self-given and self-sustaining existence and essence rather than a covenanted existence and essence not originating in itself but permanently capable of certain acts, the highest of which were intelligence and will, really knowing what is commanded in trust.[39] Pieper wrote:

> He [the one who knows that he is not himself the Divinity] also will not view the specific imperishability of the soul—although by that is meant a stability which cannot be affected either by intervention from outside or by an impairment of his own capability of being—he will not view this *incorruptibilitas* as though it were a sovereign potency which bursts the bounds of creatureliness. The individual imperishability of soul is, of course, likewise something received when the individual was created. That means that it is something given to us as really our own, which is hence forth a permanent part of our being. . . .
>
> The decisive factor, I would say, is what we mean by creation and creating. If *creatio* means that God, in creating, does not retain Being for himself so that he still remains the *Sole* reality, but truly gives and shares it, then obviously the *creatura* possesses existence and essence as

---

37. Thomas Aquinas, *On the Power of God*, trans. English Dominicans (Westminster, Md., 1952), 5, 4, ad 10.
38. Pieper, *Death and Immortality*, 119.
39. Strauss, "Progress or Return? The Contemporary Crisis," 38–39.

a veritable property, received as always from God, the ceaselessly effective Source of everything, but for this very reason a real property. Everything that man is and possesses 'by virtue of Creation' is his and possesses 'by nature'.[40]

This analysis seems to be the link between Athens, Jerusalem, and Rome that enables us to argue that, however the original sources of knowledge might immediately differ, they fall within the same range of intelligible discourse. Silence about one or the other element, however prudent, leaves one open to the Gnostic philosophical musings, which Strauss saw that the Bible used to characterize philosophy itself.

Consequently, too, the classical arguments for the immortality of the soul based on intellectual reflection—such as the proof from the existence of truth—can be arguments about the actual sort of being that a given individual—Socrates, Plato, or Mary—is, and the argument concludes to a complete happiness which would include the whole person.[41] Put negatively, no alternative meets the requirements of the being that actually exists, requirements *discovered* in authentic philosophic reflection, whether there is revelation or not.

Philosophy does not of course conclude in Christian theory to "resurrection" and cannot do so. But it can in theory recognize resurrection as the best answer to questions existentially posed at least from political philosophy about what is the final subject in which happiness is to exist, namely, not in the species, not in the polity, nor in the family, but in the complete intelligent individual, with a name such as Socrates, Plato, or Mary (Books I and X of *The Ethics* of Aristotle). Likewise, political philosophy necessarily asks about the location of the highest "city" in which this happiness is found, whether it is possibly another earthly regime like the actual Athens, Jerusalem, or Rome of history (Plato, Augustine). All other possibilities which are "thinkable," as Pieper understood, and which need to be actually thought out in argument to contradiction, are despairing and lead to

---

40. Pieper, *Death and Immortality*, 121–22.
41. See Krąpiec, *I-Man: An Outline of Philosophical Anthropology*, 127.

false philosophy, to "foolishness," to the Gnostic modern project as a substitute for genuine political philosophy and revelation.[42]

Strauss, following Aristotle, then, was correct in noting that the definition of "philosophy" in the Bible was a "philosophy" that *excluded* in principle the challenge posed by revelation, which could conceive an immortality that was not an eternal, infinite, self-made, and self-sustaining form. This is also the same point Strauss reached when he denied that "nature" and hence "philosophy" existed in the Bible while at the same time he reaffirmed that intelligence could be used to obey the divine law. This law or divinity was trustworthy and did not therefore deny in practice what it created, including the indestructible soul, in which the highest things could exist in a complete finite being, if they were presented to it. This, at the same time, saved the finiteness of the mortal being and its openness to a transcendence which it did not make.

In this sense, it is instructive that the remarks made by Paul of Tarsus, both in Athens and to the Romans, touched on these very issues. "God, who made the world and all that is in it," Paul said in Athens, recalling the Old Testament, "since He is Lord of heaven and earth, does not dwell in temples built by hands; neither is he served by human hands as if he were in need of anything, since it is he who gives all men life and breath and all things" (Acts 17:24–25). Paul indicated that there is intelligibility in the Law, that justice is to be "judged," something Plato also held, and that there would be a resurrection. At this latter affirmation, of course, the "philosophers" of Athens, listening to Paul, went away.

And to the Romans, Paul (following the Book of Wisdom, 13:1–9) expected intelligent men to know of God's existence by the use of their own reason, and like Strauss, he noted that the philosophers lapsed into vanity, into their own constructions. "For since the creation of the world his invisible attributes are clearly seen—his everlasting power also and his divinity—so that they are without excuse, seeing that,

---

42. Pieper, *Death and Immortality*, 121.

although they knew God, they did not glorify him as God or give thanks, but became vain in their reasonings, and their senseless minds have been darkened. For while professing to be wise, they have become fools, and they have changed the glory of the incorruptible God for an image made like to corruptible things" (Romans 1:20–23). What the modern project at its intellectual extreme does, if taken seriously in its radical intelligibility, is to substitute a newer and higher kind of philosophic project for the "birds and idols." The very polity itself, devoted to man as a self-forming definer of himself, becomes the "myth" or idol that is intellectually formed in the history of political philosophy, once it has been separated from the unique sources of being. "Humanity" itself, in this vision, is presupposed to no rule or norm either of nature or of revelation.

Philosophy and revelation, it would seem, need not deny categorically that no greater harmony between them is possible, provided philosophy is not defined exclusively as the basis of absolute, autonomous essences, including human nature presupposed to nothing but itself. This statement is not tantamount to denying that often philosophy is in fact defined in this extreme manner. Both Strauss's description of philosophy in the Bible and Paul's description of philosophy as tending to "foolishness" agree in recognizing that philosophy must, on its own, having rejected being as the source of truth, reformulate fantastic "entities" to substitute for the truth it ceaselessly seeks. Many, if not most, of these "entities" in the modern world have been constructions of political philosophy rooted in the modern project.

On the other hand, the relative autonomy of philosophy about its genuine integrity is necessary to guarantee to man some protection against false "theophanies" which would suggest that God is not a God of order but an arbitrary tyrant. (Pieper had noted in his *Scholasticism* that the theological definition of God, in the late Middle Ages, as *unlimited will* corresponded to and made possible the Hobbesian notion of the unlimited nature of the Leviathan and its progeny in the General Will, the Generic Being, and the Superman.)[43] The God who

---

43. Pieper, *Scholasticism*, 136–50.

does not speak of "nature," as Strauss had it, is a God, however, for whom the distinction of good and evil is absolute. For this reason revelation, as Strauss understood, often begins with repentance, something with which the New Testament likewise began.[44] The centrality of the principle of contradiction is likewise the guarantee that the God whose ways are not our ways (the guarantee therefore that the world is something more than mere human thought) is not merely arbitrary. It is the guarantee that good and evil cannot be identified even in human political acts, however difficult it may be sometimes, as Aristotle understood, to determine prudentially a given act's moral character. Consequently any universal society, even the City of God in its transcendent sense, will necessarily include the possibility of intelligent creatures who could have refused it. Otherwise, intelligent beings other than the Highest could not have existed at all.

Anton Pegis, in his *Christian Philosophy and Intellectual Freedom*, argued, moreover, that "Philosophy" as such, as deliberately separate from revelation, so that it was obliged not even to consider revelation's intelligibility, was quite different from a philosophy authentic to itself but was one also addressed *by* reason.

> Not only is it not foolish for the intellect to believe in truths above itself, it is also a fact that the truths it can know by demonstration can never be opposed to the truths of faith. The principles that guide the demonstrations of the intellect are part of the equipment with which God has endowed the nature of man. God is the author of these principles by being the author of the human nature that He made capable of knowing them. In short, the principles that direct our knowledge of our thinking originate in the same divine wisdom from which revelation has come. . . .
>
> By the same token, and in the name of the same unity of truth in God, we must likewise hold that there can be no demonstrative refutation of the truths of faith. In a word, toward divine revelation, as St. Thomas sees it, the attitude of the intellect is twofold. Truths that are

---

44. See especially Leo Strauss, "Introductory Essay for Hermann Cohn," in *Studies in Platonic Political Philosophy*, 233–47. For the theme of repentance, see especially Chap. 1 of the Gospel of Mark.

above the intellect, and that the intellect therefore holds by faith, can never be demonstrated but they can never be demonstratively refuted. This means that, in principle, all supposed refutations of supernatural truths are answerable. With regard to the truths about God that the intellect can hold by demonstration, the situation is perfectly clear-cut: being able to reach such truths by demonstration, the intellect is in principle capable of maintaining its full autonomy in their presence by its own light.[45]

Pegis went on to suggest, then, that revelation has the function of actually "promoting" the intellect's rationality, which said that revelation is not served by "defending it badly or by reasoning badly in its name."[46] It would seem that Strauss's problem with the "Divine Message of the City of Righteousness" and philosophy must go in this direction to retain the valid points about reason and revelation and to recognize a relation or harmony between them, which in no way would deny the limits of particularly human intelligence or the unfathomability of the divine knowledge, including its capacity to communicate somehow (revelation) with the finite intelligence.

Interestingly, Strauss himself reviewed Pegis's edition of the English translation of Aquinas's *Summa theologiae*. In so doing Strauss faulted Pegis for suggesting that Aquinas did not go against Aristotle's principles in the matter of creation because he (Aristotle) did not, in Pegis's view, specifically deny creation. But Aquinas instead gave another solution to the problem of the eternity of the species, one that was not Aristotle's but had the same premises. Aquinas's position was reached because of the intelligibility of revelation. Strauss, contrary to Pegis, felt that Aristotle left no room for "a revealed teaching which could be added to his rational teaching."[47]

On the other hand, Strauss defended Aquinas from what he considered to be Pegis's implied historicism, which missed the true import

---

45. Anton C. Pegis, *Christian Philosophy and Intellectual Freedom* (Milwaukee, 1955), 53–54. See McInerny, *St. Thomas Aquinas*; Krąpiec, *I-Man: An Outline of Philosophical Anthropology*, 120–69; Josef Pieper, *Reality and the Good*, trans. S. Lange (Chicago, 1967).
46. Pegis, *Christian Philosophy and Intellectual Freedom* (Milwaukee, 1955), 54–55.
47. Strauss, *What Is Political Philosophy?* 285.

of the Aristotelian-Thomist criticism of science. Strauss remarked that Pegis should have said that "Thomas studied the teachings of his predecessors with an exclusive regard to their truth or falsehood, or that for Thomas only argument, and not history, could legitimately decide the fate of any philosophic thesis."[48] This "Thomistic" position was clearly also that of Strauss.

Strauss had argued in *Natural Right and History* that Christian philosophy was unacceptable because its conclusions were reached through the impetus of natural and finally revealed theology. At any rate, the ultimate consequence of the Thomistic view of natural law was, in Strauss's view, that the natural law was practically inseparable from natural theology, "that is, from a natural theology which is, in fact, based on belief in Biblical revelation, but even on revealed theology."[49]

But Strauss's analysis of the biblical and the Platonic view of philosophy, both as the "quest for wisdom" and not as a closed circuit of answers, would not be in contradiction if this quest for wisdom of the philosopher were held to a strict accounting from reason.[50] Reason can be incited by a revelation seeking to make itself intelligible or at least noncontradictory. So in his analysis of the biblical view of philosophy and of the very results of the modern project, Strauss hinted that the sort of philosophy that resulted from revealed religion might be the very intelligence that reached truth. This is certainly the tenet of Christian philosophy, and it did not imply that the human intellect could duplicate the divine intellect. But still, it did not deny that truth was one for each intellect, according to its respective mode of knowing. The relation of divine and human knowledge was, in Aquinas's sense, analogous, not equivocal.

Classical political philosophy clearly presented nine issues: (1) the obligation of the philosopher to pursue the truth in spite of the commands of the particular polity to forbid him *(Antigone,* Socrates); (2) the need to construct at least in the mind the outlines of the perfectly

---

48. *Ibid.*
49. Strauss, *Natural Right and History,* 164.
50. Strauss, "Progress or Return? The Contemporary Crisis," 24.

just city, its conditions, and its connection with the proper functioning of the thinking human being himself, and the relation of this thinking to his happiness *(The Republic);* (3) the problem of the loneliness of the First Mover, or God, that thought thinking itself was deprived of the highest of goods known in creation in the human experience (Aristotle); (4) the desire at least of a proper happiness to each individual as an individual, not merely a member of a collectivity down the ages, as a Socrates, Plato, or Mary (Aristotle); (5) the question of the possible friendship with God, since mutual friendship is the highest of human realities (Plato, Aristotle, Cicero); (6) the immortality of the human soul, both as a location of the complete achievement of justice and friendship and of the faculty which could grasp *what is,* what is present, truth itself (Plato, Aristotle, Cicero); (7) the fact that we do not want to achieve the highest things on condition that we do not remain ourselves (Aristotle); (8) the fact that the highest faculty of man is his reason, through which he is open to all being as something properly his own in knowledge and the possession of which does not destroy him or absorb him into something else (Aristotle); (9) the fact that man must still choose to remain reasonable and open to truth, so that even the highest knowledge exists in risk and jeopardy; the City of Man or foolishness in philosophy, thus, remains ever possible in the search for the highest things both for the philosopher and for the common man (Paul, Augustine).

To return to classical political thought is to return to these very questions, in the light of which all theory about man must formulate some adequate response. Such questions pose the highest subtlety of argument. Jerusalem, Athens, and Rome (Mecca, as Strauss noted, presents also a valid but somewhat different problem) are the three intellectual traditions in which the questions persist. When they do not occur, proper human civilization has not begun in that society. For this reason philosophy relates to any city; for this reason, in other words, when the city kills the philosopher, it cuts its citizens off from the highest things. Yet these intellectual traditions do not simply imply a series of doctrines or answers, though these must be addressed. In this sense, mystery, however ultimately unfathomable, must not be posed as a contradiction to or an impossibility for the proper functioning of intellect to think and make proper distinctions. Voegelin sometimes hints that this opposition exists. Strauss, however, seemed to appreciate the issue.

> Here, we are touching on what, from the point of view of the sociology of philosophy, is the most important difference between Christianity on the one hand, and Islam as well as Judaism on the other. For the Christian, the sacred doctrine is revealed theology; for the Jew and the Muslim, the sacred doctrine is, at least primarily, the legal interpretation of the Divine Law (*talmud* or *fiqh*). The sacred doctrine in the latter sense has, to say the least, much less in common with philosophy than the sacred doctrine in the former sense. It is ultimately for this reason that the status of philosophy was, as a matter of principle, much more precarious in Judaism and in Islam than in Christianity: in Christianity philosophy became an integral part of the officially recognized and even required training of the student of the sacred doctrine. This difference explains partly the eventual collapse of philosophical inquiry in the Islamic and in the Jewish world, a collapse which has no parallel in the Western Christian world.[51]

It is instructive to recognize that this to Strauss as yet unanticipated decline in the study of particularly Thomistic philosophic philosophy within Christian circles, the major exception, significantly, being Poland, led directly to an effort, in many areas, to make Christianity into a political religion, into itself an expression of Strauss's "modern project" or Voegelin's "Gnosticism."

Henri de Lubac's remarks, it seems, are pertinent here in regard to Strauss's comments on the difference between "the religions of the Book" and Christianity:

> Christian faith can be—and history shows that it was indeed—the promoter of reason; but it is not itself, a science or a revealed philosophy; such expressions are devoid of meaning. . . . This does not mean that faith does not have a light proper to itself, nor that it completely

---

51. Strauss, *Persecution and the Art of Writing*, 18–19; see also 8–9. In this context the two chapters on "The Maniac" and "The Suicide of Thought" in G. K. Chesterton, *Orthodoxy* are worth reading.

lacks all rational justification, nor (and this is the point which interests us here) that it excludes all objectivization. On the contrary, from the beginning faith spontaneously expressed itself in symbols and concepts; the abundant riches of the texts of the New Testament bear witness to this. . . .

To wish to limit oneself strictly to biblical formulas in explaining the faith is a snare. *Scriptura sola* may have been brandished like a battle flag at one time; it still remains an untenable position, in fact as well as in principle. The ancients were not deceived. Not only did the faith of the Church precede all the writings of the New Testament and guide the interpretation of the Old Testament—our faith is not a "religion of the book", and these writings are anything but a manual or a code—but one cannot fail to inquire about the meaning of formulas, to compare them with one another, to juxtapose them, to assimilate them. . . . Now, if one disregards the necessarily abstract precisions laid down by the Councils, how will one avoid the deviations and perversions due to the invasion of "hellenism" which these clarifications were supposed to correct? . . . The human mind is made in such a way that it cannot hold to a truth, cannot maintain it, unless it seeks and seeks continually.[52]

This passage is, perhaps, exactly the sort of balanced statement that a Christian philosophy should reach in its efforts to maintain in political philosophy a mutual influence of theology and philosophy, faith and reason, one loyal to the evidence of both as open to each other in one whole.

Political philosophy, however, remains its own enterprise, however open it must leave man also to what is not politics. Pegis remarked that the articulators of revelation ought to recognize Aristotle's implication by practical reason, that "their pilgrimage to the heavenly Jerusalem includes the building of a human Athens on earth."[53] This statement cannot, however, entail a reversal of Augustine to suggest that it is possible to produce the Kingdom of God itself on earth.[54] But rather with Strauss and Aquinas, it is advisable to recall that the

52. de Lubac, *Nature and Grace*, 66–70; see also 112–13.
53. Pegis, *Christian Philosophy and Intellectual Freedom*, 72–73.
54. de Lubac, *Nature and Grace*, 106–108.

tyrannies can be rejected by reason, and the less perfect regimes can be somewhat reformed. Yet philosophy must remain open within that leisure transcendent to the polity itself, even when it is not called on to reflect on the death of a Socrates in Athens, or a Christ in Jerusalem, or a Cicero or a Paul in Rome. The ultimate questions remain to be asked and wondered about even in the best of regimes.

Strauss put the matter this way, finally, in his "Three Waves of Modernity": "The theoretical crisis does not necessarily lead to a practical crisis, for the superiority of liberal democracy to communism, Stalinist or post-Stalinist, is obvious enough. And above all, liberal democracy, in contradistinction to communism and fascism, derives powerful support from a way of thinking which cannot be called modern at all: the pre-modern thought of our Western tradition."[55] With this statement Strauss suggested a way to interpret the positive values of Western intellectual, political, and economic history—Jerusalem and Athens, Rome and Aachen, *The Federalist* and *The Wealth of Nations*—which would confront the philosophical disorders of the modern project. This reasoning could confront the philosophical disorders of the modern era while at the same time accepting the values of a moderate republic which has learned about prosperity and freedom for actual human beings. This argument has the advantage of starting at the very real roots from which these values originated, from Aristotle's realization that the particular also contains signs of wisdom.

The engagement of the three elements of this tradition, Jerusalem, Athens, and the acceptable elements in modern liberal philosophy, with the philosophic tradition of Augustine and Aquinas seems to be the positive contribution that revelation can make both to the incompleteness of the classic and Old Testament position and to the understanding of and correction of the aberrations of the modern project which Strauss and Voegelin rightly described. But it is not a one-way street. Rome itself, however valuable its addition to the complete answer to classic questions, is not itself safe without the handmaid of political philosophy, nor without Jerusalem, nor without the lived ex-

---

55. Strauss, "Three Waves of Modernity," 98.

perience of wealth production and civil freedom, nor even, in a sense, without the lived-out Gnostic systems of the modern era, which show clearly what is at stake when we think and act erroneously.

These latter therefore suggest that there is a right natural order which is not merely indifferent to whatever men do and think. The fundamentals of political philosophy require the proper positing of authentic questions from political experience, the complete experience of life in a human polity, including its life of leisure, as Aristotle used that term. These very questions and their philosophic reflections are in turn open to meaning from whatever source, insofar as it is directed to actual experience made intelligible beyond the polity. This openness included the answers posed by revelation and the alternative ideological answers that have sought to confront such questions in another fashion. The completeness of political philosophy, even in its own order, then, is not indifference to the fashion and manner in which ultimate questions are posed and answered by philosophy itself, by revelation, and, not least, by the Gnostic formulations of the modern project.

CONCLUSION

The foundation of political philosophy consists in the discovery of those accurate responses to the central questions that arise naturally and normally within human political experience whenever and wherever it occurs. This experience is the same whether it exists in an unsophisticated fashion among the great majority of the people or in an articulated manner in the philosophers. The effect of these responses, if they are adequately understood, is to prevent men, particularly the philosophers themselves, the politicians, and the theologians, from making politics and those disciplines that are related to it in the classics, especially economics, into a "substitute metaphysics," that is, into a full explanation in their own terms, of *all that is*.

To argue that politics in particular is a prime, perhaps *the* prime candidate for this dangerous role, to be sure, need not constitute an attack on or an undermining of politics as such. Indeed, the major burden of the argument presented here is that the defense of politics requires an understanding of why politics is liberated from the temptation to become itself an explanation of *all that is*. Classical political philosophy was right to distinguish the highest of the practical sciences from the speculative sciences, action from contemplation. Those more contemporary writers, such as Strauss or Voegelin or Arendt, who have sought to save politics from modern political Gnosticism in its various forms, are therefore correct to call for a return to arguments found in the classical writers in order to prevent this dangerous turn to political metaphysics.[1] But since the classics were not in fact themselves adequate to prevent a radical deviation from their own funda-

---

1. See James V. Schall, "Metaphysics, Theology, and Political Theory," *Political Science Reviewer*, XI (Fall, 1981), 1–25.

mental principles, which an accurate analysis of the meaning of post-Aristotelian philosophy and its Enlightenment revivals proves, it is not enough to return to the classics, though this first step is illuminating. We must also see why the classics were not able to answer the questions they themselves posed in their own order. The primary locus of this discussion in the history of Western political philosophy has been found in the manner in which revelation was addressed to philosophy.

The question is, then: how, in theory, can politics be limited to itself? How is its own self-moderation to be conceived so that politics can leave open to philosophy and perhaps to revelation, if it occurs, a source of responses to the highest things, which the human mind necessarily seeks, even in politics when it is cut off from finding them elsewhere? The initial fact is that, because of practical, political life, certain basic questions, already clearly asked in the classical experience, do arise. Every subsequent response to these formulated questions, from either philosophy or revelation, must in some sense relate to the manner in which these questions were or could be answered. Such questions can be answered badly or even ignored, but they remain present within any existing city and will either undermine it or force it to exist by coercion alone if they are not confronted in that freedom and openness to truth which is the leisured end of the polity and that to which it ought freely and intelligently to conform in order to be itself.

In retrospect, then, one of the fundamental aspects of political philosophy in particular is clearly the accurate philosophical description, not only of regimes and their root differences, but of the intelligibility of what happens if the fundamental principles of *what is* are at any major point rejected or confused. The human intellect, of course, does not possess its own separate "form," or as some medieval thinkers held, a common "agent intellect," existing outside the unique individual human being in whom intelligence exists concretely as a personal property. On the other hand, human beings can understand the arguments and positions of other thinkers from any time.

Thus political chaos (or sanity) in one age or society may very well be caused by arguments or considerations made two or five or twenty centuries earlier. An argument unresolved or resolved improperly can appear in some other philosopher to continue as vigorously as before, or it can be carried to new, more logical consequences. Moreover, there is objectively nothing to prevent the good or the true from being voluntarily rejected even if known, so that one cannot argue to the "untruth" of a position merely on the basis of the time in which it appeared. "Modernity," in this sense (or "antiquity"), states not merely a "now" but a series of ideas or principles explaining *what is*.

Thinking, in other words, also involves the possibility of thinking rightly and does so unavoidably. The rejection of Cynicism and skepticism also constitutes the basis on which to begin any political philosophy that claims to be able to distinguish tyranny from the actual regimes that are in fact better. What is particularly important about political thinking is that by its very nature, it is ordered to action, to being put into effect in the world. The "moderation" of political philosophy therefore becomes something quite different if the theoretical reasons for this very moderation, which consist in the reasons why life in some existing city is not the highest life open to man as such, are denied. Political philosophy must therefore be particularly sensitive to the tenor and tone of those proposals, made in the language of politics most often, which are designed to respond to questions of happiness, meaning, and the good, which a profound reflection on actual political living persistently formulates within the human condition.

Toward the end of his study *Thoughts on Machiavelli,* Leo Strauss wrote: "To return to that manifestation of the new notion of philosophy which appears clearly in Machiavelli's books, the new philosophy takes its bearings by how men live as distinguished from how they ought to live; it despises the concerns with imagined republics and imagined principalities. . . . Since man is not by nature ordered toward fixed ends, he is infinitely malleable."[2] Of course, the "imagined

---

2. Leo Strauss, *Thoughts on Machiavelli* (Glencoe, Ill., 1958), 296–97. See Michael Jackson, "Leo Strauss' Teaching: A Study of *Thoughts on Machiavelli*" (Ph.D. dissertation, Georgetown University, 1985). (This dissertation contains a complete bibliography of works by and about Leo Strauss to date.)

republics and imagined principalities," from Plato to Augustine, were endeavors to account for all reality, particularly that which was not political, so that actual republics would *not* conceive themselves capable of forming man and the city in any way the philosopher or politician chose. Thus the "imagined republics" of the political philosophers were more than mere "myths." They were perennial exercises of the human intellect and corresponded to that understanding of reality which saw its wholeness in something more than what man could fashion for himself.

This presumed "infinite malleability" of man, a being said to be presupposed to no fixed ends from nature, is, of course, what one line of political philosophy has sought to establish as the basis of reality, as its own intellectual self-justification. The steps in this development and their understanding have been followed here. They constitute one basic side of political philosophy as such, which must account for why crucial changes in man's understanding of himself came about and what constituted their essence. No political philosophy is adequate without this account, which, in effect, establishes why it is possible, at least, to strive to make politics into a "substitute metaphysics," an explanation of *all that is,* presupposed to no standards from nature and revelation. Once these steps have been seen, which lead finally to the Generic Man and the revolutionary endeavor of radical modernity to replace man himself as he was described philosophically in the classics and revelation, the brilliance of this effort cannot be underestimated, nor less its attraction, why it has come to be tempting even for many adherents of revelation itself.

Once the philosophic position has been established, namely, that there are no intelligible ends in reality save those implanted there by the exercise of the human will guiding its own intelligence to produce the "intelligible" forms in things, the highest exercise of human will acting outside itself will obviously be politics, not the directing of the intellect to contemplation or revelation. At this point it becomes theoretically possible to impose man's political images or myths, his Gnostic speculations and radical projects, onto reality, since literally nothing stands in the way of intelligence, either substitutional or actual, to

Conclusion

resist it. The very purpose of activity removing every sign of this given order from nature or revelation, on which Marx so shrewdly insisted, was to define man's being as exclusively subject only to the human will. This constituted a volitional act to reject, both politically and personally, that order of things, which, as Aristotle held, men found but did not make.

Ellis Sandoz's description of Eric Voegelin's conclusions on these points is likewise pertinent:

> The discontinuity of Plato's Vision . . . is embodied in the saving tale that "reveals revelation as an event of transfiguration; reality is really moving toward the *'eschaton'* of immortality." In Saint Paul the discontinuity induced by the overwhelming revelation of pleromatic presence in Christ tends to become more than the epochal event in history that it is. Rather, it tempts the pneumatic visionaries into the deformation of expecting the transfiguration of reality in the near future, thereby proclaiming the end of history at the expense of the balance of consciousness. It clearly sounds the theme of annihilating break signalled in the *"alle bisherige Geschichte"* of Marx's *Manifesto* 2,000 years later and of the other second realities of the modern centuries in the mode of deformed existence.
>
> The balance of consciousness requires that "struggle" be held at the center of the meditative's quest as the lot of man in history. The Vision of the Whole comprehends the truth of disorder no less than of order in human existence. Hence, the philosopher "is obliged to recognize the *machte athanatos* (undying struggle) as the movement toward the experienced *eschaton* of immortality and yet not to indulge in the dreamer's fantasy of an eschatological transformation to be pleromatically accomplished by his own dreams and actions."[3]

In addition to Strauss's "infinite malleability" of human nature, however, Voegelin recognized the possibility of locating those ideas and truths, discovered legitimately in revelation, in the politics of this world. He understood correctly that this constituted the corrup-

---

3. Ellis Sandoz, *The Voegelinian Revolution* (Baton Rouge, 1981), 250–51. See James V. Schall, "The Abiding Significance of Gnosticism," *American Ecclesiastical Review,* CXLVII (September, 1962), 164–73.

tion of both politics and revelation. The argument of these reflections has not been, of course, to deny either the reality or the danger of this possibility. But the "pneumatic visionaries" are not the center of the classical revelational tradition but precisely alien to it, so that Voegelin's valid warning ought not to be taken as if the whole revelational answer were somehow a "vision" or a "myth." The central issue, as it has been argued here, is that the "dreamers' fantasies" become powerful particularly when they are cut off from political philosophy as that is addressed by revelation but valid nevertheless in itself.

Thus the protection of both normal political life and authentic revelation depends upon a political philosophy which recognizes *what is* and the given distinctions in things. Particularly, this protection depends on a political philosophy in which the proper life of man as a unique "political" being, his life as a mortal, is seen as legitimate but not as itself the complete explanation of all that is in man. Once reality and particularly man are seen as "infinitely malleable," a notion from Rousseau, the "dreams and actions" of the mystics and revolutionaries will seem as probable as those of classical political philosophy and revelation. Such politico-religious visionaries will demand, furthermore, that their "projects" for human cities be put into the only kind of existence that seems available to them, namely, political existence. The *esse* of being thus becomes the *esse* of politics. Aristotle was quite right, then, that, "if man were the highest being, politics would be the highest science"—only, on this supposition, politics would be no longer a practical science but a complete metaphysics whose "truth" could only be the artistic one of whether it conformed to the willed intelligible form of what controlled the political order.

The foundations of political philosophy, then, must include an account of the record of human thought, as it were, "thinking on itself," a thinking which becomes automatically political once the highest things are said to be those practical virtues unique to man in the cosmos and not those things which transcend even man's own given, and good, being. But if political philosophy is to protect the polity from the modern Gnostic projects, which present answers to questions initially posed by political living in parodies seeking existence, parodies of immortality, resurrection, charity, and friendship, it must include an account of political philosophy which does not in principle exclude the sorts of reflections posed by revelation to the questions that arise in political philosophy.

The relation of reason and revelation, in this regard, as Thomas Pangle sensed in Strauss, is a most fundamental one in political philosophy.[4] Voegelin had suggested why political philosophy must be critical of any revelational claim because of the temptation, even of the cleric, perhaps especially of the cleric, to want to change the dimensions of revelation into a program for political order, for structuring the City of God on earth, a position which is the direct denial of both Plato and Augustine, not to mention Aquinas. However "open" political philosophy ought to remain to whatever is directed to it from a presumed revelation, still in the tradition of Thomas Aquinas, reason seems both more critical and more important than in either Strauss or Voegelin because, in Aquinas, the relation of reason and revelation was one of noncontradiction. Politics, in other words, could legitimately decide about false theophanies or the "arbitrary" will of even God's law. On the contrary, this same principle suggested that revelation addressed to reason could expand reason itself in the direction not of myth but of intelligence.

In this context, however, it is likewise necessary to see in this whole issue something more than a sort of subtle flexibility before the normally expected changes that happen in any society. Paul Sigmund argued:

> It would be unfortunate if Thomistic thought no longer gave rise to new social and political formulations, because, along with Marxism and the liberal humanism of the Enlightenment, Christianity has been a principal source of symbols and motivation for the transformation of society, especially in times of crisis, and the Thomistic formulation of Christian social and political theory remains one of the most appealing, moderate, and flexible ways to relate the Christian message to

---

4. See Thomas Pangle, "Introduction," to Strauss, *Studies in Platonic Political Philosophy*, 18–23. See also Jaffa, "The Legacy of Leo Strauss."

contemporary politics and society. More fundamentally, the belief that it exemplifies that human beings can perceive a purposive life in community is one that has attracted man throughout the ages—and if that belief disappears, one has reason to fear for the future of democracy—or even of our civilized life together."[5]

But the question is not just whether Thomistic political philosophy is another system alongside Marxism or liberal humanism, but whether, at a deeper level, as Strauss and Voegelin argued, it addresses the fundamental relation of the latter two positions to the modern Gnostic project itself and whether this dedication to "purposive order" was rooted in a reason open to revelation which can address the questions that limit politics itself. In other words, any "transformation of society" ought itself to be limited by a reason open to revelation, not merely to change itself.

Political philosophy by itself cannot conceive all the answers to its own ultimate questions. Yet it is capable of at least suspecting that answers once presented are answers that allow its own order, politics, to be itself and not some ideological description imposed on reality. Political philosophy presents a series of questions for which there are no adequate *political* answers. This fact is the reason why there is a possibility that political philosophy can be presented as an alternate metaphysics. Yet this latter result has the paradoxical effect of eliminating the moderation and limited nature of politics itself. That political philosophy should, by strict logical argument, lead to its own destruction seems, on the surface, improbable. Yet if politics is finally held to bear the burden of explaining all of the questions of reality, there seems to be no alternative. This characteristic in part explains the deep passion and enthusiasm that often exist in the modern ideologies based in the modern Gnostic project, since they are more than merely abstract philosophical analyses.

In his dicussion of Rabbi Yahuda Helevi, Leo Strauss again referred to the notion of a "philosophy" closed to reason (the biblical view of

---

5. Paul Sigmund, "Thomistic Natural Law and Social Theory," *Calgary Aquinas Studies*, ed. Anthony Parel (Toronto, 1979), 76.

Conclusion

philosophy for Strauss) and one open to it, by contrasting Marsilius of Padua and Aquinas, wherein the view that natural law is merely opinion (Marsilius) is opposed to Aquinas, wherein it is a reason placed in things (substitute intelligence) and a participation by the creature in the eternal law.[6] Strauss continued:

> One has not to be naturally pious, he has merely to have a passionate interest in genuine morality in order to long with all his heart for revelation: moral man as such is the potential believer. Halevi could find a sign for the necessity of the connection between morality and revelation in the fact that the same philosophers who denied the Divine Lawgiver, denied the obligatory character of what we would call the moral law. In defending Judaism, which, according to him, is the only true revealed religion, against the philosophers, he was conscious of defending morality itself and therefore the cause, not only of Judaism, but of mankind at large. His basic objection to philosophy was then not particularly Jewish, nor even particularly religious, but moral.[7]

Whatever the fact of it is, Strauss understood that revelation could be a defense of reason and morality (practical reason) because the philosophers, who in principle denied the obligation of the moral law, since they saw no cause or authority behind it to enforce or reward it (the problem of immortality), did not defend properly, as did revelation, what was in fact "reasonable," even though this reasonableness had to be stimulated by Old Testament revelation before this could be seen in the case of the second section of the Decalogue, in its description of normal morality.

We can perhaps in this context understand the reasons for Strauss's insistence on a radical separation of faith and reason if we recognize that "philosophy" can mean that thought which in principle rejects revelation (and hence morality). In the *City and Man*, however, Strauss spoke of philosophy by itself, to open the political philosopher to the limits of finite reason itself. On this basis, then, the revelational re-

---

6. Leo Strauss, "The Law of Reason in the *Kuzari*," in *Persecution and the Art of Writing*, 96–98.
7. *Ibid.*, 140–41. See also Pangle, "Introduction," 20; James V. Schall, "Natural Law in the Medieval Intellectual Context," *Modern Age*, XXVIII (Spring–Summer, 1984), 228–35.

sponses to certain impasses in political philosophy, itself already aware of problems connected with immortality, friendship, and happiness, need not exclude the revelational responses as at least feasible answers, with the realization that these too can become, as Voegelin saw, politicized to become a threat to the city itself.

To call the revelational answers in principles strictly "necessary"—Aquinas at times used the word "necessary" for "suasive"—responses would be, as Pieper pointed out, to make the human intellect in some instances capable of fathoming all the mysteries in finite terms, which is to make the human intellect equivalent to the divine intellect.[8] This latter conclusion, be it noted, is the conclusion not of classical or medieval political theory before Joachim of Flora or Marsilius but precisely of "modern" political theory, that which proposes that human nature is infinitely malleable and therefore subject to nothing but itself in its highest science—politics, that is.

The argument here, however, has been that, within political philosophy, both in principle and in practice, a studied, considered openness to revelation in its major forms is an essential aspect of political philosophy itself. Without this openness, political philosophy will invariably go in the Gnostic direction in which it will impose, whatever the form of regime, even liberal democracy, some myth onto the city as the only reality to be allowed in practice, if not even in theory.[9] To know that the ultimate questions are not necessarily posed "in vain" is sufficient to undermine the Gnostic projects. These latter seek to refashion the world and man to respond to these legitimate questions, particularly the highest ones, but in a fashion that has turned out to be in practice highly dangerous, ideological, innerworldly utopian.

In his essay "St. Thomas and Nietzsche," Frederick Copleston wrote:

> Once man has been set free (in modern philosophy), i.e., has set himself free, from subjection to God and the moral law, once he has asserted his independence of the transcendental by denying its existence,

---

8. Pieper, *Scholasticism*, 55–76, 136–51.
9. Eric Voegelin, *Science, Politics, and Gnosticism*, 97–110.

Conclusion

once he has declared himself to be 'man the creator', what results? No doubt there is at first a sense of boundless freedom—Nietzsche speaks of the infinite vistas that open out when God is dead—of limitless opportunity for creative action, for the end and purpose of a man's life is no longer fixed and clear, something given from a source outside man and above man; but, if there is to be creative activity at all, if human nature is to be developed, if human society is to be formed in a new way, there must be some clear conception of the end to be achieved, the model to be realized in concrete fact. Who is to fix this end, who is to delineate the model? Man himself. Yes, but there is no individual man-in-himself, there are only individual men and women. The inevitable result is, then, that some men, those who have the ability, the opportunity, and power and drive and energy, take it upon themselves to fix the end of man and the ideal nature of human society, not only for themselves, but also for others: they may do this ostensibly in the name of Mankind, but actually they speak in their own names, they express their own subjective wills.[10]

This has indeed been the direction of specifically modern political philosophy in its own autonomy.

And writing similarly of the exact same issue within the history of literature, Marion Montgomery wrote in his insightful *Reflective Journey Toward Order:*

Through the imagination, the soul confuses its own awareness with an existing God or an existing soul in nature. The imagination may subversively lead the self to suppose that it sees things feel, and the subversiveness is unsettling. . . . Recognizing the possibility of such illusion, the soul comes upon doubt: has imagination indeed led the soul to create a world in its own image? What if that rebellious "creative" power be intent upon making the soul its own Heaven, thus removing itself from all else except itself? . . .

One may shift that early humanist position that "nothing human is alien to me" to read "nothing is alien to me," and by a metamorphosis elevate oneself while obscuring the essential distinction between the

---

10. Frederick C. Copleston, *St. Thomas and Nietzsche* (London, 1955), 21–22 (paper read before the Aquinas Society of London on April 15, 1944).

human and non-human, between the Self and the Other. The hubris of such a seeming elevation makes one initially suppose man equal to the gods. The final effect, however, may be to destroy distinctions by the mind, and thereby destroy the distinctiveness of mind itself. The final victim is individuality. The mind is left in a state of uncomfortable awareness: it is aware of its particular existence but is not able to explain or justify it. That is, one becomes an awareness alienated from all else except self-awareness.[11]

The parallels of the artistic mind and the political mind are not accidental, once we recall the distinction between art and prudence in the Aristotelian analysis. That is to say, once fixed ends in human nature are denied, there is no difference between art and politics. Truth is merely the conformity of the reality with what the artist (or politician) wanted to make. The suspicion that there is no longer individuality but only a kind of general self-awareness is, no doubt, the point at which Marx arrived from another angle with his generic being, in which all individual distinctions disappeared and only the individual as species remained.

The defense of moderate political philosophy must grasp why this "creativity" presupposed only to will cannot produce the proper description of those answers to political questions that would free politics from the burden of establishing the world itself. Thomas Aquinas, in his commentaries on Aristotle, had recognized that the Philosopher, while not anticipating the peculiar nature of the responses of revelation presented to the questions that he had already formulated, did leave open to reason an intelligible alternative that could arise on the basis of the questions properly posed in the classics. In this sense, reason and revelation are to be perennial in all subsequent political philosophy, both as the practical way to prevent various endeavors to establish Gnostic modern projects in this world on the basis of only human will ("better" answers were available) and as the means to suggest properly why it is right for politics not to become a substitute

---

11. Marion Montgomery, *The Reflective Journey Toward Order: Essays on Dante, Wordsworth, Eliot, and Others* (Athens, Ga., 1973), 172, 192–93.

metaphysics, that is, why politics to be merely politics can remain itself.

On the other hand, if something more "reasonable" than merely human reason functions also in our cities, it follows that reason, in its effort to understand what kind of being is required to be capable of revelation that corresponds to speculative knowledge, indirectly fosters the kind of city in which the "sights" are aimed high enough to sustain man as something more than a sophisticated animal who functions by a calculus of pleasure and pain alone. Strauss was correct that "moral man is a potential believer," because the philosopher is able to understand that virtue, from whatever source, is in fact contributing to the good of the existing cities, though in even the best existing city, there are questions not adequately answered by politics alone or by philosophy that do have feasible answers proposed by revelation.

The foundations of political philosophy, then, are to be found in the questions posed by politics and the answers posed by philosophy, revelation, and the alternatives of the modern Gnostic projects. None of these will eliminate the other unless the political philosopher and the citizen come to understand how much of the City of Divine Righteousness man can come to understand by himself. The proposals of more adequate answers, even from a revelation, will always strike man with surprise. But these ought not to cause either rejection or lack of further thought as to what such answers must mean. For they occasion the necessary moderation that protects the city from the political will subject to no end but itself or from the this-wordly enthusiasm of the believers demanding the formation of the City of God on Earth.

Understanding the meaning of political philosophy itself, how it came to propose what it did in intellectual terms, what alternatives are available to it, is the necessary initial philosophic exercise in political philosophy. Modern political philosophy reached an impasse in its own order that resulted in the greatest actual deformation in existing cities because of the manner in which it answered these questions. The rethinking of the foundation of political philosophy from the classics, but including the revelational philosophical tradition as addressed to reason found in the experience of politics, can restore the fullness to political theory. This rethinking it has lacked since it "lowered its sights" to deal with what man does do while retaining in itself, unconsciously perhaps, those very higher ends that were proposed by revelation but were argued in modern political thought to be susceptible of achievement by technical or political means, by a refashioning of the city and man.

Since these ends—happiness, friendship, generosity, mercy, a complete life, and the attainment of the common good of the universe—could not be achieved by political or even philosophical means, their very experience left the civil order open to Gnostic projects proposing alternative descriptions of the highest things. These descriptions, however, are in no wise as complete or as responsive (on philosophic, not religious, terms) to questions as they arose in reason and were responded to by revelation. The meaning of political philosophy is not complete without a consideration of all that is presented as intelligible to the human reason on the basis of its own experiences and questions. It is one thing for a moral and political man to be a "potential" believer. It is another for the believer to be a philosopher with full awareness of the questions posed by the experience of politics. In this sense, political philosophy is the handmaiden of theology.

The location of the City of God, the Kingdom of Righteousness, remains apart from the existing cities, even though the actual members of existing cities seek an explanation of and participation in *all that is*, by themselves, for their own sakes. Civil life cannot be opposed to the highest good on the grounds that the location of this highest good is not and cannot be in this life. Quite the contrary, for there even to be a finite civil good, it must first be understood that politics is no substitute metaphysics or embodiment of revelation. Once this point is clear, it can follow that the same people, who live in the cities of the world, are the very ones for whom these questions about the ultimate good and happiness arise, something that is evident even in Book I of *The Republic* of Plato or *The Ethics* of Aristotle.

The moderation of politics, then, depends finally on the "wisdom" of the answers given to intelligence also in revelation. These "unexpected" responses ought not to be ignored or placed outside the realm of human intellect simply because of their source. Rather they should be accepted or rejected only because they may or may not address the questions presented to all mankind as formulated in the classical political books and commented on by philosophers, who also recognized that intelligence was broader than finite reason, without ceasing to be reason. When Strauss, in *Natural Right and History,* implied that the political philosopher did not need to address natural law insofar as it was itself stimulated by revelation, he did a disservice to his own contribution to political philosophy, a contribution which he corrected, as we have suggested (Chapter 8), in his analysis of the meaning of philosophy in the Bible.[12] Revelation was instructive in inciting the political philosophers to think about what political experience actually proposed about friendship, about destiny, about justice, and happiness. In this sense, moral and political man was able to long "for revelation," which could confirm the "fixed ends" required to limit that "infinite malleability" so destructive of any purely man-made civil order.

On the other hand, on the principle that "grace builds on nature," political philosophy demanded that revelation, to be known, propose solutions to it, questions of the limits of law, of the limits of justice, of the limits of pride, which in fact undermined the peace of the city. What has been argued, in short, is merely that the fullness of political philosophy in its integrity requires a reconsideration of revelation (and what has in turn happened to it in isolation from this very project of political philosophy), not merely as a means to revive the classics, but as a response to the classics and to the record of modern political metaphysics itself. This is no mere esoteric exercise or obscure religious contention but an enterprise upon which depends the possibility of a human city that has in fact openness to a true morality, even in the political world, one recognized as such by intelligence, wisdom, and experience. Yet, in the end, this does not deny that the highest things,

12. Strauss, *Natural Right and History,* 164.

wondered about in the classics, cannot be available even to the least citizen, even in the worst regime, but not as a result of politics alone. Reason and revelation both stand at the foundation of political philosophy because the ultimate questions are posed to everyone in every regime.

BIBLIOGRAPHY

Alberti Magni [Albert the Great]. *Opera omnia*. Edited by A. Borgenet. Vols. V, VI, VII of 39 vols. Paris, 1890.
Allers, Rudolf. *The Psychology of Character*. London, 1934.
Allers, Ulrich S. "Rousseau's Second Discourse." *Review of Politics*, XX (January, 1958), 91–120.
Arendt, Hannah. *Between Past and Future*. New York, 1968.
——. *The Human Condition*. Garden City, N.Y., 1959.
——. *On Revolution*. New York, 1963.
——. *The Origins of Totalitarianism*. New York, 1973.
Aristotle. *The Basic Works of Aristotle*. Edited by Richard McKeon. New York, 1941.
Armstrong, A. H. *An Introduction to Ancient Philosophy*. Westminster, Md., 1957.
——. *Plotinus*. London, 1952.
Arnold, E. Vernon. *Roman Stoicism*. New York, 1958.
Arquillière, H. X. *L'Augustinisme politique*. Paris, 1934.
Auerbach, Maurice. "The Philosophical Politics of Leo Strauss." *Teaching Political Science,* XII (Winter, 1984–85), 52–60.
Augustine. *The Basic Writings of St. Augustine*. Edited by Whitney J. Oates. 2 vols. New York, 1948.
——. *The City of God*. Edited by Vernon J. Bourke. Garden City, N.Y., 1958.
Bailey, Cyril. *The Greek Atomists and Epicurus*. 2nd ed. Oxford, 1957.
Barker, Ernest. "The Roman Conception of Empire." In *Church, State, and Education*, edited by Ernest Barker. Ann Arbor, 1957.
Baynes, Norman H. *The Political Ideas of St. Augustine's 'De civitate Dei.'* London, 1949.
Becker, Carl. *The Heavenly City of the Eighteenth-Century Philosophers*. New Haven, 1931.
Bevan, Edwyn. *Stoics and Skeptics*. Oxford, 1913.
Bochenski, J. M. *Philosophy—An Introduction*. New York, 1972.
Bréhier, Emile. *Chrysippe et l'ancien Stoïcisme*. Paris, 1951.
——. *The Philosophy of Plotinus*. Translated by Joseph Thomas. Chicago, 1958.
Briefs, Goetz A. *The Proletariat*. New York, 1937.
——. "The Solidarist Economics of Goetz A. Briefs," edited by Walter R. Waters. *Review of Social Economy*, XLI (December, 1983).

Brinton, Crane. *The Shaping of the Modern Mind*. New York, 1959.
Brown, Oscar. *Natural Rectitude and Divine Law in Aquinas*. Toronto, 1981.
Buber, Martin. *Between Man and Man*. Translated by Roland Gregor Smith. Boston, 1955.
Burnyeat, M. F. "Sphinx Without a Secret." Review of *Studies in Platonic Political Philosophy*, by Leo Strauss. *New York Review of Books*, May 30, 1985, pp. 30–36.
Burtt, E. A. *The Metaphysical Foundations of Modern Science*. Garden City, N.Y., 1954.
Bury, J. B. *The Idea of Progress*. New York, 1955.
Carey, George, and James V. Schall, eds. *Essays in Christianity and Political Philosophy*. Lanham, Md., 1984.
Carlyle, A. J., and R. W. Carlyle. *A History of Mediaeval Political Thought in the West*. Vol. I of 6 vols. London, 1950.
Cassirer, Ernst. *An Essay on Man*. Garden City, N.Y., 1944.
———. *The Myth of the State*. New Haven, 1946.
———. *The Philosophy of the Enlightenment*. Translated by Fritz C. Koelin and James P. Pettegrove. Boston, 1951.
Cayré, F. *Initiation à la philosophie de Saint Augustin*. Paris, 1947.
Chesterton, G. K. *Orthodoxy*. London, 1909.
———. *St. Thomas Aquinas*. New York, 1933.
Cicero. *De officiis*. Translated by Walter Miller. Loeb ed. London, 1921.
———. *De re publica* and *De legibus*. Translated by Clinton Walker Keys. Loeb ed. Cambridge, Mass., 1948.
Collins, James. *A History of Modern European Philosophy*. Milwaukee, 1954.
Cooper, John M. *Reason and Human Good in Aristotle*. Cambridge, Mass., 1975.
Copleston, Frederick C. *St. Thomas and Nietzsche*. London, 1955. (Paper read to the London Aquinas Society on April 15, 1944.)
Dawson, Christopher. *Beyond Politics*. London, 1939.
———. *Dynamics of World History*. Edited by John J. Mulloy. Lasalle, Ill., 1978.
———. *The Making of Europe*. New York, 1957.
———. "The Politics of Hegel." *Dublin Review*, CCXIII (October, 1943), 97–107.
———. *Religion and the Rise of Western Culture*. London, 1950.
Deane, Herbert. *The Political and Social Ideas of St. Augustine*. New York, 1956.
de Lubac, Henri. *Nature and Grace*. San Francisco, 1984.
———. *The Sources of Revelation*. Translated by Luke O'Neill. New York, 1968.
Dennehy, Raymond. *Reason and Dignity*. Lanham, Md., 1981.
Douglass, Bruce. "The Break in Voegelin's Program." *Political Science Reviewer*, VII (Fall, 1977), 1–21.
———. "The Gospel and Political Order: Eric Voegelin on the Political Role of Christianity." *Journal of Politics*, XXXVIII (Fall, 1976), 25–45.
East, John. "The Political Relevance of St. Augustine." *Modern Age*, XVI (Spring, 1972), 167–81.

Edel, Abraham. *Aristotle and His Philosophy*. Chapel Hill, N.C., 1982.
Eterovich, Francis. *Aristotle's Nicomachean Ethics*. Lanham, Md., 1980.
Fears, J. Rufus. "The Cult of Jupiter and Roman Imperial Ideology." In *Aufstieg und Niedergang der Römischen Welt*, edited by Hildegard Temporini and Wolfgang Hasse. Vol. II of 4 vols. Berlin, 1981.
Feuerbach, Ludwig. *The Essence of Christianity*. Translated by George Eliot. New York, 1957.
Finnis, John. *Natural Law and Natural Right*. New York, 1980.
Fortin, Ernest. "Comment." *This World*, II (Spring–Summer, 1984), 97–103.
———. *Political Idealism and Christianity in the Thought of St. Augustine*. Villanova, Pa., 1972.
———. "Rational Theologians and Irrational Philosophers: A Straussian Perspective." *Interpretation*, XII (May–September, 1984), 349–56.
Foster, Michael. *Masters of Political Thought*. Vol. I of 4 vols. Boston, 1941.
Germino, Dante. *Political Philosophy and the Open Society*. Baton Rouge, 1982.
———. "Voegelin, Christianity, and Political Philosophy: *The New Science of Politics* Reconsidered." Paper presented at the annual meeting of the American Political Science Association. Chicago, 1983.
Gilson, Etienne. *A Gilson Reader*. Edited by Anton C. Pegis. Garden City, N.Y., 1957.
———. *God and Philosophy*. New Haven, 1941.
———. *A History of Christian Philosophy in the Middle Ages*. New York, 1955.
———. *Introduction à l'étude de Saint Augustin*. Paris, 1943.
———. *The Unity of Philosophical Experience*. New York, 1937.
Green, F. C. *Rousseau and the Idea of Progress*. Oxford, 1950.
Grisez, Germain C. "Kant and Aquinas: Ethical Theory." *Thomist*, XXI (January, 1958), 44–78.
Hallowell, John. *Main Currents in Modern Political Thought*. New York, 1950.
———. "Obstacles to the Recovery of a Christian Perception on Human Nature." *Modern Age*, XXVII (Winter, 1983), 2–14.
Hegel, Georg Wilhelm Friedrich. *The Philosophy of History*. Translated by J. Sibree. New York, 1956.
———. *The Philosophy of Right*. Translated by T. M. Knox. Oxford, 1942.
Henry, Paul. *Plotin et l'Occident*. Louvain, 1934.
Himmelfarb, Gertrude. "Denigrating the Rule of Reason." *Harper's*, CCLXVIII (April, 1984), 84–90.
———. *The Idea of Poverty*. New York, 1983.
Hook, Sidney. *Marx and the Marxists: The Ambiguous Legacy*. New York, 1955.
Hughes, Philip. *A History of the Church*. Vol. I of 3 vols. New York, 1952.
Jackson, Michael. "Leo Strauss' Teaching: A Study of *Thoughts on Machiavelli*." Ph.D. dissertation, Georgetown University, 1985.

Jaffa, Harry. *The Conditions of Freedom: Essays in Political Philosophy.* Baltimore, 1975.
———. "The Legacy of Leo Strauss." *Claremont Review of Books,* III (Fall, 1984), 14–21.
———. "Leo Strauss' Churchillian Speech and the Question of the Decline of the West." *Teaching Political Science,* XII (Winter, 1984–85), 61–67.
———. *Thomism and Aristotelianism.* Westport, Conn., 1952.
Jaki, Stanley. *The Road of Science and the Ways to God.* Chicago, 1978.
Kant, Immanuel. *The Philosophy of Kant.* Edited by Carl J. Friedrich. New York, 1949.
Katz, Joseph. *Plotinus' Search for the Good.* New York, 1950.
Knox, Ronald. *Enthusiasm.* New York, 1950.
Kohn, Hans, ed. *The Making of the Modern French Mind.* New York, 1955.
Kossel, Clifford G. "The Moral Views of Thomas Aquinas." In *The Encyclopedia of Morals.* Edited by Virgilius Ferm. New York, n.d.
———. "Some Problems of Truth in Ethics." In *Proceedings of the Jesuit Philosophical Association.* Woodstock, Md., 1957.
Krąpiec, Mieczyław A. *I-Man: An Outline of Philosophical Anthropology.* Translated by Francis Lescoe, Andrew Woznicki, et al. New Britain, Conn., 1983.
Lottin, Odon, "La définition classique de la loi." *Revue Néoscholastique de Philosophie,* XXVII (1925), 129–45.
McCoy, Charles N. R. "The Logical and the Real in Political Theory: Plato, Aristotle, and Marx." *American Political Science Review,* XLVIII (December, 1954), 1058–66.
———. "Ludwig Feuerbach and the Formation of the Marxian Revolutionary Idea." *Laval Théologique et Philosophique,* VII, No. 2 (1951), 218–48.
———. "The Meaning of Jean-Jacques Rousseau and the Structure of Political Theory." In *Proceedings of the American Catholic Philosophical Association.* Washington, D.C., 1956.
———. "The Place of Machiavelli in the History of Political Thought." *American Political Science Review,* XXXVII (August, 1943), 626–41.
———. *The Structure of Political Thought.* New York, 1963.
———. "The Turning Point in Political Philosophy." *American Political Science Review,* XLVI (September, 1950), 678–88.
Machiavelli, Niccolo. *The Prince and Discourses.* New York, 1950.
McIlwain, Charles Howard. *Growth of Political Thought in the West.* New York, 1932.
McInerney, Ralph. *St. Thomas Aquinas.* Notre Dame, 1982.
MacIntyre, Alasdair. *After Virtue.* Notre Dame, 1981.
Maritain, Jacques. *Man and the State.* Chicago, 1951.
———. *Scholasticism and Politics.* Garden City, N.Y., 1960.
Marx, Karl. *Capital.* Translated by Samuel Moore and Edward Aveling. New York, 1936.

———. *A Contribution to the Critique of Political Economy.* Translated by N. I. Stone. Chicago, 1904.
———. *Die Frühschriften.* Edited by von Siegfried Landshut. Stuttgart, 1953.
———. *Oeuvres philosophiques.* Translated by J. Moliter. 6 vols. Paris, 1937.
———. *The Poverty of Philosophy.* Translated by H. Quelch. Chicago, 1920.
———. *Selected Writings in Sociology and Social Science.* Edited by T. B. Bottomore and Maximilian Rubel. London, 1956.
Marx, Karl, and Friedrich Engels. *Basic Writings on Politics and Philosophy.* Edited by Lewis S. Feuer. Garden City, N.Y., 1959.
———. *Correspondence, 1846–95.* Translated by Dona Torr. London, 1934.
———. *The German Ideology.* Translated by R. Pascal. New York, 1939.
Mattingly, Sir Herold. *Roman Imperial Civilization.* Garden City, N.Y., 1959.
Midgley, E. B. F. "Authority, Alienation, and Revolt." *Aberdeen University Review,* XLVI (Autumn, 1976), 372–83.
———. "Concerning the Modernist Subversion of Political Philosophy." *New Scholasticism,* LIII (Spring, 1979), 168–90.
———. "On 'Substitute Intelligences' in the Formation of Atheistic Ideology." *Laval Théologique et Philosophique,* XXXVII (October, 1980), 239–53.
Montesquieu, Baron de. *The Spirit of the Laws.* Edited by Franz Neumann. Translation by Thomas Nugent. New York, 1949.
Montgomery, Marion. *The Reflective Journey Toward Order: Essays on Dante, Wordsworth, Eliot, and Others.* Athens, Ga., 1973.
Morrall, John. *Aristotle.* New York, 1977.
Mulgen, Robert. *Aristotle's Political Theory.* Oxford, 1977.
Murray, Gilbert. *The Stoic Philosophy.* New York, 1915.
Nichols, James H. *Epicurean Political Philosophy.* Ithaca, 1976.
Niebuhr, Reinhold. "Augustine's Political Realism." In *Perspectives in Political Philosophy.* Edited by J. Downton. New York, 1971.
Nisbet, Robert. *History of the Idea of Progress.* New York, 1980.
Novak, Michael. *Freedom with Justice.* San Francisco, 1984.
———. *The Spirit of Democratic Capitalism.* New York, 1982.
Ortega y Gasset, José. "The Past and Future of Western Thought." *Modern Age,* II (September, 1958), 251–56.
Pegis, Anton C. *Christian Philosophy and Intellectual Freedom.* Milwaukee, 1955.
———. *St. Thomas and Philosophy.* Milwaukee, 1964.
———. *St. Thomas and the Problem of the Soul in the Thirteenth Century.* Toronto, 1934.
Pieper, Josef. *Death and Immortality.* Translated by R. and C. Winston. New York, 1969.
———. "On the 'Negative' Element in the Philosophy of Thomas Aquinas." *Cross Currents,* IV (Fall, 1953), 46–56.

———. *Reality and the Good.* Translated by S. Lange. Chicago, 1967.
———. *Scholasticism.* New York, 1972.
———. *The Silence of St. Thomas.* Chicago, 1957.
Pistorius, Philippus Villiers. *Plotinus and Neoplatonism.* Cambridge, 1952.
Plato. *Alcibiades.* Translated by W. R. M. Lamb. Loeb ed. London, 1927.
———. *The Laws.* Translated, with an interpretative essay, by Thomas L. Pangle. New York, 1980.
———. *Phaedo.* Translated by F. J. Church. New York, 1951.
———. *The Republic.* Translated, with notes and an interpretative essay, by Allan Bloom. New York, 1968.
———. *Statesman.* Translated by J. B. Skemp. New York, 1957.
———. *Theaetetus.* Translated by Benjamin Jowett. Oxford, 1931.
———. *Timaeus.* Translated by R. G. Bury. Loeb ed. Cambridge, Mass., 1952.
Plotinus. *Enneads.* Translated by Stephen Mackenna. Boston, n.d.
Popper, Karl. *The Unended Quest.* London, 1979.
Pozzo, Gianni M. "L'Etica e la politica di Epicuro." *Humanitas,* X (Agosto, 1955), 789–93.
Reesor, Margaret. *The Political Theory of the Old and Middle Stoa.* New York, 1951.
Rist, John, ed. *The Stoics.* Berkeley, 1977.
Rommen, Heinrich. "The Genealogy of Natural Rights." *Thought,* XXIX (Spring, 1954), 403–25.
———. *The Natural Law.* St. Louis, 1947.
———. *The State in Catholic Thought.* St. Louis, 1945.
Rousseau, Jean-Jacques. *De L'Inégalité parmi les hommes.* Geneva, 1946.
———. *The Social Contract.* An eighteenth-century translation, revised, edited, and with an introduction, by Charles Frankel. New York, 1955.
Sabine, George. "Hegel's Political Philosophy." *Philosophical Review,* XLI (May, 1932), 261–82.
———. *A History of Political Theory.* Rev. ed. New York, 1953.
St. Augustine. Edited by M. C. D'Arcy. New York, 1957.
Sambursky, S. *The Physics of the Stoics.* London, 1959.
Sandoz, Ellis. *The Voegelinian Revolution.* Baton Rouge, 1981.
Schall, James V. "The Abiding Significance of Gnosticism." *American Ecclesiastical Review,* CXLVII (September, 1962), 164–73.
———. "Cartesianism and Political Theory." *Review of Politics,* XXIV (April, 1962), 260–82.
———. *Christianity and Life.* San Francisco, 1981.
———. *Christianity and Politics.* Boston, 1981.
———. "Classical Politics." Review of *Studies in Platonic Political Philosophy,* by Leo Strauss. *Reflections* (Summer, 1984), 12.

———. *The Distinctiveness of Christianity*. San Francisco, 1983.
———. *Human Dignity and Human Numbers*. Staten Island, N.Y., 1971.
———. "Immortality and the Foundations of Political Theory." Ph.D. dissertation, Georgetown University, 1960.
———. "Immortality and the Political Life of Man in Albertus Magnus." *Thomist*, XLVIII (October, 1984), 535–65.
———. *Liberation Theology*. San Francisco, 1982.
———. "Luther and Political Philosophy." *Faith and Reason*, VIII (Summer, 1982), 7–31.
———. "Metaphysics, Theology, and Political Theory." *Political Science Reviewer*, XI (Fall, 1981), 1–25.
———. "Natural Law in the Medieval Intellectual Context." *Modern Age*, XXVIII (Spring–Summer, 1984), 228–35.
———. "Plotinus and Political Philosophy." *Gregorianum*. No. 3, Vol. LXVI (1985), 687–707.
———. *The Politics of Heaven and Hell: Christian Themes from Classical, Medieval, and Modern Political Philosophy*. Lanham, Md., 1984.
———. "Post-Aristotelian Philosophy and Political Theory." *Cithara*, III (November, 1963), 56–77.
———. "Reason, Revelation, and Politics: Catholic Reflections on Strauss." *Gregorianum*, LXII, Nos. 2 and 3 (1981), 349–65, 467–97.
———. *Redeeming the Time*. New York, 1968.
———. Review of *St. Thomas Aquinas* by Ralph McInerny. *Teaching Political Science*, X (Summer, 1983), 195–97.
———. "Theory in American Politics." *Modern Age*, IV (Spring, 1960), 150–159.
———. "The Totality of Society: From Justice to Friendship." *Thomist*, XX (January, 1957), 1–26.
Schumacher, E. F. *A Guide for the Perplexed*. New York, 1977.
Sentroul, Charles. *Kant et Aristote*. Paris, 1913.
Sigmund, Paul. "Thomist Natural Law and Social Theory." In *Calgary Aquinas Studies*, edited by Anthony Parel. Toronto, 1979.
Simon, Julian. *The Ultimate Resource*. Princeton, 1980.
Solterer, Josef. "Toward the Humanizing of Economics." *Review of Social Economy*, XXX (September, 1972), 394–400.
Spanneut, Michel. *Le Stoïcisme des pères de l'église*. Paris, 1957.
Stoic and Epicurean Philosophers. Edited, with a general introduction, by Whitney J. Oates. New York, 1940.
Strauss, Leo. *City and Man*. Chicago, 1964.
———. "The Mutual Influence of Philosophy and Theology." *Independent Journal of Philosophy*, III (1979), 111–18.

———. *Natural Right and History.* Chicago, 1953.
———. *Persecution and the Art of Writing.* Glencoe, Ill., 1952.
———. *The Political Philosophy of Hobbes.* Translated by Elsa M. Sinclair. Chicago, 1952.
———. *Political Philosophy: Six Essays.* Edited by Hilail Gildin. Indianapolis, 1975.
———. *The Predicament of Modern Politics.* Edited by Harold J. Spaeth. Detroit, 1964.
———. "Progress or Return? The Contemporary Crisis in Western Civilization." *Modern Judaism,* I (1981), 17–45.
———. *Spinoza's Critique of Religion.* New York, 1965.
———. *Studies in Platonic Political Philosophy.* Edited by Thomas L. Pangle. Chicago, 1983.
———. *Thoughts on Machiavelli.* Glencoe, Ill., 1958.
———. *What Is Political Philosophy?* Glencoe, Ill., 1959.
Strauss, Leo, and Joseph Cropsey, eds. *History of Political Philosophy.* Chicago, 1972.
Sullivan, Roger J. *Morality and the Good Life in Aristotle.* Memphis, 1977.
Tarn, W. W. *Hellenistic Civilization.* 3rd ed. rev. London, 1952.
Thomas Aquinas. *Compendium of Theology.* Translated by Cyril Vollert. St. Louis, 1947.
———. *De physico.* Edited by A. Pirotta. Naples, 1953.
———. *In Aristotelis librum de anima, Commentarium.* Turin, 1936.
———. *In decem libros ethicorum Aristotelis ad Nicomachum expositio.* Turin, 1934.
———. *In Metaphysicam Aristotelis, Commentaria.* Turin, 1935.
———. *In octo libros politicorum Aristotelis expositio seu De rebus civilibus.* Quebec, 1940.
———. *On Kingship to the King of Cyprus.* Translated by Gerald B. Phelan. Revised, with an introduction and notes, by I. Th. Eschmann. Toronto, 1949.
———. *On the Power of God.* Translated by the English Dominicans. Westminster, Md., 1952.
——— [Sancti Thomae Aquinatis]. *Opera omnia.* 25 vols. Parma, 1875; rpr. New York, 1948–50.
———. *St. Thomas Aquinas.* Selected and translated, with notes and introduction, by Thomas Gilby. Vol. I. *Philosophical Texts.* Vol. II. *Theological Texts.* Durham, N.C., 1982.
———. *Summa contra Gentiles.* Rome, 1934.
———. *Summa theologiae.* 3 vols. Turin, 1948.
Veatch, Henry. *Aristotle.* Indianapolis, 1974.
Voegelin, Eric. *From the Englightenment to Revolution.* Edited by John Hallowell. Durham, N.C., 1975.
———. *The New Science of Politics.* Chicago, 1952.
———. *Order and History.* 4 vols. Baton Rouge, 1974.

———. *The Philosophy of Order*. Edited by P. J. Opitz and George Sebba. Stuttgart, 1981.
———. *Science, Politics, and Gnosticism*. Chicago, 1968.
von Balthasar, Hans Urs. *A Theological Anthropolgy*. New York, 1967.
Whittaker, Thomas. *The Neo-Platonists*. Cambridge, 1928.
Wilhelmsen, Frederick D. *Christianity and Political Philosophy*. Athens, Ga., 1978.
Wiser, James L. *Political Philosophy: A History of the Search for Order*. Englewood Cliffs, N.J., 1983.
Wojtyla, Karol. *The Acting Person*. Translated by Andrej Potecki. Dordrecht, Netherlands, 1979.
Wolin, Sheldon. *Politics and Vision: Continuity and Innovation in Western Political Thought*. Boston, 1960.
Zeller, Eduard. *Stoics, Epicureans, and Skeptics*. Translated by Oswald J. Reichel. London, 1890.

INDEX

Aachen, 223
Adams, John, 5
Albert the Great (Albertus Magnus), 16, 20, 22, 23, 61, 143, 144
Alienation, 38, 63, 89, 135, 139, 142, 146, 164, 171, 176, 180, 235
Allers, Rudolf, 5
Allers, Ulrich, 134
Antigone of Sophocles, 219
Aquinas, Thomas: on Aristotle, 12, 114–17, 120, 123; on Augustine, 93; on friendship and political philosophy, 121–28; on medieval political philosophy, 105–21; in Strauss, 185, 192, 197, 207, 218–19, 222; *Summa contra Gentiles*, 93, 94, 115, 119, 127; *Summa theologiae*, 115, 122, 123, 218; on rethinking political philosophy, 186, 187, 192, 211, 231, 236; mentioned, 185–87, 190–92, 196, 218, 231–32, 234, 236, and *passim*
Arendt, Hannah, 5, 12, 79, 199, 225
Aristotle: on First (Prime, Unmoved) Mover, 35, 36, 38, 40, 41, 45–47, 50, 55, 57, 58, 60, 62, 66, 70, 71, 82, 101, 109, 125, 127, 133, 139, 141, 142, 148, 162, 171, 179, 201, 211, 220; on happiness, 48–55; on human and divine activity, 42–49; on immortality, 55–62; on sensory and theoretic knowledge, 29–37; *The Ethics*, 10, 16, 18, 39, 48, 49, 81, 97, 112, 113, 114, 116, 117, 121, 125, 127, 128, 201, 214; *The Metaphysics*, 10, 18, 92, 116; *The Politics*, 9, 49, 92, 97, 110, 113, 116, 118, 128, 194, 210, and *passim*
Arquillière, H. X., 79
Art, 32, 47, 98, 111, 129, 191, 230, 236
Athens, 14, 26, 42, 72, 188, 192, 193, 194, 203, 206, 207, 214, 215, 220, 222, 223
Augustine, Aurelius (St.), 2, 6, 7, 11, 73, 75–92, 94, 100, 112, 113, 192, 197, 201, 203, 206, 214, 220, 223, 228, and *passim*

Autonomy, 5, 33, 35, 65, 66, 71, 75, 100, 105, 138, 139, 140, 155, 165, 171, 208, 216, 218, 235
Averroes, 61, 94, 105, 194, 197, 205
Avicenna, 61

Barbarism, 19
Bevan, Edwyn, 69
Bible: New Testament, 19, 109, 188, 191, 192, 200, 201, 205, 222; Old Testament, 109, 118, 191, 192, 208, 213, 215, 222, 223, 233; mentioned, 188, 207, 209, 210, 213, 214, 215, 216, 239
Bloom, Allan, 18
Bréhier, Emile, 76
Briefs, Goetz A., 5
Brinton, Craine, 131
Burke, Edmund, 5, 193

Carlyle, A. J., and R. W., 63, 71
Cassirer, Ernst, 41–42, 66, 130
Cause, 39, 41, 85, 109, 111, 149, 162
Charity, 69, 207
Chesterton, Gilbert K., 82
Christ, Jesus, 82, 87, 110, 203, 208, 223
Church, 79, 110, 104
Cicero, Marcus Tullius, 2, 22, 68–71, 84, 99, 201, 220, 223
City of God, 77–85, 87, 92, 128, 197, 202, 203, 217, 237, 238
Coercion, 113, 114, 121
Communism, 172, 175–76, 223
Condorcet, Marquis de, 131
Contemplation, 9, 16, 18, 21, 23, 25, 35, 37, 45, 46, 47, 49, 50, 51, 52, 53, 54, 60, 71, 75, 88, 91, 100, 171, 197, 208, 228
Copleston, Frederick C., 234
Creation, 14, 19, 21, 86, 109, 118, 147, 164, 207, 209, 211, 213, 214, 215, 218
Cynicism, 59, 64, 73, 227

Darwin, Charles, 41
Dawson, Christopher, 78, 199, 210
Death, 39, 52, 109, 131, 144, 163, 206, 212
Decalogue (Commandments), 200, 208, 233
de Lubac, Henri, 204, 221
Democracy, 223
Democritus, 63
Descartes, Rene, 12, 89, 129, 130, 141, 146, 157, 189

Engels, Friedrich, 169
Enlightenment, 131, 212, 226, 231
Epicurus, 63
Epicureans, 59, 63, 65, 66, 67
Equity, 122, 123
Evil, 20, 81, 85, 95, 113, 114, 115, 120, 133, 146, 163, 164, 191, 203, 207, 212
Evolution, 41

Fall, The (original sin), 85, 112, 113, 131, 174
Fascism, 223
Feuerbach, Ludwig, 165–68, 169, 170, 171, 172
Finality (teleology), 41, 42, 43, 58, 88, 109, 111, 133, 153
Forms, 23, 24, 25, 26, 29, 32, 34, 175, 226
Fortin, Ernest, 91, 188
Foster, Michael, 80
Freedom, 33, 66, 67, 91, 135, 142, 146, 147, 150, 154, 161, 190, 207, 223, 226
Friendship, 9, 20, 22, 73, 116, 121, 123–28, 168, 180, 202, 220, 234, 238, 239
Futility, 93, 94, 95, 118, 234

Generic being (man), 179, 181, 182, 183, 198, 199, 203, 216, 228, 236
Germino, Dante, 11
Gilson, Etienne, 10, 87, 88, 203
Gnosticism, 6, 124, 125, 145, 186, 189, 190, 192, 193, 195, 200, 203, 204, 206, 214, 221, 224, 225, 228, 230, 232, 234, 236, 237, 239
Good, 23, 25, 27, 29, 32, 36, 37, 38, 44, 46, 49, 50, 54, 75, 82, 85, 97, 98, 99, 100, 116, 124, 125, 126, 127, 129, 143, 157, 159, 163, 191, 199, 200, 203, 217, 227

Grace, 77, 95, 107, 108, 110, 144, 164, 197, 239
Grotius, Hugo, 148

Happiness, 9, 29, 39, 47, 48, 49–55, 62, 65, 90, 96, 100, 115, 117, 119, 126, 175, 227, 234, 239
Hegel, Georg W. F., 133, 142, 148, 157–62, 169, 170, 180, 198
"Highest Things," 10, 18, 20, 32, 47, 48, 119, 125, 182, 196, 197, 198, 200, 205, 220, 239
Hobbes, Thomas, 60, 100, 113, 129, 130, 136, 137, 181, 189, 205, 216
Humanity, 134, 162, 165, 177, 216
Hume, David, 149, 150, 152

Ideology, 5, 12, 13, 18, 93, 145, 185, 187, 203, 234
Immortality, 11, 16, 17, 18–22, 39, 40, 41, 44, 58, 59, 61, 73, 84, 88, 94, 102, 110, 131, 141, 145, 147, 150, 163, 164, 165, 167, 168, 195, 199, 201, 203, 206, 211, 212, 229, 231, 233, 234
Incarnation, 2, 72, 76, 77, 78, 87, 109, 127
Individual, 11, 19, 23, 25, 29, 31, 34, 40, 44, 61, 71, 85, 90, 96, 99, 101, 108, 109, 115, 124, 125, 135, 139, 140, 147, 148, 150, 155, 162, 163, 167, 172, 177, 182, 183, 194, 201, 206, 208, 234, 236

Jaffa, Harry V., 185
Jerusalem, 188, 192, 193, 194, 203, 206, 207, 214, 220, 222, 223
Joachim of Flora, 234
Justice, 27, 95, 96, 121, 122, 123, 125, 215, 239

Kant, Immanuel, 133, 138, 139, 142–57, 160, 161, 162, 165, 205
Katz, Josef, 77
Knowledge, 25, 26, 28–37, 42, 43, 55, 56, 57, 59, 60, 61, 62, 68, 89, 91, 103, 125, 149, 151, 176, 179, 180, 189, 218, 219, 237
Kossel, Clifford G., 4

Index

Law, 70, 107, 108, 113, 115, 116, 121, 131, 133, 134, 136, 142, 148, 151, 154, 185, 194, 207, 209, 214, 215, 221, 229, 231
Leibnitz, G. W., 130
Life, 16, 51, 52, 79, 89, 91, 95, 98, 107, 109, 125, 126, 141, 163
Locke, John, 130
Luther, Martin, 138

McCoy, Charles N. R., 4, 31, 138
Machiavelli, Niccolo, 12, 100, 105, 113, 129, 131, 146, 157, 171, 189, 197, 199, 200, 201, 203, 227
Malleability, 141, 145, 227, 228, 229, 234, 239
Maritain, Jacques, 6, 193
Marsilius of Padua, 106, 129, 136, 233, 234
Materialism, 170, 180
Marx, Karl, 32, 60, 63, 71, 138, 139, 140, 169–81, 198, 229, 236
Mercy, 122
Metaphysics, 1, 4, 7, 11–13, 15, 18, 27, 32, 33, 34, 38, 58, 64, 65, 87, 109, 125, 146, 147, 150, 174, 195, 202, 205, 225, 228, 232, 237, 239
Midgley, E. B. F., 186
Moderation (limits), 7, 11, 36, 62, 63, 64, 109, 123, 128, 145, 190, 192, 199, 205, 227, 232, 233
"Modern Project," 6, 72, 100, 106, 139, 187, 188, 189, 190, 193, 194, 199, 201, 202, 203, 204, 216, 219, 221, 224, 236
Money, 48, 50, 175
Montesquieu, Charles Louis de Secondat, Baron de, 132, 133, 134, 136, 157
Montgomery, Marion, 235

Nature, 10, 29, 33, 38, 42, 43, 44, 59, 71, 86, 89, 95, 107, 111, 119, 138, 141, 145, 151, 160, 161, 168, 171, 176, 177, 178, 197, 207, 211, 213, 215, 217, 239
Neuman, Franz, 132
Newton, Isaac, 130
Nietzsche, Friedrich, 183, 198, 235

Ortega y Gasset, José, 132

Pangle, Thomas, 231
Paul of Tarsus (Saint), 81, 185, 200, 203, 210, 215, 216, 220, 229
Pegis, Anton C., 217, 218, 222
Phaleas, 120
Philosophy, 19, 20, 21, 36, 68, 78, 85, 99, 102, 103, 104, 111, 112, 128, 130, 141, 171, 188, 202, 208, 210, 214, 216, 217, 220, 224, 226, 232, 233
Pieper, Josef, 211, 212, 213, 214, 216, 234
Plato: and Augustine, 73, 78–79, 86–87, 90; *The Apology*, 10, 17, 101; *The Laws*, 35; political thought, 22–29, and *passim; The Republic*, 17, 18, 25, 27, 28, 29, 37, 39, 95, 96, 102, 153, 208, 212, 220, 238
Plotinus, 73–77, 79, 84, 86, 87, 90, 91, 158
Political Philosophy: as subject, 5, 9, 11, 13, 16, 21, 36, 92, 95, 114, 128, 129, 147, 195, 223; American, 4, 5, 21, 202; Christian, 5, 19, 59, 61, 65, 66, 72, 99, 106, 145, 182, 184, 185, 190, 194; classical, 9, 12, 17, 21, 63, 100, 146, 206, 219–20, 230, 239; medieval, 12, 13, 100, 102, 105–21, 144; modern, 3, 4, 5, 6, 8, 12, 13, 21, 32, 33, 38, 63, 84, 94, 96, 100, 102, 125, 128, 129, 144, 145, 164, 184, 186, 191, 198, 200, 201, 204, 234, 235, 237; Post-Aristotelian, 17, 59, 62–74, 144, 226; Roman, 17, 31, 63, 67–81, 82
Polybius, 99
Practical sciences (reason, order), 1, 4, 13, 22, 35, 68, 79, 97, 98, 102, 106, 109, 111, 112, 128, 160, 193
Pride (*superbia*), 67, 185
Progress, 131, 132, 146, 170
Pyrrho, 66

Reesor, Margaret, 68
Reason: and faith, 95, 104, 141, 217; and revelation, 14, 15, 36, 94, 95, 103, 104, 109, 123, 148, 182, 186, 200, 201, 202, 203, 209, 211, 213, 215, 217–19, 237, 240
Regime, 99, 100, 101, 106, 197
Religion, 2, 3, 12, 17, 21, 106, 136, 137, 164, 171, 189, 205
Resurrection, 11, 17, 19, 58, 76, 83, 110,

115, 116, 143, 144, 163, 164, 206, 214, 231
Revelation: and political philosophy, 1, 6, 7, 14, 19, 34, 54, 62, 63, 66, 67, 96, 101, 106, 107, 181, 191, 195, 197, 201–24, 226, 228, 229, 230, 231, 236, 237, 239; Hebrew (Jewish), 1, 6, 196, 221, 233
Rights, 39, 207
Rome, 5, 71, 82, 188, 194, 203, 214, 220, 223
Rommen, Heinrich A., 4
Rousseau, Jean Jacques, 7, 133–42, 160, 181, 183, 230

Sabine, George H., 63, 71
Sandoz, Ellis, 229
Sciences, 23, 39, 98, 100, 178, 189, 191, 230
Self-liberation, 47, 72
Sensation, 24, 26, 27, 30, 57, 60, 171, 178, 179, 180
Sentroul, Charles, 156
Sigmund, Paul E., 231
Singulars, 107, 123
Socrates, 10, 23, 39, 95, 119, 199, 203, 206, 219, 223
Solterer, Josef, 5
Soul, 9, 41, 45, 53, 56, 57, 58, 60, 61, 75, 87, 95, 96, 102, 109, 212, 214, 235
Species, 43, 96, 115, 124, 140, 146, 148, 160, 161, 165, 166, 167, 171, 172, 181, 182, 218
Spinoza, Benedict, 130
Stoicism, 59, 64–71, 74, 84, 156
Strauss, Leo, 5, 6, 12, 106, 148, 189–93, 198, 202, 204–11, 215–19, 221, 222, 223, 227, 233, 239, and *passim*
"Substitute Intelligence" (metaphysics), 59, 139, 140, 171, 211, 225, 228, 233, 237
Superabundance, 121, 122, 125

Tarn, W. W., 63
Theology, 4, 13, 79, 103, 163, 188, 203, 205, 206, 210, 211, 219, 222, 238
"Thought Thinking Itself," 46, 125, 127, 230
Thucydides, 22, 201
Transcendence, 9, 11, 15, 108, 126, 138, 162, 197, 214, 223
Trinity, 2, 79, 88, 109, 110, 127, 165, 209
Truth, 18, 19, 33, 39, 89, 90, 94, 95, 98, 100, 105, 116, 119, 124, 126, 145, 189, 191, 197, 200, 202, 205, 206, 216, 218, 219, 222, 226, 229, 236
Tyranny, 7, 195, 216, 223, 227

Voegelin, Eric, 5, 6, 12, 106, 183, 184, 185, 197, 201, 221, 223, 225, 229, 230, 231, 232, 234, and *passim*

"What is" (All that is), 9, 11, 12, 14, 37, 38, 47, 58, 65, 97, 98, 99, 100, 103, 104, 107, 109, 112, 126, 127, 133, 143, 146, 148, 156, 165, 183, 190, 191, 195, 198, 202, 225, 226, 227, 228, 230, 238
Wisdom, 125, 223, 239

Zeller, Eduard, 65, 67
Zeno, 67